Missouri Genealogical Gleanings

1840 and Beyond
Volume 4

Sherida K. Eddlemon

HERITAGE BOOKS
2009

HERITAGE BOOKS
AN IMPRINT OF HERITAGE BOOKS, INC.

Books, CDs, and more—Worldwide

For our listing of thousands of titles see our website at
www.HeritageBooks.com

Published 2009 by
HERITAGE BOOKS, INC.
Publishing Division
100 Railroad Ave. #104
Westminster, Maryland 21157

Copyright © 1997 Sherida K. Eddlemon

All rights reserved. No part of this book may be reproduced or transmitted in any form or by any means, electronic or mechanical, including photocopying, recording or by any information storage and retrieval system without written permission from the author, except for the inclusion of brief quotations in a review.

International Standard Book Numbers
Paperbound: 978-0-7884-0805-2
Clothbound: 978-0-7884-7581-8

DEDICATION

To the biggest surprise of my life, my daughter, Rhena Ann Victoria South, born September 14, 1995

PREFACE

Missouri was a gateway to the west. Both the Santa Fe Trail to the southwest and the Oregon Trail to the northwest began at Independence, Missouri. Settlers and new immigrants from Germany, Switzerland, Ireland, England, Poland, Bohemia and Italy flooded into Missouri when statehood was granted in 1821. Many of these new arrivals often did not list a destination on the ship passenger list. If a destination was indicated, it may mean that their were other relatives already there or that the family had already purchased property in advance.

Kansas was part of the Missouri Territory until 1821, but it was not until 1854 that the territory of Kansas was created luring new immigrants and settlers from Illinois, Ohio, Indiana and Missouri. So many Missourians relocated to Kansas that in 1855 Kansas was voted into the Union as a slave state.

Missouri was plagued with outlaws and raiders that had their beginnings even before the Civil War. The 1857 Dred Scott Decision helped to inflame the anti-slavery feelings in Missouri. During the Civil War, raiders and outlaws such as William Clarke Quantrill, Frank and Jesse James and the Cole Younger gangs terrorized Missouri. In the eyes of some these outlaws were heroes, but the law prevailed in the end.

Each new Gold Rush lured more people to Missouri on their way to make their fortune. There was a California Gold Rush in 1848; the Colorado Gold Rush in 1858 and the Klondike Gold Rush in the Yukon in 1896-1897. Many lost sons went to look for gold as well as whole families with only a child born in Missouri to show their passing through the state.

St. Joseph, Missouri was the starting point for the Pony Express. It promised delivery of the mail to Sacramento, California in eight to ten days. Although it was only in operation for eighteen months, these riders gained a glamorous spot in Missouri history.

Dr. Perry Nichols' Sanitarium began operation in Savannah, Andrew County, Missouri in 1912. In 1956 the Sanitarium was sold to the Sisters of St. Francis. The Andrew County Historical Society has some, but not all of the yearbooks for the Sanitarium. If anyone is interested in more complete information on the Nichols Sanitarium, please contact the Andrew County Historical Society, P. O. Box 12, Savannah, MO 64485-0012. Please include an SASE with all correspondence.

Although there are extant census records for Missouri starting in 1830 many travelers and pioneering settlers were missed in the census years or only lived in the state between the census years. The purpose of this collection is to help the researcher pinpoint his ancestor between the census years.

All names appear as written on the records including the abbreviations of given names. The surnames appearing in the parentheses are included in the index. No attempt has been made to make corrections in spelling. Cemetery listings and mortality schedules include only persons born in 1840 or later.

In some instances it was necessary to use abbreviations. They are as follows:

- m - Month
- d - Day/Died
- b - Born
- D - Date
- GE - Grantee
- P - Page
- R - Range
- AP - Application
- MOC - Missouri Connection
- TWP - Township
- A - Age
- BP - Birth Place
- OC - Occupation
- MD - Marriage Date
- CMTS - Comments

- y - Year
- RD - Recorded Date
- CLK - Clerk
- GR - Grantor
- IN - Instrument
- I - Issue
- C - Court Cases
- Dis - Dismissed
- SUS - Suspended
- APP - Appraiser
- St - Martial Status
- RES - Residence
- ADM/AD - Admission
- MG - Minister
- SVC - Service

Good luck in finding your ancestors within these pages.

DATES TO REMEMBER

1821	Missouri became the 24th state.
1835	Samuel K. Clemens or Mark Twain was born.
1837	Missouri gained six northwestern counties with the Platte Purchase.
1846	Mexican War
1848	California Gold Rush
1849	St. Louis Cholera Epidemic
1854	Kansas Territory was created.
1855	So many Missourians moved to Kansas that it was voted in as a slave state.
1857	Dred Scott Decision
1858	Colorado Gold Rush
1858	Butterfield Stage Line ran from St. Louis, MO to San Francisco, CA.
1860 - 1861	Pony Express mail run from St. Joseph, MO to Sacramento, CA.
1863	Some State registration of births and deaths began, but very scattered.
1861 - 1865	Civil War
1865	New Missouri constitution was created with a "Test Oath" clause denying southern sympathizers the right to vote.
1865	Wm. C. Quantrill, guerilla raider, was killed.
1870	Great Mississippi steamboat race between the "Robert E. Lee" and the "Natchez" from St. Louis to New Orleans.
1870 - 1872	Missouri-Kansas-Texas Railroad in operation.
1875	Sixty-eight men were elected to draft a new

Missouri constitution.

1883 - 1893   County Clerks were required to register births and deaths, but not enforced.

1889   Oklahoma Land Rush

1896 - 1897   Gold Rush to the Klondike District of the Yukon.

1911   Full compliance for the State registration of births and deaths.

TABLE OF CONTENTS

                                                                         Page

ANDREW COUNTY
(Founded 1841 from the Platte Purchase)

Testimonials Dr. Perry Nichols' Sanitarium,
Patients from Iowa, 1935 56

AUDRAIN COUNTY
(Founded 1843 from Monroe County)

Appleman Cemetery 138

BOONE COUNTY
(Founded 1820 from Howard County)

Stephen's Female College, Faculty and Students,
1879-1880 145

BUCHANNAN COUNTY
(Founded 1838 from the Platte Purchase)

Bartlett Trust Company, Officers, 1920 141

CARTER COUNTY
(Founded 1859 from Ripley and Shannon Counties)

Aldrich Cemetery 78
Marriage Records, 1860 - 1881 130

CASS COUNTY
(Founded 1835 from Jackson County)

Poll Book, Pleasant Hill Township, Mar. 31, 1885 53

CLAY COUNTY
(Found 1822 from Ray County)

WPA Sketch Grandma Handy, Field Oct. 10, 1940 7

GRUNDY COUNTY
(Founded 1841 from Livingston County)

Register of Births, 1864 - 1870 122

HICKORY COUNTY
(Founded 1845 from Benton and Polk Counties)

Antioch Cemetery 184

HOWELL COUNTY
(Founded 1857 from Oregon and Ozark Counties)

Willow Spring High School Graduates, 1895 - 1913 178

JACKSON COUNTY
(Founded 1826 from Lafayette County)

Kansas City Police Officers Killed in the line of duty,
1881 - 1949 120

MACON COUNTY
(Founded 1837 from Randolph County)

Ballinger Cemetery 137

MARIES COUNTY
(Founded 1855 from Osage and Pulaski Counties)

Wm. S. Thompson's Will, filed Jan. 24, 1892 194

PLATTE COUNTY
(Founded 1838 from Platte Purchase)

Original Land Record 79

RANDOPLH COUNTY
(Founded 1829 from Chariton County)

Pensioners on the Roll of Jan. 1, 1883 173

REYNOLDS COUNTY
(Founded 1845 from Shannon County)

Marriage Records, 1870 - 1891 11

ST. LOUIS COUNTY
(Founded 1812, Original District)

Coleman Cemetery, Babler State Park 53
Mississippi Valley Trust Company, Officers, 1920 141
St. Louis Women's Exchange Members, 1884 - 1886 150

TANEY COUNTY
(Founded 1837 from Greene County)

Wolf Cemetery 128

MISCELLANEOUS MISSOURIANA

"*Licking Valley Register,*" Covington, Kentucky
   Issues: Apr. 10, 1844, Nov. 23, 1844, Jun. 1, 1844,
      Jun. 14, 1844, May 3, 1845, Oct. 25, 1845 1
Missouri Graduates from West Point, NY Military
   Academy 1
Medal of Honor Recipents, Civil War 1
WPA Autobiographical Sketch of Rose Wilder Lane,
   Received Oct. 10, 1940 4
"*Weekly Kansas Chief,*" Issues: Jan. 7, 1892, Feb. 25, 1892,
   Mar. 17, 1892, Mar. 31, 1892, Apr. 21, 1892,
   Jun. 9, 1892, Jun. 30, 1892, Jul. 21, 1892, Nov. 3, 1892,
   Nov. 17, 1892, Dec. 15, 1892, Mar. 23, 1893,
   Apr. 13, 1893, Apr. 27, 1893, May 18, 1893,
   Jun. 15, 1893, Jun. 22, 1893 9
Missourians Listed on the Vietnam War Memorial,
   Surnames, A - C 153
Registered Coal Oil Inspectors, 1903 179
Emigrates from Europe designating Missouri as
   their destination. Ships: Wierra, May 31, 1887; City
   of Richmond, Aug. 19, 1887; Marsala, Sep. 22, 1887;
   Sorrento, Oct. 27, 1887; Waesland, Feb. 11, 1888;
   England, Dec. 23, 1888; The Queen, Mar. 15, 1888;
   Rhein, May 9, 1888; America, May 20, 1888; The
   Queen, Jun. 6, 1888; Donau, Jun. 13, 1888 143

"Licking Valley Register," Covington, Kentucky, April 10, 1844
Married on the 6th inst. By Rev. Asa Drury, Nathaniel Price, Jr., of St. Louis, MO and Miss Jane E. Randall, of KY.

"Licking Valley Register," Covington, Kentucky, November 23, 1844
Married at St. Louis, MO on the 25th ult., Joseph Corlay, of St. Louis to Miss Donna Maria del Refugio Antonia Mucia Isodora Johanna Bernarda de Jesu Solares Covian, of New Mexico.

"Licking Valley Register," Covington, Kentucky, Jun. 1, 1844
Married on Thursday morning, 30th ult. By Rev. A. Drury, Alfred W. Hughey of Hannibal, MO and Miss Margaret Martin of this city.

"Licking Valley Register," Covington, Kentucky, May 3, 1845.
On Thursday evening, April 17th, at the residence of Major E. E. Dobyns, of St. Louis, MO, Peter Burns, merchant of that city, married Miss Mary T. Burgess. Rev. Ebenezer Rogers performed the marriage ceremony. The bride is the daughter of John D. Burgess of Mason Co., KY

"Licking Valley Register," Covington, Kentucky, June 14,1845.
Died in St. Louis, MO at the home of F. T. Woolfolk on the 1st inst. William E. Price, age eight months and twenty-one days. He was only ill two days. He was the son of Wm. M. and Mary E. Price.

"Licking Valley Register," Covington, Kentucky, Oct. 25, 1845.
In Palmyra, MO on Sunday morning, September 14th, Mrs. Pocahontas Sloan died after an illness of six days. She was the widow of the late Dr. S. C. Sloan.

Military Academy at West Point, NY, Graduates.
James P. Major: (BP) Missouri, (APT) Missouri, (CMTS) Brigadier-General, July 21, 1863, Commanding cavalry brigade in the District of Western Louisanna, Graduated 1856.
Charles Campbell: (BP) Missouri, (APT) Missouri, (CMTS) Captain of Artillary and Major First Missouri Infantry, Graduated May, 1861.

Medal of Honor Recipent, Civil War
Ayers, John G. K.: Rank and organization: Private, Company H, 8th Missouri Infantry, Place and date: At Vicksburg, MS., 22 May 1863. Entered service at. Pekin, Tazwell County, IL.; Birth: Washlinaw, MI. Date of issue: 31 August 1895. Citation: Gallantry in the charge of the "volunteer storming party."

Bickford, Matthew: Rank and organization: Corporal, Company G, 8th Missouri Infantry. Place and date: At Vicksburg, MS., 22 May 1863. Entered service at: Trivolia, Peoria County, Ill. Birth: Peoria County, IL. Date of issue: 31 August 1894. Citation: Gallantry in the charge of the "volunteer storming party."

Bieger, Charles: Rank and organization: Private, Company D, 4th Missouri Cavalry. Place and date: At Ivy Farm, MS., 22 February 1864. Entered service at: St. Louis, MO. Birth: Germany. Date of issue: 8 July 1897. Citation: Voluntarily risked his life by taking a horse, under heavy fire, beyond the line of battle for the rescue of his captain, whose horse had been killed in a charge and who was surrounded by the enemy's skirmishers.

Blodgett, Welis H.: Rank and organization: First Lieutenant, Company 37th IllinoisInfantry. Place and date: At Newtonia, MO., 30 September 1862. Entered service at: Chicago, Ill. Born: 29 January 1839, Downers Grove, Ill. Date of issue: 15 February 1894. Citation: With a single orderly, captured an armed picket of 8 men and marched them in prisoners.

Cunningham, James S.: Rank and organization: Private, Company D, 8th Missouri Infantry. Place and date: At Vicksburg, MS., 22 May 1863. Entered service at: Bloomington, McLean County, IL. Birth: Washington County, Pa. Date of issue: 30 July 1894. Citation: Gallantry in the charge of the "volunteer storming party."

Flynn, James E.: Rank and organization: Sergeant, Company G, 6th Missouri Infantry. Place and date: At Vicksburg, MS., 22 May 1863. Entered service at: St. Louis, Mo. Birth: Pittsfield, IL. Date of issue: 19 June 1894. Citation: Gallantry in the charge of the "volunteer storming party."

Follett, Joseph L.: Rank and organization: Sergeant, Company G, 1st Missouri Light Artillery. Place and date: At New Madrid, Mo., 3 March 862; at Stone River, Tenn., 31 December 1862. Entered service at: St. Louis, Mo. Birth: Newark, N.J. Date of issue: 19 September 1890. Citation: At New Madrid, Mo., remained on duty though severely wounded. While procuring ammunition from the supply train at Stone River, Tenn., was captured, but made his escape, secured the ammunition, and in less than an hour from the time of his capture had the batteries supplied.

Frizzell or Frazell, Henry F.: Rank and organization: Private, Company B, 6th Missouri Infantry. Place and date: At Vicksburg, Miss., 22 May 1863. Entered service at: Pilot Knob, Iron County, Mo. Birth: Madison County, Mo. Date of issue: 30 July 1894. Citation: Gallantry in the charge of the "volunteer storming party."

Grebe, M. R. William: Rank and organization: Captain, Company F, 4th

Missouri avalry. Place and date: At Jonesboro, Ga., 31 August 1864. Entered service at: St. Louis, Mo. Born: 4 August 1838, Germany. Date of issue: 24 February 1899. Citation: While acting as aide and carrying orders across a most dangerous part of the battlefield, being hindered by a Confederate advance, seized a rifle, took a place in the ranks and was conspicuous in repulsing the enemy.

Guerin, Fitz W.: Rank and organization: Private, Battery A, 1st Missouri Light Artillery. Place and date: At Grand Gulf, MS., 28 and 29 April 1863. Entered service at: St. Louis, MO. Birth: New York, N.Y. Date of issue: 10 March 1896. Citation: With two comrades voluntarily took position on board the steamer Cheeseman, in charge of all the guns and ammunition of the battery, and remained in charge of the same for a considerable time while the steamer was unmanageable and subjected to a heavy fire from the enemy.

Gwynne, Nathaniel: Rank and organization: Private, Company H, 13th Ohio Cavalry. Place and date: At Petersburg, Va., 30 July 1864. Entered service at: Fairmount, MO. Birth: Champaign County, Ohio. Date of issue. 27 January 1865. Citation: When about entering upon the charge, this soldier, then but 15 years old, was cautioned not to go in, as he had not been mustered. He indignantly protected and participated in the charge, his left arm being crushed by a shell and amputated soon afterward.

Hammel, Henry A.: Rank and organization: Sergeant, Battery A, 1st Missouri Light Artillery. Place and date: At Grand Gulf, MS, 28 and 29 April 1863. Entered service at: St. Louis, Mo. Birth: Germany. Date of issue: 10 March 1896. Citation: With two comrades voluntarily took position on board the steamer Cheeseman, in charge of all the guns and ammunition of the battery, and remained in charge of the same for considerable time while the steamer was unmanageable and subjected to a heavy fire from the enemy.

Hunt, Louis T.: Rank and organization: Private, Company H, 6th Missouri Infantry. Place and date: At Vicksburg, MS., 22 May 1863. Entered service at: Jefferson County, Mo. Birth: Montgomery County, IN. Date of issue: 12 July 1894. Citation: Gallantry in the charge of the "volunteer storming party."

Kirby, Dennis T.: Rank and organization: Major, 8th Missouri Infantry. Place and date: At Vicksburg, MS., 22 May 1863. Entered service at: St. Louis, Mo. Born: 14 September 1838, Niagara, County, NY. Date of issue: 31 January 1894. Citation: Seized the colors when the color bearer was killed and bore them himself in the assault.

Porter, Ambrose: Rank and organization: Commissary Sergeant, Company D, 12th Missouri Cavalry. Place and date: At Tallahatchie River, Miss., 7 August 1864. Entered service at: Rockport, Atchison County, MO. Birth:

Allegany County, MD. Date of issue: 24 August 1905. Citation: Was 1 of 4 volunteers who swam the river under a brisk fire of the enemy's sharpshooters and brought over a ferry boat by means of which the troops crossed and dislodged the enemy from a strong position.

Schofield, John M.: Rank and organization: Major, 1st Missouri Infantry. Place and date: At Wilson's Creek, MO., 10 August 1861. Entered service at: St. Louis, MO. Born: 29 September 1831, Gerry, NY. Date of issue: 2 July 1892. Citation: Was conspicuously gallant in leading a regiment in a successful charge against the enemy.

Stockman, George H.: Rank and organization. First Lieutenant, Company C, 6th Missouri Infantry. Place and date: At Vicksburg, MS., 22 May 1863. Entered service at: Chicago, IL. Birth. Germany. Date of issue: 9 July 1894. Citation: Gallantry in the charge of the "volunteer storming party."

Wherry, William M.: Rank and organization: First Lieutenant, Company D, 3d U.S. Reserve Missouri Infantry. Place and date: At Wilsons Creek, Mo., 10 August 1861. Entered service at: St. Louis, Mo. Born: 13 September 1836, St. Louis, Mo. Date of issue: 30 October 1895. Citation: Displayed conspicuous coolness and heroism in rallying troops that were recoiling under heavy fire.

Accession no. W7263: Date received; Oct. 10, 1940; Consignment No. 1; WPA. PROJECT; Writers' Unit; Form—3; Folklore Collection; Autobiographical sketch of Rose Wilder Lane; Place of origin: Missouri; Date: Missouri 1938-39

I was born in Dakota Territory, in a shanty, forty-nine years ago come next December. It doesn't seem possible. My father's people were English family; his ancestors came to America in 1630 and, farming progressively westward, reached Minnesota during my father's boyhood. Naturally, he took a homestead farther west. My mothers ancestors were Scotch and French; her father's cousin was John J. Ingalls, who, "lie a lonely crane, swore and swore and stalked the Kansas plain." She is Laura Ingalls Wilder, writer of books for children. Conditions had changed when I was born; there was no more free land. Of course, there never had been free land. It was a saying in the Dakotas that the Government bet a quarter section against fifteen dollars and five years' hard work that the land would starve a man out in less than five years. My father won the bet. It took seven successive years of complete crop failure, with work, weather and sickness that wrecked his health permanently, and interest rates of 36 per cent on money borrowed to buy food, to dislodge us from that land. I was then seven years old. We reached the Missouri at Yankton, in a string of other covered wagons. The ferryman took them one by one, across the wide yellow river. I sat between my parents in the wagon on the river bank, anxiously hoping to get across before dark. Suddenly the rear end of the wagon jumped into the air and came down with a terrific crash. My mother seized the lines; my father leaped over the wheel and in desperate haste tied the wagon to the ground, with ropes to picket pins deeply driven in. The loaded wagon kept lifting off the ground, straining at the ropes; they creaked and stretched, but held. They kept wagon and horses from being blown into the river. Looking around the edge of the wagon covers I saw the whole earth behind us billowing to the sky. There was something savage and terrifying in the howling yellow swallowing the sky. The color came, I now suppose, from the sunset.

"Well, that's our last sight of Dakota," my mother said. "We're getting out with a team and wagon; that's more than a lot can say," my father answered cheerfully.

This was during the panic of '93. The whole Middle West was shaken loose and moving. We joined long wagon trains moving south; we met hundreds of wagons going north; the roads east and west were crawling lines of families traveling under canvas, looking for work, for another foothold somewhere on the land. By the fires in the camps I heard talk about Coxey's army, 60,000 men, marching on Washington; Federal troops had been called out. The country was ruined, the whole world was ruined; nothing like this had ever happened before. There was no hope, but everyone felt the courage of despair. Next morning wagons went on to the north, from which we had been driven, and we went on toward the south, where those families had not been able to live. We were not starving. My mother had baked quantities of hardtack for the journey; we had salt meat and beans. My father tried to sell the new--and incredible--asbestos mats that would keep food from burning; no one had ten cents to pay for one, but often he traded for eggs or milk. In Nebraska we found an astoundingly prosperous colony of Russians; we could not talk to them. The Russian women gave us -- outright gave us -- milk and cream and butter from the abundance of their dairies, and a pan of biscuits. My mouth watered at the sight. And because my mother could not talk to them, and so could not politely refuse these gifts, we had to take them and she to give in exchange some cherished trinket of hers. She had to, because it would have been like taking charity not to make some return. That night we had buttered biscuits. These Russians had brought from Russia a new kind of wheat -- winter wheat, the foundation of future prosperity from the Dakotas to Texas.

Three months after we had ferried across the Missouri, we reached the Ozark hills. It was strange not to hear the wind any more. My parents had great good fortune; with their last hoarded dollar, they were able to buy a piece of poor ridge land, uncleared, with a log cabin and a heavy mortgage on it. My father was an invalid, my mother was a girl in her twenties, I was seven years old. Good fortune continued. We had hardly moved in to the cabin, when a stranger came pleading for work. His wife and children camped by the road, were starving. We still had a piece of salt pork. The terrible question was, "Dare we risk any of it?" My father did; he offered half of it for a day's work. The stranger was overjoyed. Together they worked from dawn to sunset, putting down trees, sawing and splitting the wood, piling into the wagon all it would hole. Next day my father drove to town with the wood. It was dark before we heard the wagon coming back. I ran to meet it. it was empty. My father had sold that wood for fifty cents in cash. Delirious, I rushed into the house shouting the news. Fifty cents! My mother cried for joy.

That was the turning point. We lived all winter and kept the camper's family alive till he got a job; he was a hard worker. He and my father cleared land, sold wood, built a log barn. When he moved on, my mother took his place at the cross-cut saw. Next spring a crop was planted; I helped put in the corn, and on the hills I picked green huckleberries to make a pie. I picked ripe huckleberries, walked a mile and a half to town, and sold them forten cents a gallon. Blackberries too. Once I chased a rabbit into a hollow log and barricaded it there with rocks; we had rabbit stew. We were prospering and cheerful The second summer, my father bought a cow. Then we had milk, and I helped churn; my mother's good butter sold for ten cents a pound. We were paying ? per cent interest on the mortgage and a yearly bonus for renewal. That was forty years ago. Rocky Ridge Farm is now 200 acres, in meadow, pasture and field; there are wood lots, but otherwise the land is cleared, and it is clear. The three houses on it have central heating, modern plumbing, electric ranges and refrigerators, garages for three cars. This submarginal farm, in a largely submarginal but comfortably prosperous county, helps support some seven hundred families on relief. They live in miserably small houses and many lack bedsteads on which to put the mattresses, sheets and bedding issued to them. The men on work relief get only twenty cents an hour, only sixteen hours a week. No one bothers now to pick wild berries; it horrifies anybody to think of a child's working three or four hours for ten cents. No farmer's wife sells butter; trucks for the cream cans, and butterfat brings twenty-six cents. Forty years ago I lived through a world-wide depression; once more I am living through a depression popularly believed to be the worst in history because it is world-wide; this is the ultimate disaster, the depression to end all depressions. On every side I hear that conditions have changed, and that is true. They have.

Meanwhile I have done several things. I have been office clerk, telegrapher, newspaper reporter, feature writer, advertising writer, farmland salesman. I have seen all the United States and something of Canada and the Caribbean; all of Europe except Spain; Turkey, Egypt,

Palestine, Syria, Iraq as far east as Bagdad, Georgia, Armenia, Azerbaijan. California, the Ozarks and the Balkans are my home towns.

Politically, I cast my first vote -- on a sample ballot -- for Cleveland, at the age of three. I was an ardent if uncomprehending Populist; I saw America ruined forever when the soulless corporations in 1896, defeated Bryan and Free Silver. I was a Christian Socialist with Debs, and distributed untold numbers of the Appeal to Reason. From 1914 to 1920 -- when I first went to Europe -- I was a pacifist; innocently, if criminally, I thought war stupid, cruel, wasteful and unnecessary. I voted for Wilson because he kept us out of it. In 1917 I became convinced, though not practicing communist. In Russia, for some reason, I wasn't and I said so, but my understanding of Bolsdevism? made everything pleasant when the Cheka arrested me a few times.

I am now a fundementalist American; give me time and I will tell you why individualism, laissez faire and the slightly restrained anarchy of capitalism offer the best opportunities for the development of the human spirit. Also I will tell you why the relative freedom of human spirit is better -- and more productive, even in material ways -- than the communist, Fascist, or any other rigidity organized for material ends.

Personally, I'm a plump, Middle-Western, Middle-class, middle-aged woman, with white hair and simple tastes. I like buttered popcorn, salted peanuts, bread-and-milk. I am, however, a marvelous cook of foods for others to eat. I like to see people eat my cooking. I love mountains, the sea -- all of the seas except the Atlantic, a rather dull ocean -- and Tschaikovsky and Epstein and the Italian primatives. I like Arabic architecture and the Moslem way of life. I am mad about Kansas skies, Cedar Rapids by night, Iowa City any time, Miami Beach, San Francisco, and all American boys about fifteen years old playing basketball. At the moment I don't think of anything I heartily dislike, but I can't understand sport pages, nor what makes radio work, nor why people like to look at people who write fiction.

"But aren't you frightfully disappointed?" I asked a stranger who was recently looking at me.

"Oh, no," she said. "No, indeed. We value people for what they do, not for what they look like."

No. 7517; Date Received: Oct. 10, 1940; Consignment No. 1; Shipped from
Wash. Office; WPA L. C. PROJECT; Writers' Unit; Folklore Collection; I have talked with Grandma Handy; Place of origin: Clay County, Mo. Date 1938 or 39
Mrs. Pansy Powell, Gower, Missouri.
Dear Mrs. Powell:

I have talked with Grandma Handy, and have gathered a little more information, some of which you may be able to use. I will repeat it in her words.

"In our family, the Dennis Parsons family, there were five negro slaves, four men and one negro cook. We had owned them for a long time. "The men all had wives at other homes in the vicinity and on Saturday nights they spruced up and visited their wives and some of them had children also.

"We gave out negroes a holiday of one week, from Christmas Day to New Years. Sometimes they used that time making brooms to sell. We paid our negro woman $1.00 to get two meals a day during the holiday, and the rest of the time was her own. It was our custom for everyone to do a large amount of work on New Years' Day "Slaves in Clinton County very often ran away, but they didn't go far. The pad-a-rollers, men hired to hunt them in the woods at nigh soon brought them back. We had one man to run off. I was much frightened when they tied him up to lash him, but they never whipped him and he never ran away again.

"We sold one young negro boy, I remember, to George Huffaker for $700. And another, our cook's boy, a good boy, died of heart trouble and we buried him in our private cemetery.

"During the war we sent the slaves to the south, and then the Emancipation Proclamation gave them their freedom and they all came back. But they were not much account to work any more. Our cook settled in an old house one fourth mile away and died there.

"Just after the Civil War flour was $5.00 for twenty-five pounds and we ate cornbread mostly. We bought a cook stove--One of the first in the community. We set in the fireplace and let the pipe extend up through the chimney. We used it only in the summer and set it back in the winter to make it last longer.

"There were not Indians in Clinton County. In fact, I never in my life saw but one Indian. I was six years old and saw him traveling, riding a little pony, on the Lathrop road. "I was at church one spring morning, and when we came outside, the air was full of grasshoppers, in brown herds. They ate everything bare as they went, the grass, gardens, leaves from the trees, and all the young corn. They finally passed on but everything had to be planted over."

I might add that Grandma Handy will be 87 years old next Tuesday and I am sending a little story of her life to the Star which I hope they can use-- you can watch for it.

Hoping this little bit more way help you some.
Sincerely,
Dela Handy.

Weekly Kansas Chief

January 7, 1892.

At Knob Noster, Missouri, Mrs. A. H. Miller, resident of Horton, received that her two sisters, Mrs. Beatty and Mrs. Shafer, and her brother-in-law, Mr. Beatty died of pneumonia Her father, age 96 or 97 died of old age following her Mother who died a few years earlier.

February 25, 1892.

Robert O'Brien from Boonville, Missouri is visiting his sister, Mrs. Van Buskirk.

March 17, 1892

On Thursday, March 10th, Judge J. A. Daugherty died at his residence in Union Star, Andrew County, Missouri. He was one of the early pioneer settlers at Petersburg, Marion Township. It is believed that he is the father of Mrs. William Rappelye.

George W. Lindley died last Friday at his farm on Roy's Creek. George came to Roy's Creek with Ed and Robert Buchanan from Penssylvania. Mr. Lindley stopped in Orgeon, Missouri, where he wed a sister of the Springer family and of Mrs. John Beeler.

March 31, 1892

Milton E. Bryant, born Bryant's Station, Kentucky, died at his residence near Wathena Sunday last. He was 86. He came to Missouri as a young man of 21 and lived near Lexington or Boonville. In 1828 he accompanied a trading expedition to Santa Fe. He later went to St. Joseph and in 1854 he came over and helped to found the town of Wathena.

April 21, 1892

B. O. Cowen sold some cattle in Holt County, Missouri.

Henry T. Alkire, Oregon, Missouri, was nominated for Missouri Secretary of State. He was raised in the Missouri Bottoms opposite of White Cloud on Elijah Alkire's, his Father, farm.

June 9, 1892

Mrs. William Quick and her son, of Stewartsville, Missouri, visited Mrs. Henderson of Troy.

William Hambleton will be teaching at Trenton, Missouri.

June 30, 1892

Mrs. R. Brown was visited by her daughter, Mrs. Elmer Schock, of Parnell, Missouri.

July 21, 1892

Nellie Carter died on Tuesday. She is one of the oldest colored residents of Troy. She came over after the outbreak of the Civil War.

November 3, 1892

Frederick S. Rostock, Oregon, Missouri, died there on October 21st. He was 83.

November 17, 1892
Mrs. Derina Collins died in Washington, Kansas on November 22th. She was born in Jackson County, Tennessee on June 16, 1817. In 1844 she married Lawson Collins and moved to Mt. Vernon, Missouri in 1855. In 1863 the couple decided to move to Doniphan. After her husband's death, Mrs. Collins moved to Washington, Kansas. She was buried in Fanning cemetery.

December 15, 1892
Rev. Joshua Bowman, age 86 and former resident of Oregon, Missouri, died at Pueblo, Colorado on November 30th. He was the father of the printers, Charley and Cy Bowman.

March 23, 1893
William Mailler on March 17th died at St. Joseph at age 83. He arrived here about 1856 where he lived until after the end of the Civil War. After the war he moved back to St. Joseph. He is the father of Robert C. and John H. Mailler.

Miss Beeler was visited by her sister, Mrs. Kelly, the wife of Dr. Kelly of Oregon, Missouri.

Mrs. Bertha Burrett, 27, died on March 16th at Campbell, Missouri. She was the daughter of Fred Hahn of Doniphan. Mrs. Burret was buries at Doniphan cemetery. The funeral was attended by Lou Hahan, brother, and Mr. and Mrs. Ed Lyons, sister and brother-in-law.

April 13, 1893
Miss Cynthia Beeler, Oregeon, Missouri attended graduation excerises last night.

April 27, 1893
Anton Burnevick, former resident of Troy, was cowhided Friday evening last in St. Joseph by his brother, Henry's wife. The dispute was over the estate of Mr. Burnevick's father.

Thomas C. Monson, former resident of Troy, is the school principal of Warsaw, Missouri.

May 18, 1893
Friday last Herman Ferking died in St. Joseph. He was the son of Mrs. Charles Ferking, former citizen of Troy.

June 15, 1893
Fred Arygle, a St. Joseph gambler, died last week in Maitland, Missouri.

June 22, 1893
Notice was received from Helena, Montana that William Mann died on June 16th. He was a citizen of Troy and was born in Buchanan County. After his Father died, his mother wed Isaac Fleek. Early in the Civil war, he traded his land in Missouri to Cary B. Whitehead for a farm in Peter's Creek.

John Morgan, Independence, Missouri, was in town visiting. His sister is the wife of Sam Dittemore and his wife is the sister of Pryor Plank.

Reynolds County, Missouri Marriage Records,1870-1891

Daniel Lester and Mrs. Martha Jane Leadbetter, (MD) 10 March 1870, (MG) A .A. Rudy, J. P.

James H. George and Elizabeth Stigall, (MD) 11 April 1874, (MG) A. A. Rudy, J. P.

William Aron Hill and Nancy Isabel Onsbee, (MD) 9 May 1872, (MG) J. C. Gross, J. P.

Lanis Willy and Julett Butcher, (MD) 3 March 1873, (MG) J. C. Gross, J.P.

William Bay and (?) Duncan, (MD) 1 September 1872, (MG) J. C. Gross, J. P.

William J. Ferrewld and Manda Hannings, (MD) 7 April 1872, (MG) William H. Morgan, Minister

William O. Camden and Mary Parker, (MD) 26 January 1873, (MG) William H. Morgan, Minister

William A. Pogue and Maria A. Slade, (MD) 10 March 1872, (MG) Isaac Lane, Minister

J. W. Price and Latisha C. Harris, (MD) 24 December 1882, (MG) Isaac Lane, Minister

J. F. Rayfield and Laura B. Laws, (MD) November 1882, (MG) Isaac Lane, Minister

Henry Baker and M. E. J. Reed, (MD) 18 November 1886, (MG) Isaac Lane, Minister.

Sutton W. Willhelmes and Mary H. Chitwood, (MD) 10 February 1887, (MG) Isaac Lane, Minister

J. W. Vanarsdall and Milly J. Skiles, (MD) 27 October 1887, (MG) Isaac Lane, Minister

Eddie Fox and Anne J. Harris, (MD) 15 November 1887, (MG) Isaac Lane, Minister

Reed and Julia E. Copeland, (MD) 17 November 1887, (MG) Isaac Lane, Minister

J. F. Taylor of St. Francois Co and Mattie Hunt, (MD) 11 December 1887, (MG) Isaac Lane, Minister

William Barnes and Lura Copeland, (MD) 20 September 1888, (MG) Isaac Lane, Minister

Wiley Pogue and Parzilla Chitwood, (MD) 12 September 1888, (MG) Isaac Lane, Minister

James W. Shrum and Isabel Strickland, (CMTS), both of Iron Co., (MD) 2 October1872, (MG) Robert A. Rich, Minister

E.J. Gasten and Louisa Shrum, (MD) 2 October 1872, (MG) Robert A.

Rich, Minister

John Fitzgerald and Elisa Shrum, (MD) 1 September 1872, (MG) Robert A. Rich, Minister

Henry James (?) and Nancy Sullivan, (MD) 13 May 1873, (MG) Robert A. Rich, Minister

Jasper N. Shrum and Amelia McKinnis, (MD) 21 June 1873, (MG) Robert A. Rich, Minister

Charles Vleoxey and Mercy L. Wilson, (MD) 26 October 1873, (MG) Robert A. Rich, Minister

Peter Rapp and Mary Weever, (MD) 5 March 1876, (MG) Robert A. Rich, Minister

William Alexander Rutledge and Lucy Adkins, (MD) 15 February 1877, (MG) Robert A. Rich, Minister

Monroe Wilson and Lavida Richmond, (MD) 1 March 1877, (MG) Robert A. Rich, Minister

Henry M. Light and Mary E. Hasty, (MD) 26 November 1884, (MG) Robert A. Rich, Minister

John J. Williams and Sarah Johnston, (MD) 27 February 1890, (MG) Robert A. Rich, Minister

W. Wilson and Laura O'Brien, (MD) 29 October 1890, (MG) Robert A. Rich, Minister

R.M. Gumut and Betsy Taylor, (MD) 13 July 1872, (MG) James C. Asher, Minister

James F. Rayfield and Lucy A. Goggin, (MD) 5 December 1872, (MG) James C. Asher, Minister

Elisha W. Allen and K. Judrier Black, (MD) 16 April 1872, (MG) James C. Asher, Minister

Foreman F. Gallaher and Nancy C. Goggin, (MD) 30 May 1872, (MG) James C. Asher, Minister

Alexander Robinson and Josephine Sloan, (MD) 5 November 1872, (MG) James C. Asher, Minister

Joseph Black and Sarah J. Smith, (MD) 26 February 1874, (MG) James C. Asher, Minister

Thomas James and Rebecca Worley, (MD) 19 November 1873, (MG) James C. Asher, Minister

John H. Trolinger and Tyldiann Anderson, (MD) 13 September 1875, (MG) James C.Asher, Minister

Boston Miers and Elutishey C. Dunn, (MD) 10 June 1876, (MG) James C. Asher, Minister

Wesley Gunnett and Elsie Brown, (MD) 20 March 1877, (MG) James C. Asher, Minister

William Barton and Polly Montgomery, (MD) 29 March 1877, (MG) James C. Asher, Minister

Albert Smith and Armilda Barton, (MD) 3 September 1887, (MG) James C. Asher, Minister

William Moore and Mandy Lawson, (MD) 27 March 1879, (MG) James C. Asher, Minister

John Miller and Elizabeth Summers, (MD) 10 December 1879, (MG) James C. Asher, Minister

Joseph Lawson and Margaret Duglas, (MD) 1 July 1880, (MG) James C. Asher, Minister

Jeff Rains and Adaline Bone, (MD) 20 November 1881, (MG) James C. Asher, Minister, (PM) Marriage occured at the Rain's home.

Francis Marion Strickland and Sarah Emaline Hasty, (MD) 18 December 1881, (MG) James C. Asher, Minister, (PM) Married at the Union Church

William Riley Black and Jane Foster, (MD) 11 January 1883, (MG) James C. Asher, Minister

Jeff Campbell, of Shannon Co., and Deliala Melvina Clements, (MD) 11 December 1882, (MG) James C. Asher, Minister

Kinsy Camden, of Dent Co., and Minnie White, (MD) 13 November 1884, (MG) JamesC. Asher, Minister, (PM) Married at the brides home

Taylor Black, of Shannon Co., and Sarah Camden, (MD) 12 October 1872, (MG) James Bowen, Minister

George W. Conley and Josephine Bounds, of Shannon Co., (MD) 19 March 1883, (MG) James Bowen, Minister

Robert Mills and Angeline Johnson, (MD) 22 August 1872, (MG) William A. Pogue, Minister

Matthew G. Dinkens and Mary Rutter, (MD) 8 July 1874, (MG) William A. Pogue, Minister

John L. Miller and Sarah P. Coil, (MD) 6 September 1883, (MG) William A. Pogue, Minister

Peter Wright and Lydia M. Miller, (MD) 28 February 1884, (MG) William A. Pogue, Minister

James Cook and Martha Boyd, (MD) 4 April 1884, (MG) William A. Pogue, Minister

James Miller and Mary Barnes, (MD) 21 December 1884, (MG) William A. Pogue, Minister

Samuel Vinson and Ella Dicas, (MD) 2 August 1885, (MG) William A. Pogue, Minister, (PM) Married at the residence of Mr. Pogue

George N. Cook, of Iron Co., and Mrs. Sarah Wilson, (MD) 6 August 1885, (MG) William A. Pogue, Minister

W. P. Brown and Lizzie Faulkenberry, (MD) 18 November 1886, (MG) William A. Pogue, Minister

William T. Santhuff and Dorothy Warner, (MD) 16 April 1890, (MG) William A. Pogue, Minister

Jonathan L. Baker and Elizabeth Carter, (MD) 27 February 1873, (MG) B .S. McNail, Minister

John Parker Cain and Joramiah Manny Carty, (MD) 26 September 1873, (MG) B. S. McNail, Minister

Thomas D. Shy and Margret Carty, (MD) 23 April 1874, (MG) B. S. McNail, Minister

William H. Shy and Nancy Annis January, (MD) 16 July 1875, (MG) B. S. McNail, Minister

George W. Fedder and Amanda J. Rayfield, (MD) 26 October 1876, (MG) B. S. McNail, Minister

H. Hodges, of Iron Co., and Sidia Catharine Gallaher, (MD) 17 December 1862, (MG) B. S. McNail, Minister

Giles G. Henderson, of Washington Co., and Emma A. January, (MD) 15 October 1878, (MG) B.S. McNail, Minister

Maes M. Pickens and Francis Jane Farris, (MD) 3 July 1879, (MG) B. S. McNail, Minister

John S. Ward and Nancy Talbert, (MD) 5 May 1879, (MG) B.S. McNail, Minister

Samuel A. Imboden, of Iron Co., and Elizabeth Irvin, (MD) 1 February 1881, (MG) B. S. McNail, Minister

Joseph McGlothlin and Celeste I. Lowry, (MD) 25 October 1872, (MG) Lewis Orrick, Minister

Joel Cora, of Iron Co., and Jane Sutton, (MD) 27 June 1875, (MG) Lewis Orrick, Minister

James C. Asher and Mary Jane Barton, (MD) 10 January 1876, (MG) Lewis Orrick, Minister

Brown George Cook and Mary McMahan, of Iron Co., (MD) 20 February 1876, (MG) Lewis Orrick, Minister

Thomas Elliot and Elizabeth Marloe, (MD) 30 May 1876, (MG) Lewis Orrick, Minister

Henry Van Down and Nancy E. Sherall, (MD) 17 September 1876, (MG) Lewis Orrick, Minister

James Marlow and Elizabeth Asher, (MD) 11 April 1878, (MG) Lewis Orrick, Minister

Marion Ledbetter and Mary E. Williams, (MD) 13 October 1878, (MG) Lewis Orrick, Minister

Jefferson Raines, of Iron Co., and Permina Sherrelle, (MD) 3 April 1879, (MG) Lewis Orrick, Minister

S. E. Miner and Nancy J. Williams, (MD) 12 March 1879, (MG) Lewis Orrick, Minister

Thomas Williams and Rebecca Edmons, (MD) 6 November 1879, (MG) Lewis Orrick, Minister

Moses Edmonds and L. B. Sherill, (MD) 20 July 1890, (MG) Lewis

Orrick, Minister

James Hiram Chronister and Charity Chitwood, (MD) 11 February 1873, (MG) Caswell Warren, Minister

Louis C. Hart and Cary Ann Page, both of Shannon Co., (MD) 9 August 1874, (MG) Caswell Warren, Minister

George Dillard and Adline Conway, (MD) 9 July 1874, (MG) Caswell Warren, Minister

William Riley Counts and Eliza Jane Nash of Shannon Co., (MD) 8 November 1874, (MG) Caswell Warren, Minister

Michael Cavanagh and Nancy Jane Sargent, (MD) 21 November 1874, (MG) Caswell Warren, Minister

Lewis Williams and Martha Jane Goforth, (MD) 4 December 1875, (MG) Caswell Warren, Minister

Alfred Nickles Tripp and Elizabeth Cox, (MD) 16 September 1875, (MG) Caswell Warren, Minister

Thomas C. Edmonds and Josephine C. Williams, (MD) 26 December 1875, (MG) Caswell Warren, Minister

Martin V. Wadkins and Sarah R. Hardcastle, (MD) 10 July 1876, (MG) Caswell Warren, Minister

Aaron Chitwood and Sarah Adeline Conway, (MD) 10 May 1877, (MG) Caswell Warren, Minister

Person Smith and Rebecah J. Swiers, (MD) 27 September 1877, (MG) Caswell Warren, Minister

John R. Smith and Martha Wesley, (MD) 12 January 1878, (MG) Caswell Warren, Minister

Joshua H. Randolph and Anna Mooney, (MD) 20 January 1879, (MG) Caswell Warren, Minister

George W. Randolph and Harriet Mooney, (MD) 14 March 1879, (MG) Caswell Warren, Minister

Ephram Dillard and Arminda J. Randolph, (MD) 18 March 1880, (MG) Caswell Warren, Minister

George W. Sullivan and W. Elizabeth Davis, (MD) 23 February 1882, (MG) Caswell Warren, Minister (PM) Married at the Davis home.

William R. Gober and Sarah E. Wadkins, (MD) 27 June 1882, (MG) Caswell Warren, Minister

John Lawson and Nancy Hardcastle, (MD) 25 December 1882, (MG) Caswell Warren, Minister

W. D. Tucker and Sintha Johnston, (MD) 26 July 1883, (MG) Caswell Warren, Minister

J. S. Swiers and Martha Jones, (MD) 4 October 1883, (MG) Caswell Warren, Minister

John T. Hicks and Martha J. Radford, (MD) 13 February 1884, (MG) Caswell Warren, Minister

James H. Sullivan and Nancy Anderson, (MD) September 1884, (MG) Caswell Warren, Minister, (PM) Married at the residence of J. W. Widger

C. C. Callahan and Mrs. Sarah A. Neill, (MD) 26 October 1884, (MG) Caswell Warren, Minister, (PM) Married at the ministers home

John Ellis Tripp and Ruth Sullivan, (MD) December 1884, (MG) Caswell Warren, Minister, (PM) Married at the brides home

Maes A. Radford and Mary E. Willis, (MD) 18 December 1884, (MG) Caswell Warren, Minister

William A. Crownover and Rebecca Dillard, (MD) 1 January 1885, (MG) Caswell Warren, Minister, (PM) Married at the residence of Allen Sutterfield

Henderson Chitwood, Jr. and Emma Arminda Edmonds, (MD) 24 September 1886, (MG) Caswell Warren, Minister

W. G. Hart and Sarah Jane Willis, (MD) 16 December 1886, (MG) Caswell Warren, Minister

James Tripp and Matilda Bruden, of Shannon Co., (MD) 15 January 1887, (MG) Caswell Warren, Minister

Albert Chitwood and Sarah E. McNail, (MD) July 1887, (MG) Caswell Warren, Minister

Andy Lawsen and Delaina Counts, (MD) 21 July 1887, (MG) Caswell Warren, Minister

William H. Lay and Lucinda B. Tripp, (MD) 29 September 1887, (MG) Caswell Warren, Minister

Thomas Beck and Rosa Mullins, (MD) 20 October 1887, (MG) Caswell Warren, Minister

Calvin G. Frye and Luzety Eviline Warren, (MD) 19 December 1887, (MG) CaswellWarren, Minister

John Bruden, of Shannon Co., and Martha M. Bush, (MD) 2 January 1890, (MG) Caswell Warren, Minister

Andrew W. Patterson and Caroline Swyers, (MD) 23 January 1890, (MG) Caswell Warren, Minister

G. (?) F. Rosa and Martha E. Randolph, (MD) 27 November 1890, (MG) Caswell Warren, Minister

W. C. Widger and Mary J. Tripp, (MD) 23 December 1890, (MG) Caswell Warren, Minister

George Gibbs, of Wayne Co., and Paulina Rion, (MD) 25 December 1890, (MG) Caswell Warren, Minister

Samuel F. Larue, of Wayne Co., and Bell Dora Keathley, (MD) 6 March 1887, (MG) Caswell Warren, Minister

George Derin and Martha Murry, (MD) 14 November 1872, (MG) John Crowley, Minister

John R. Mann and Sarah Seal, (MD) 16 January 1873, (MG) John

Crowley, Minister
(?) Dean and Catharan Johnston, (MD) 1 March 1873, (MG) John Crowley, Minister
William C. Webb and Sarah Ann Carter, (MD) 14 January 1875, (MG) John Crowley, Minister
Thomas Seal and Maelia C. Rayfield, (MD) 16 July 1874, (MG) John Crowley, Minister
A. Sweezy and Mira Farris, (MD) 14 April 1875, (MG) John Crowley, Minister
Green Webb and Emetier Farris, (MD) 29 December 1875, (MG) John Crowley, Minister
William O. Sutterfield and July A. Wallen, (MD) 9 February 1873, (MG) Samuel Black, Minister (PM) Married at the home Allen Sutterfield
Henry Asher and Leaner Asher, (MD) 3 May 1876, (MG) Samuel Black, Minister
Robert A. Jennings and Edith Asher, (MD) 28 May 1874, (MG) Samuel Black, Minister
Boston Ollis and Giney Jane Lauson, (MD) 30 June 1874, (MG) Samuel Black, Minister
Green Anderson and Easter Jane Johnson, (MD) 27 August 1874, (MG) Samuel Black, Minister
William Jo Walker and Elizabeth Jarvice, (MD) 13 August 1874, (MG) Samuel Black, Minister
William Johnson and Elizabeth Wigger, (MD) 23 July 1874, (MG) Samuel Black, Minister
Thomas Parker and Barbara Malisa Parks, (MD) 30 November 1875, (MG) Samuel Black, Minister
Rhode Barton and Missouri Jane Montgomery, (MD) 9 December 1875, (MG) Samuel Black, Minister
Henry F. Shaw and Lusinda Parker, (MD) 20 January 1876, (MG) Samuel Black, Minister
Thomas Tompson and Adeline Kee, (MD) 28 March 1876, (MG) Samuel Black, Minister
William Hodges and Susan Parker, (MD) December 1871, (MG) Samuel Black, Minister
John Francis Montgomery and Rebecca Barton, (MD) 29 March 1877, (MG) Samuel Black, Minister
Levi Tharp and Elizabeth Black, (MD) 6 December 1866 Samuel Black, Minister
George R. Barton and Fannie Conway, (MD) 4 September 1878, (MG) Samuel Black, Minister
Samuel E. Barton and Elizabeth J. Lewis, (MD) 8 August 1878, (MG) Samuel Black, Minister

Joseph Conley and Mahuldy Kiserier Tilley, (MD) 16 February 1880, (MG) Samuel Black, Minister

Samuel Holmes and Mary Ann Carty, (MD) 19 February 1880, (MG) Samuel Black, Minister

William Smith and Rosa Belle Carty, (MD) 19 February 1880, (MG) Samuel Black, Minister

Samuel E. Strickling and Clary E. Sutterfield, (MD) 19 August 1880, (MG) Samuel Black, Minister

William M. Gunnett and Jane Barton, (MD) 24 May 1880, (MG) Samuel Black, Minister

John E. Barton and Sarah Asher, (MD) 21 September 1880, (MG) Samuel Black, Minister

F. E. Webb and Elizabeth Bartlett, (MD) 14 January 1881, (MG) Samuel Black, Minister

Louis Copeland and Sarah Jane Homes, (MD) 5 October 1882, (MG) Samuel Black, Minister

Charles Shaw and Martha Livingston, (MD) 5 December 1882, (MG) Samuel Black, Minister

R. V. Sumpter, of Iron Co., and Mrs. Betty Baker, (MD) 12 April 1883, (MG) Samuel Black, Minister

Joseph Linson and Jane Miers, (MD) 30 August 1883, (MG) Samuel Black, Minister

John H. Strickland and Catharine G. Troutman, (MD) 13 December 1883, (MG) Samuel Black, Minister

John R. Wolf and Nancy E. Bowen, (MD) 19 November 1890, (MG) Samuel Black, Minister

John C. McMillin and Rebecca M. Kuthly (?), (MD) 16 January 1873, (MG) William H. Meyers, Minister

Daniel Mitchell and Letishey Jane Hackworth, (MD) 30 April 1874, (MG) William H. Meyers, Minister

Preston Hackworth and Elizabeth Colyoutt, (MD) 6 July 1873, (MG) William H. Meyers, Minister

Alexzander Nimrod Colyoutt and Mary Elizabeth Keethly, (MD) 23 April 1874, (MG) William H. Meyers, Minister

James K. P. Asberry and Ketty Ratliff, (MD) 4 January 1874, (MG) William H. Meyers, Minister

Levy Marrler and Elizabeth Barber, (MD) 14 March 1874, (MG) William H. Meyers, Minister

William H. Asberry and Margaret Jane Keethley, (MD) 9 July 1874, (MG) William H. Meyers, Minister

Richard Vickrey and Susan Lidy E. McMillin, (MD) 13 October 1874, (MG) William H.Meyers, Minister

Hugh Mulligan and Mary Ellen Grayham, (MD) November 1874, (MG)

(MG) William H. Meyers, Minister
Hugh Mulligan and Mary Ellen Grayham, (MD) November 1874, (MG) William H. Meyers, Minister
George J. Kemp and Mary Elizabeth Warmick, (MD) 20 June 1875, (MG) William H. Meyers, Minister
William C. Wadlow and July Maria Dunnagan, (MD) 9 December 1875, (MG) William H. Meyers, Minister
J. L. Barton and Margaret Montgomery, (MD) 18 March 1884, (MG) William H. Meyers, Minister
Robert Bell, of Dent Co., and Nancy E. Dennison, (MD) 28 March 1884, (MG) William H. Meyers, Minister
James W. Dunn and Mary A. Wer (?), (MD) 9 October 1884, (MG) William H. Meyers, Minister, (PM) Married at the residence of Boss Myers
John Larson (?) and Margaret Larson, (MD) 20 January 1885, (MG) William H. Meyers, Minister
John H. Werley and Martha L. Dunn, (MD) 6 August 1885, (MG), William H. Meyers, Minister, (PM) Married at the residence of W.W. Dune
R. Goggin and Lydia A. Dennis, (MD) 1 September 1885, (MG) William H. Meyers, Minister
Joel J. Barton and Susan Asher, (MD) 4 March 1886, (MG) William H. Meyers, Minister
John W. Cay and Melvina L. Bowen, (MD) 25 February 1886, (MG) William H. Meyers, Minister
James Cay and Rebecca E. Barton, (MD) 18 March 1886, (MG) William H. Meyers, Minister
Amos Ownesby and Rachael Mathis, (MD) 23 August 1886, (MG) William H. Meyers, Minister
George W. Barton and Lozzie Mason, (MD) 15 October 1886, (MG) William H. Meyers, Minister
General W. Radford and Vicy Barton, (MD) 10 February 1887, (MG) William H. Meyers, Minister
John T. Barton and Mary A. Camden, (MD) 27 October 1887, (MG) William H. Meyers, Minister
James H. Moore and Miley Jane Lawson, (MD) 13 August 1888, (MG) William H. Meyers, Minister
Wilson Caulley and Mary Foster, (MD) 21 November 1889, (MG) William H. Meyers, Minister
John H. Reynolds and Hattie Miner, (MD) 3 February 1890, (MG) William H. Meyers, Minister
Louis Conley and Matilda Fortner, (MD) 6 March 1890, (MG) William H. Meyers, Minister
Andrew Jackson Meser and Catharine Clemintine Cueasey, (MD) 18 July

Thomas Barnes, Minister
Frances M. Price and Mary Ann Casey, (MD) 20 May 1874, (MG) Thomas Barnes, Minister
William C. Lane and Sarah J. Crague, (MD) 21 May 1874, (MG) Thomas Barnes, Minister
James H. Lones and Margaret Snodgrass, (MD) 21 June 1874, (MG) Thomas Barnes, Minister
Charles C. Ford and Delana Baker, (MD) 16 August 1875, (MG) Thomas Barnes, Minister
Winifield Scott Stevenson and Dart Elizabeth Edmonds, (MD) 12 November 1876, (MG)Thomas Barnes, Minister
Samuel Copeland and Virginia Bowers, (MD) 26 November 1876, (MG) Thomas Barnes, Minister
James Piles and Elizabeth Copeland, (MD) 28 March 1878, (MG) Thomas Barnes, Minister
Carrel Frank Dinkens and Julia A. Dickson, (MD) 30 October 1879, (MG) Thomas Barnes, Minister
Addison Hood and Artenia Asberry, (MD) 16 December 1880, (MG) Thomas Barnes, Minister
Clinton Davis and Elizabeth Dill, (MD) 30 November 1880, (MG) Thomas Barnes, Minister
George Dallas Johnson and Mary J. Thornton, (MD) 13 December 1876, (MG) Thomas Barnes, Minister
John T. Copeland and Sarah E. Carpenter, (MD) 14 September 1881, (MG) Thomas Barnes, Minister
Dr. William A. Copeland and Mayme E. Moore, (MD) 27 August 1882, (MG) ThomasBarnes, Minister
J. M. Pogue and Sarah E. Thornton, (MD) 1 March 1883, (MG) Thomas Barnes, Minister
Anderson Webb and Lucy A. Chilton, (MD) 1 June 1884, (MG) Thomas Barnes, Minister
James H. Parks and Matilda Rayfield, (MD) 13 October 1873, (MG) J. R. Pratt, Minister
Benjamin Stewart and Emeline Miner, (MD) 15 June 1873, (MG) R. C. Williams, Minister
Isaiah Radford and Margaret M. Stiwert, (MD) 15 June 1873, (MG) R. C. Williams, Minister
Jessee Ellis Heeton and May E. Asher Ware, (MD) 24 April 1879, (MG) R. C. Williams, Minister
James Baker and Tennessee Smith, (MD) 3 April 1873, (MG) A. M. Robinson, Minister
George Baker of Shannon Co and Elizabeth Chitwood, (MD) 28 August 1873, (MG) A. M. Robinson, Minister

George Baker of Shannon Co and Elizabeth Chitwood, (MD) 28 August 1873, (MG) A. M. Robinson, Minister

William H. Patterson and Polly Piles, (MD) 28 June 1874, (MG) A. M. Robinson, Minister

David Cowin of Carter Co and Charity Baker, of Shannon Co., (MD) 5 March 1882, (MG) A. M. Robinson, Minister

Thomas Barnes and Sarah G. Snodgrass, (MD) 20 April 1873, (MG) John F. Cowan, Minister

F. M. Blankenship and Mary A. McDaniels, (MD) 23 December 1875, (MG) John F. Cowan, Minister

John Turner Jens and Catharine Trollinger, (MD) 29 August 1873, (MG) James H. Bowers, Minister

Samuel Johnson and Eliviney Mason, (MD) 4 November 1873, (MG) James H. Bowers, Minister

George Baxter and Jane Sargen, (MD) 22 May 1873, (MG) Morris M. Adams, Minister

James Reedman and America Gaskin, (MD) 5 March 1878, (MG) Morris M. Adams, Minister

Levi Dalton and Mary J. Bell, (MD) 31 August 1876, (MG) Morris M. Adams, Minister

A. D. Maxwell, of Dent Co. Mo. and Mary J. Davis, (MD) 21 May 1885, (MG) Morris M. Adams, Minister

James H. McLarney and Dorsie A. Smith, (MD) 19 January 1888, (MG) Morris M. Adams, Minister

James C. Lee and Sarah E. Sprow, (MD) 5 August 1888, (MG) Morris M. Adams, Minister

Green B. Napper, of Shannon Co., Mo, and Osa Botkin, (MD) 17 January 1890, (MG)Morris M. Adams, Minister

Philip A. Carty and Martha E. Fitts, (MD) 26 December 1890, (MG) Morris M. Adams, Minister

William H. Ellis and Nancy E. Murey, (MD) 8 September 1873, (MG) John W. Allen, Minister

Elizabeth A. Daniels and William C. Pennington, (MD) 23 February 1876, (MG) John W. Allen, Minister

John Copeland and Miranda Moore, (MD) 17 August 1876, (MG) John W. Allen, Minister

George Gallaher and Lettie Baxter, (MD) 17 February 1881, (MG) C. T. Fortune, Minister, (PM) Married at Green Goggins home

Charles Dagner and Mary Stabb, (MD) 9 September 1873, (MG) C. T. Fortune, Minister

John B. Goggin, of Iron Co. and Vianna May Hartman, (MD) 8 August 1883, (MG) C. T. Fortune, Minister

A. J. Miner and Emma Goforth, (MD) 5 April 1885, (MG) C. T. Fortune,

Minister
F. E. Stafford and Sarah Goggin, (MD) 20 August 1887, (MG) C. T. Fortune, Minister
Marvin M. Munger and Sarah E. Shy, (MD) 5 September 1887, (MG) C. T. Fortune, Minister
Charles T. Carty and Anna Kline, (MD) 19 September 1887, (MG) C. T. Fortune, Minister
T. J. Stevens and Sarah A. Carty, (MD) 10 November 1887, (MG) C. T. Fortune, Minister
James K. Bunyard and Florida McDanell, (MD) 4 March 1873, (MG) Isaac Copeland, Minister
Rev. Thomas H. Brooks and Obedience Flippo, (MD) January 1875, (MG) Isaac Copeland, Minister
Benjamin L. Tabor and Trisely Thornton, (MD) December 1875, (MG) Isaac Copeland, Minister
William Yates and Tennessee Sheets, (MD) 9 March 1876, (MG) Isaac Copeland, Minister
Isam Yates and Jane Sheets, (MD) 24 February 1878, (MG) Isaac Copeland, Minister
Elija W. Bruster and Margaret A. Barker, (MD) 28 January 1878, (MG) Isaac Copeland, Minister
William L. Mills and Malinda J. Allen, (MD) 19 October 1879, (MG) Isaac Copeland, Minister
Alonzo C. Carpenter and Martha A. Dearing, (MD) 9 November 1879, (MG) Isaac Copeland, Minister
John W. Croner and Sarah E. Hedrick, (MD) 5 April 1880, (MG) Isaac Copeland, Minister
John Reed and Martha J. Coleman, (MD) 17 November 1880, (MG) Isaac Copeland, Minister
James A. Stuart and Roda Bowere, (MD) 18 November 1880, (MG) Isaac Copeland, Minister
Jefferson Nicholas Scaggs and Marget Catharine Eads, (MD) 20 November 1873, (MG) G. W. Carpenter, J. P.
Gestz Lane and Leucean Piles, (MD) 24 September 1874, (MG) G. W. Carpenter, J. P.
Louis Fears and John (?) Francis Dunigan, (MD) 6 August 1874, (MG) G. W. Carpenter, J. P.
Jesse R. Harrison and Theodosia E. Mann, (MD) 8 December 1875, (MG) G. W. Carpenter, J. P.
Jessie Vinson and Mary Ann Dunnagan, (MD) 6 January 1876, (MG) G. W. Carpenter, J. P.
Sarah Jane Thorton and George W. Rayfield, (MD) 23 March 1876, (MG) G. W. Carpenter, J. P.

Francis Caroline Copeland and John Steen, (MD) 1 October 1877, (MG) G. W. Carpenter, J. P.

John Sanders Jordan and Manervy L. Farris, (MD) 24 February 1878, (MG) G. W. Carpenter, J. P.

George F. Pearson and Amanda A. Gowen, (MD) 10 March 1883, (MG) G. W. Carpenter, J. P.

J. J. S. Farris and Nettie S. Pile, (MD) 15 November 1883, (MG) G. W. Carpenter, J. P.

J. M. Pyrtle and R. Elizabeth Scaggs, (MD) 9 January 1884, (MG) G. W. Carpenter, J. P.

(?) F. Piles and Mrs. Mary A. Vinson, (MD) 2 March 1884, (MG) G. W. Carpenter, J. P.

H. B. Mills and Caroline Angel, (MD) 31 May 1885, (MG) G. W. Carpenter, J. P., (PM) Married at the residence of Almira Angel

Calvie Radford and Easter Albert, (MD) 27 March 1867, (MG) Joseph McGlothlin, Minister

John Seal and Francis E. Angel, (MD) 9 Oct. 1873, (MG) Samuel Beard, Minister

John Dill and Marthy Elizabeth O'Dell, (MD) 14 March 1875, (MG) Samuel Beard, Minister

Joel Lewis of Wayne Co. and Allie Winchell, (MD) 17 September 1875, (MG) Samuel Beard, Minister

John W. Hargroves and Margaret C. Mann, (MD) 21 December 1875, (MG) Samuel Beard, Minister

Franklin J. Smith and Mary J. Roberts 19 April 1876, (MG) Samuel Beard, Minister

T. M. McClung and Elisabeth Fitzgerald, (MD) 31 December 1876, (MG) Samuel Beard, Minister

George W. Camel and Jane Chitwood, (MD) 10 January 1878, (MG) Samuel Beard, Minister

D. B. Newton and Sariah Miller, (MD) 27 December 1877, (MG) Samuel Beard, Minister

William H. Hanger and Nancy Ann Green of Carter Co., (MD) 18 August 1878, (MG) Samuel Beard, Minister

Wesley Copeland and Sarah Ann Sexton, (MD) 19 December 1879, (MG) Samuel Beard, Minister

B. C. VanDyke and Mattie A. McGee, (MD) 17 October 1879, (MG) Samuel Beard, Minister

S. M. Burnham and Sarah Homey, (MD) 18 February 1880, (MG) Samuel Beard, Minister

S. H. Burnham and C. A. Chitwood, (MD) 3 January 1884, (MG) Samuel Beard, Minister

Thomas Grigg and Louisa Dunigin, (MD) 23 October 1887, (MG) Samuel

Beard, Minister

John Clark and Mary J. Lewis, (MD) 30 October 1873, (MG) Z. T. Cavender, Minister

James W. Brooks, of Dent Co and Nella M. Adams, (MD) 14 October 1888, (MG) Z. T. Cavender, Minister

Charles H. Copeland and Josephine Trammell, (MD) 25 December 1873, (MG) J. W. Myrick, Minister

William B. Hoskins, of Carter Co., and Rebeca J. Dunklin, (MD) 31 November 1873, (MG) J. C. O'Dell, Minister

A. R L. Medor of Wayne Co and Cicily Dixon of Reynolds Co., (MD) 17 September 1874, (MG) J. C. O'Dell, Minister

Alexander Sanders and Mary Hewette, (MD) 30 October 1875, (MG) J. C. O'Dell, Minister

Bennet Tilly and Margaret Hewette, (MD) 14 September 1875, (MG) J. C. O'Dell, Minister

Henry Hampton and Rhody Merrill, (MD) 6 January 1876, (MG) J. C. O'Dell, Minister

Lewis Vetile Smith and Margaret L. Hampton, (MD) 3 February 1876, (MG) J. C. O'Dell, Minister

John T. Mann and Permelia Hampton, (MD) 23 August 1876, (MG) J. C. O'Dell, Minister

Pinkney H. Helvy and Mary J. Merril, (MD) 4 January 1876, (MG) J. C. O'Dell, Minister

George McAlister and Lucy Margaret Seal, (MD) 1 December 1877, (MG) J. C. O'Dell, Minister

Absalom Roberts and Liza Carter, (MD) 11 January 1877, (MG) J. C. O'Dell, Minister

Henry C. Duncan and Meartha (Martha) L. Chilton, (MD) 25 January 1877, (MG) J. C. O'Dell, Minister

Jacob Mann and Elvina Carter, (MD) 1 March 1877, (MG) J. C. O'Dell, Minister

William Webb and Louisa Copeland, (MD) 11 October 1877, (MG) J. C. O'Dell, Minister

Isaac Chilton and Mary Carter, (MD) 16 January 1878, (MG) J. C. O'Dell, Minister

William Skiles and Liza E. Thornton, (MD) 27 March 1878, (MG) J. C. O'Dell, Minister

Jones B. Rutledge and Nancy C. Duncan, (MD) 4 July 1878, (MG) J. C. O'Dell, Minister

Ferman Hanger and Nancy J. Skile, (MD) 12 September 1878, (MG) J. C. O'Dell, Minister

Louis G. Scaggs and Ellen G. Hanger, (MD) 3 October 1878, (MG) J. C. O'Dell, Minister

Henderson Freeze and Mary Holland, (MD) 22 December 1878, (MG) J. C. O'Dell, Minister

James M. Harrison and Mary C. Carter, (MD) 20 July 1879, (MG) J. C. O'Dell, Minister

Joseph A. Bohnert and Sarah E. Carnahan, (MD) September 1879, (MG) J. C. O'Dell, Minister

James F. Skiles and Jane Elington, (MD) 28 September 1879, (MG) J. C. O'Dell, Minister

John West and Nancy Hanger, (MD) December 1879, (MG) J. C. O'Dell, Minister

Charles F.Carter and Mary A. Roberts, (MD) 18 December 1879, (MG) J. C. O'Dell, Minister

Clark Mann and Lucinda M. Wallis, (MD) 29 February 1880, (MG) J. C. O'Dell, Minister

Thomas W. Cole and Hester Ann Strong, (MD) 15 August 1880, (MG) J. C. O'Dell, Minister

William B. Cosgrove and Betty Ann Elington, (MD) 22 August 1880, (MG) J. C. O'Dell, Minister

Arnold Mann and Malissa Hampton, (MD) 6 October 1880, (MG) J. C. O'Dell, Minister

John W. Wadlow and Sallie Chitwood, (MD) 16 October 1880, (MG) J. C. O'Dell, Minister

Henry S. Stewart and Ann Carnahan, (MD) 16 October 1880, (MG) J. C. O'Dell, Minister

William A. Piles and Ida B. Cook of Carter Co.,, (MD) 20 March 1881, (MG) J. C. O'Dell, Minister, (PM) Married at J. C. O'Dells home

Daemon J. Taylor, of Wayne Co. and Liza Ann Holland, (MD) 24 March 1881, (MG) J. C. O'Dell, Minister

James I. Miller and Margaret J. Ward, (MD) 30 November 1881, (MG) J. C. O'Dell, Minister

Eli Lewis and China Chitwood, (MD) 9 August 1881, (MG) J. C. O'Dell, Minister

James Copeland and Mary Ann Carter, (MD) 22 September 1881, (MG) J. C. O'Dell, Minister

Charles Carter and Nancy E. Babb, (MD) 5 December 1881, (MG) J. C. O'Dell, Minister, (PM) Married at the bride's home.

Vetile Smith and Margarette S. Hampton, (MD) 24 January 1882, (MG) J. C. O'Dell, Minister

William Henry Carter and Dee Jones, (MD) 25 June 1882, (MG) J. C. O'Dell, Minister

Lysander Webb and Samantha S. Pile, (MD) 27 August 1882, (MG) J. C. O'Dell, Minister

Willis W. Smith and Emma Underhill, (MD) 19 August 1882, (MG) J. C.

O'Dell, Minister, (PM) Married at Mary Underhill's home.
Thomas H. Boston and Ida Lee Farris, (MD) 3 September 1882, (MG) J. C. O'Dell, Minister
H. (?) Dorton, of Craighead Co., Arkansas and Mrs. Edney Campbell, (MD) 5 April 1883, (MG) J. C. O'Dell, Minister
William Jake Hampton and Adeline Cowin, of Carter Co., Mo., (MD) 12 April 1883, (MG) J. C. O'Dell, Minister
W. T. Berry and Clementine Carter, (MD) 5 April 1883, (MG) J. C. O'Dell, Minister
Lee Webb and Fannie Dorris, (MD) 29 April 1883, (MG) J. C. O'Dell, Minister
William W. Dickson and Mary E. Reed, (MD) 26 April 1883, (MG) J. C. O'Dell, Minister, (PM) Married at the residence of John Carter
Daniel M. Smith and Sarah E. Boyer, (MD) 3 June 1883, (MG) J. C. O'Dell, Minister
James Spears and Ella L. Goodman, (MD) 15 June 1883, (MG) J. C. O'Dell, Minister
John L. Pratt and Louiza J. Botkins, (MD) 20 December 1880, (MG) J. C. O'Dell, Minister
James M. McAllister and Mary E. Duncan, (MD) 20 March 1884, (MG) J. C. O'Dell, Minister
George Dershan of Wayne Co and Rohesa Boston, (MD) September 1884, (MG) J. C. O'Dell, Minister
James W. Chilton and B. J. Vineyard, (MD) 14 December 1884, (MG) J. C. O'Dell, Minister, (PM) Married at the residence of James Vineyard
J. H. Haley and Mrs. Mary E. Brown, (MD) May 1885, (MG) J. C. O'Dell, Minister, (PM) Married at the residence of J. Baker
J. H. Stone and Lucy Powell, (MD) 28 June 1885, (MG) J. C. O'Dell, Minister
T. J. Shy and Leonara N. Parks, (MD) 6 August 1885, (MG) J. C. O'Dell, Minister
James Vineyard and Jane Chitwood, (MD) 27 September 1885, (MG) J. C. O'Dell, Minister
F. M. Copeland and Sarah J. Pratt, (MD) 13 May 1886, (MG) J. C. O'Dell, Minister
Robert Benson and Sophrona Sweazea, (MD) 25 July 1886, (MG) J. C. O'Dell, Minister
Harvey Huett and Kate Slusher (Stusher), (MD) 25 July 1886, (MG) J. C. O'Dell, Minister
G. McDonald and Laura B. Howell, (MD) 26 August 1886, (MG) J. C. O'Dell, Minister
M. M. Bingmam and Maria C. Morris, (MD) 4 September 1886, (MG) J. C. O'Dell, Minister

B. Parker and Mandie E. Hanger, (MD) 16 September 1886, (MG) J. C. O'Dell, Minister

James W. Mann and Mollie D. Hogan, (MD) 23 September 1886, (MG) J. C. O'Dell, Minister

S. P. Chitwood and Mary J. Angle, (MD) 8 May 1887, (MG) J. C. O'Dell, Minister

Richard Webb and F.L. Bowers, (MD) 13 November 1887, (MG) J. C. O'Dell, Minister

T. M. Angel and Nancy R. Freeman, (MD) 29 December 1887, (MG) J. C. O'Dell, Minister

Joseph Pevril and Martha J. Bearden, (MD) 25 December 1887, (MG) J. C. O'Dell, Minister

William H. Botkin and Cynthia E. Carter, (MD) 8 April 1888, (MG) J. C. O'Dell, Minister

P. N. Pile, of Jefferson Co., and Suda Rayfield, (MD) 5 April 1888, (MG) J. C. O'Dell, Minister

James Hines and Martha Allen, (MD) 23 September 1888, (MG) J. C. O'Dell, Minister

T. P. Conway and Ella Sagasture, (MD) 10 November 1889, (MG) J. C. O'Dell, Minister

William H. Johnson and M.C. Bowers, (MD) 15 December 1889, (MG) J. C. O'Dell, Minister

E. C. Haywood and Alma Copeland, (MD) 6 November 1890, (MG) J. C. O'Dell, Minister

Newton Redman and Mary Eveline Ives, (MD) 26 Oct. 1873, (MG) W. J. Ferrell, Minister

James Helton and Mary Ellen Parker, (MD) 11 November 1873, (MG) W. J. Ferrell, Minister

Thomas Jones and Juliann Denham, (MD) 23 November 1873, (MG) W. J. Ferrell, Minister

James Jones and Isabell Redmans, (MD) 17 December 1873, (MG) W. J. Ferrell, Minister

James Stricklan and Sarah Baxter, (MD) 15 January 1874, (MG) W. J. Ferrell, Minister

William Golden and Mary Ann Greeley, (MD) 13 February 1874, (MG) W. J. Ferrell, Minister

John Holland and Mary Ellen Swaford, (MD) 23 December 1875, (MG) W. J. Ferrell, Minister

John Carter and Josi Reed of Shannon, (MD) 11 January 1880, (MG) W. J. Ferrell, Minister

Gentry Sloan and Eudora Dill, (MD) 19 November 1874, (MG) N. G. Jacks, Minister

Richard Piles and Tennessee Wood, (MD) 9 October 1873, (MG) N. G.

Jacks, Minister

W. H. Wood and Amanda Dill, (MD) 14 January 1874, (MG) N. G. Jacks, Minister

James Walker and Emily Barnes, (MD) 4 June 1874, (MG) N. G. Jacks, Minister

Martin Burnham and Elizabeth Sloan, (MD) 4 February 1874, (MG) A. W. Robinson, Minister

William Denison and Susanah Bay, (MD) 3 April 1875, (MG) William J. Davis, J. P.

Robert Smith and Anna Levingston Booth, (MD) 19 January 1874, (MG) William J. Davis, J. P.

William R. Tucker and Catharine Goforth, (MD) 5 November 1874, (MG) William J. Davis, J. P.

William R. Harrison and Susannah Little, (MD) 5 November 1875, (MG) William J. Davis, J. P.

David C. Lowell and Sarah Price, (MD) 6 June 1875, (MG) William J. Davis, J. P.

Joseph Carter and Emmaline Johnston, (MD) 4 June 1874, Both colored, (MG) John Layn, J. P., (PM) Married at the residence of Richard Johnson

John Weible and Lourenz Parker, (MD) 18 January 1874, (MG) J. K. Hawkins, Minister

George Wells and Alis Jones, (MD) 4 August 1874, (MG) J. K. Hawkins, Minister

Franklin A. Buffington and Sarah F. Adams, (MD) 15 October 1874, (MG) J. K. Hawkins, Minister

William McDonald and Nancy Whitecotton, (MD) 12 November 1874, (MG) J. M. Rop or Rapp, Minister

James N. Bowles and Jane Parks, (MD) 27 August 1874, (MG) J. M. Rop or Rapp, Minister

William Colley and Mary Barton, (MD) 29 February 1874, (MG) J. M. Rop or Rapp, Minister

William Proffitt and Lucy Miller, (MD) 10 March 1871, (MG) J. M. Rop or Rapp, Minister

Samuel Strother and Julia McNail, (MD) 12 February 1872, (MG) J. M. Rop or Rapp, Minister

Edward Shirrill and Martha Allcorn, (MD) 13 November 1873, (MG) J. M. Rop or Rapp, Minister

George W. Parks and Mary E. Larkin, (MD) 10 December 1874, (MG) J. M. Rop or Rapp, Minister

(?) and Margaret Snodgrass, (MD) 10 November 1874, (MG) J. M. Rop or Rapp, Minister, (PM) Married at the residence of William Hills

John T. Thornton and Malinda E. Talley, (MD) 31 December 1874, (MG)

John Wallen, Minister
John G. Allen of Wayne Co and Matilda O'Dell, (MD) 22 November 1874, (MG) Austin Meador, Minister
James Samuel McEntrie and Pheba Price, (MD) 13 December 1874, (MG) A. W. Kee, J. P.
Thomas G. Goggin and Sarah C. Carty, (MD) 10 January 1878, (MG) A. W. Kee, J. P.
George W. Adams and Evaline Reed, (MD) 31 January 1878, (MG) A. W. Kee, J. P.
Robert Pyrtle and Lucinda Wadlow, (MD) 8 January 1878, (MG) A. W. Kee, J. P.
John W. Slade and Elizabeth Adkins, both of Lesterville, Mo, (MD) 10 January 1875, (MG) E. H. Brown, J. P.
Joseph P. McNail and Nancy Brooks, (MD) September 1875, (MG) E. H. Brown, J. P., (PM) Married at the residence of Wm. Goggins
Davis Stevens and Charlotte Miller, (MD) 15 February 1876, (MG) E. H. Brown, J. P.
J. A. Baker and Beatrice G. Parks, (MD) 15 June 1876, (MG) E. H. Brown, J. P.
Sydney Pyrtle and Jane Wadlow, (MD) 23 December 1876, (MG) E. H. Brown, J. P.
John Tedder and Mariah Elizabeth Rayfield, (MD) 28 December 1874, (MG) E. H. Brown, J. P.
William Z. Carter and Laura C. Dobbins, (MD) 3 August 1877, (MG) E. H. Brown, J. P.
Wiilliam Robinet and Nancy Ann Boyd, (MD) 4 September 1877, (MG) E. H. Brown, J. P.
Frederick Hunt and Mary Jane Stegall, (MD) 11 October 1877, (MG) E. H. Brown, J. P.
Jesse Chapman and Manervia Asberry, (MD) 15 October 1877, (MG) E. H. Brown, J. P.
John M. Sutterfield and Mary Elans Duggan, (MD) 21 March 1878, (MG) E. H. Brown, J. P.
Joseph Jackson and Emily Crownover, (MD) 25 April 1878, (MG) E. H. Brown, J. P.
Wesley Montgomery and Sarah D. Sutterfield, (MD) 6 June 1878, (MG) E. H. Brown, J. P.
Ninian Marten and Elisia Jane Sutterfield, (MD) 24 December 1874, (MG) Wm. S. Troutman, J. P.
Azariah R. Anderson and Mary Tellitha Sutterfield, (MD) 25 February 1875, (MG) Wm. S. Troutman, J. P.
John Reace and Walean D. Smith, (MD) 12 August 1875, (MG) Wm. S. Troutman, J. P.

John Bates, of Crawford Co., and Amelia Gant, (MD) 20 December 1876, (MG) Wm. S. Troutman, J. P.

Albert Dyre and Margaret Farrell, (MD) 28 January 1877, (MG) Wm. S. Troutman, J. P.

George W. Sutterfield and Liney Adeline Crossland, (MD) 27 May 1877, (MG) Wm. S. Troutman, J. P.

William H. Bay and Sarah E. Martin, (MD) 4 October 1877, (MG) Wm. S. Troutman, J. P.

Adrian Marten and Aneally Bates, (MD) 4 November 1877, (MG) Wm. S. Troutman, J. P.

Andrew Jackson Tucker and Luetishey Asher, (MD) 18 November 1877, (MG) Wm. S. Troutman, J. P.

O. S. White and Delpha Crossland, (MD) 17 December 1877, (MG) Wm. S. Troutman, J. P.

Samuel Polk and Lucy A. Sutterfield, (MD) 23 March 1878, (MG) Wm. S. Troutman, J. P.

Ely Reace and Matildab Levingstone, (MD) 28 September 1878, (MG) Wm. S. Troutman, J. P.

Allen Callahan and Nancy Howell, (MD) 14 November 1878, (MG) Wm. S. Troutman, J. P.

John C.F. Howell and M. Nannie White, (MD) 17 April 1879, (MG) Wm. S. Troutman, J. P.

Jacob Bertwinger, of Dent Co., Mo. and Emery Beck, (MD) 22 March 1879, (MG) Wm. S. Troutman, J. P.

John Leonard and Jane Wisdom, (MD) 31 August 1879, (MG) Wm. S. Troutman, J. P., (CMTS) both of Dent Co.

Francis Montgomery and Lucinda Conway, (MD) 2 January 1880, (MG) Wm. S. Troutman, J. P.

C. P. Black, of Iron Co., and Mrs. Nancy M. Cozine, (MD) 1 December 1879, (MG) Wm. S. Troutman, J. P.

John M. Johnson and Dicey Ann Perry, (MD) 22 January 1880, (MG) William S. Troutman, J. P.

William Halk and Malisey Hienson, (MD) 18 March 1880, (MG) Wm. S. Troutman, J. P.

Green B. Goggin, Jr. and Elen Richmond, (MD) 10 April 1881, (MG) William S. Troutman, J. P.

Benjamin P. Holms and Taney Conway, (MD) 8 June 1881, (MG) William S. Troutman, J. P.

Joseph A. Estep and Sarah J. Johnson, (MD) 31 July 1881, (MG) Wm. S. Troutman, J. P.

Joseph G. Ketcherside and Mary Withro, (MD) 10 December 1881, (MG) William S.Troutman, J. P.

Elisha Bowen and Nancy Jane Kay, (MD) 22 December 1881, (MG) Wm.

S. Troutman, J. P.
J.W. Smith and Mary C. Smith, (MD) 12 March 1882, (MG) William S. Troutman, J. P., (PM) Married by Wm. S. Troutman at his home.
J. M. Byrd and Sarah D. Montgomery, (MD) 12 July 1882, (MG) Wm. S. Troutman, J. P., (PM) Married at the residence of E. H. Sutterfield
Alfred Perry and Mary Earls, (MD) 19 October 1882, (MG) Wm. S. Troutman, J. P.
Jonathan Black and Nancy Jane Hinsen, (MD) 9 November 1882, (MG) Wm. S. Troutman, J. P.
William H. Miner and Hattie Miner, (MD) 26 April 1885, (MG) Wm. S. Troutman, J. P., (PM) Married at the bride's home
John T. Linson ,of Iron Co., and Martha Johnson, (MD) 14 September 1886, (MG) Wm.S. Troutman, J. P.
S. N. Conway and Nancy A. E. Brown, (MD) 29 October 1886, (MG) Wm. S. Troutman, J. P.
W. T. Hinsen and Mary Chamberlin, (MD) 18 August 1887, (MG) Wm. S. Troutman, J. P.
Thomas Stout and Mary F. Bird, (MD) 19 February 1888, (MG) Wm. S. Troutman, J. P.
James C. Clinton and Ettama Miner, (MD) 11 September 1888, (MG) William S.Troutman, J. P.
Andy Lee and Pearley Miner, (MD) August 1888, (MG) William S. Troutman, J. P.
Lewis J. Montgomery and Nancy J. Estep, (MD) 8 November 1888, (MG) William S. Troutman, J. P.
Samuel Estep and Mary Bailey, (MD) 16 October 1890, (MG) Wm. S. Troutman, J. P.
Robert Black and Mary Montgomery, (MD) 12 February 1891, (MG) Wm. S. Troutman, J. P.
William C. Brooks and Emily E. Hill, (MD) 13 December 1874, (MG) George F. Brooks, Minister
Aaron Hill and Lucinday Lawson, (MD) 24 October 1878, (MG) George F. Brooks, Minister
James Hill and Benorah Hunter, (MD) 10 December 1879, (MG) George F. Brooks, Minister
John C. Kuntz and Mary Helen Parmer, (MD) 3 March 1887, (MG) George F. Brooks, Minister
Caswell Warren and Matilda Wadkins, (MD) 19 January 1875, (MG) Thomas H. Brooks, Minister
Noah Blankenship and Rebecca McDonald, (MD) 18 November 1877, (MG) Thomas H. Brooks, Minister
Eliha Freeman and Martha Jane McMullen, (MD) 6 March 1878, (MG) Thomas H. Brooks, Minister

William R. Stagner and Margaret E. McLearney, (MD) 26 October 1880, (MG) Thomas H. Brooks, Minister

John T. Price and Sophia Voss, (MD) 12 August 1881, (MG) Thomas H. Brooks, Minister

J. R. Moore and Mollie F. Carty, (MD) 28 June 1883, (MG) Thomas H. Brooks, Minister

William C. Bowles and Margaret E. Brooks, (MD) 1 May 1884, (MG) Thomas H. Brooks, Minister

D. H. Smith and Sarah C. Brooks, (MD) 20 August 1885, (MG) Thomas H. Brooks, Minister, (PM) Married at the residence of William Brooks

B. F. Bucher and Mary A. Moss, (MD) October 1886, (MG) Thomas H. Brooks, Minister

James M. Cundiff and Cynthia E. Barnes, (MD) 6 January 1887, (MG) Thomas H. Brooks, Minister

Franklin Barfield and Mary B. Morris, (MD) 3 March 1887, (MG) Thomas H. Brooks, Minister

S. Dugger and Amanda Miner, of Dent Co., (MD) 17 October 1887, (MG) Thomas H. Brooks, Minister

William A. Munger and Alice Moore, (MD) 11 January 1888, (MG) Thomas H. Brooks, Minister

J. D. Rouse and Aimey A. O'Dell, (MD) 3 July 1890, (MG) Thomas H. Brooks, Minister

A. M. Shriver and Allie N. Munger, (MD) 24 December 1890

George L. Parmer and Mary J. Wimpy, of Sinking Creek, (MD) 12 January 1875

Leonard T. Hackworth and Sarah Mead, (MD) 31 January 1875, (MG) Hugh E. Johnson, Minister

James Benton Jinings and Mary Elizabeth Dennison, (MD) 5 August 1875, (MG) John R. Adams, Minister

Lucy J. Carty and Huston Lathem, (MD) 9 May 1878, (MG) John R. Adams, Minister

Andrew J. Lindsay and Susan F. Parker, (MD) 3 November 1881, (MG) John R. Adams, Minister, (PM) Married at the brides home

Benjamin Williams and California Brooks, (MD) 18 June 1875, (MG) D. M. Lee, Minister

John Amsden and Manda C. Meadows, (MD) 31 January 1876, (MG) D. M. Lee, Minister

A. Laramore and Elizabeth Watson, (MD) 12 September 1875, (MG) N. J. Chance, Minister

Josiah Sutton and Jane Harrison, (MD) 14 October 1875, (MG) N. J. Chance, Minister

William VanDyke and Sarah Snodgrass, (MD) 3 February 1876, (MG) N. J. Chance, Minister

William Davis and Lucinda Jane Latham, (MD) 30 September 1875, (MG) Nelson Adams, Minister

James F. Sutterfield and Martha E. Henson, (MD) 3 October 1875, (MG) J. G. Rutter, Minister

John R. Fitts and Mary Conoway of Shannon Co., (MD) 8 November 1875, (MG) J. G. Rutter, Minister

Robert Elzander Car and Slenia E. Barnes, (MD) 18 August 1875, (MG) James Barnes, J. P.

John R. Lane and Mary E. Harrison, (MD) 30 December 1875, (MG) James Barnes, J. P.

James Kohn and Mary Hedric, (MD) 26 June 1877, (MG) James Barnes, J. P.

William B. Masters and Sarah Jane Martin, (MD) 10 December 1877, (MG) James Barnes, J. P., (CMTS) Both of Iron Co.

Abraham Vinson and Mary Voss, (MD) 12 December 1877, (MG) James Barnes, J. P.

Benjamin F. Kohn and Lucinda White, (MD) 31 May 1878, (MG) James Barnes, J. P.

William C. Lane and Parzetta C. Hill, (MD) 22 December 1878, (MG) James Barnes, J. P.

James H. Loness and Mary A. Silvey, (MD) 22 January 1880, (MG) James Barnes, J. P.

J. C. Casey and Josephine M. Maberry, (MD) 16 February 1882, (MG) James Barnes, J. P.

William M. Collyout and Leona McMillen, (MD) 28 November 1875, (MG) Elijah Johnson, Minister

Baley Chitwood and Mary Miller, (MD) 19 September 1875, (MG) James R. Trammell, Minister

Joseph Shelby Carty and Sarah Lucetta Chance, (MD) 3 February 1876, (MG) A. B. Adams, J. P.

Samuel Fears and Matilda Brawley, (MD) 6 February 1876, (MG) A. B. Winchell, Minister

Charles Wilson and Julia A. Carty, (MD) 1 March 1876, (MG) A. P. Shriver, J. P.

George Huff and Alice Blackwell, (MD) 18 May 1876, (MG) A. P. Shriver, J. P.

Jefferson Wilson and Sarah Carty, (MD) 21 February 1877, (MG) A. P. Shriver, J. P.

Richard J. January and Isabelle C. Shy, (MD) 4 July 1877, (MG) A. P. Shriver, J. P.

Barney G. Parks and Catherine Adams, (MD) 30 December 1877, (MG) A. P. Shriver, J. P.

Benjamin Bucher and Nanie E. Edmonds, (MD) 28 March 1878, (MG)

A.P. Shriver, J. P.
Fredic Wornica and Charity Brewer, (MD) February 1876, (MG) Alex S. Moore, Minister
John R. Harrison and Nancy Goggin, (MD) 4 October 1877, (MG) Alex S. Moore, Minister
Henry N. Harrison and Elvina E. Pyrtle, (MD) 19 June 1879, (MG) Alex S. Moore, Minister
Eeibe Louis, of Iron Co. and Permelia Wormicke, (MD) 8 June 1879, (MG) Alex S. Moore, Minister
James D. Henry and Deliala A. Reed, (MD) 30 May 1870, (MG) James E. Drake, J. P.
James Wombel, of Iron Co. and Margaret Hurt, (MD) 4 February 1876, (MG) M. W. Munger, J. P.
William Schreeves and Marthia Bucsten, of Iron Co., (MD) 26 September 1878, (MG) M. W. Munger, J. P.
John Riefenauer and Mary S. Taab, (MD) 13 December 1878, (MG) M. W. Munger, J. P.
Taylor Rutledge and Emma Wilson, (MD) 12 April 1883, (MG) M. W. Munger, J. P.
David F. Jaycox and Maggie Shrum, (MD) 19 December 1883, (MG) M. W. Munger, J. P.
Taylor Barton and Susan Baron, (MD) 12 May 1876, (MG) J. H. Somers, J. P.
James Dennison and Louisa Lane, (MD) 28 July 1876, (MG) G. M. Piles, Minister
Calvin Bowen (Bower) and Rettie E. Lane, (MD) 22 February 1877, (MG) G. M. Piles, Minister
William Taylor and Fox Alice A. Sabin, (MD) 21 September 1879, (MG) G. M. Piles, Minister
John C. Wood and Emma J. Rice, (MD) 2 September 1880, (MG) G. M. Piles, Minister
William F. Sabin and Elizabeth Watson, (MD) 21 July 1884, (MG) G. M. Piles, Minister
W. A. Wimpy and Tennessee L. Dickson, (MD) 3 March 1887, (MG) G. M. Piles, Minister
George Gowin and Gergority Johnson, (MD) 4 October 1876, (MG) J. P. McNail, Minister
James C. Paulus and Sarah A. McCampbell, (MD) 17 February 1878, (MG) J. P. McNail, Minister
Robert Thomason and Cynthia Mills, (MD) 3 November 1878, (MG) J. P. McNail, Minister
Berry Barnes and Martha Mills, (MD) 27 May 1879, (MG) J. P. McNail, Minister

Jesse Lester and Angeline Mills, (MD) 28 December 1879, (MG) J. P. McNail, Minister

William Stefner and Adlade Rutter, (MD) 1 February 1880, (MG) J. P. McNail, Minister

William Walker and Jane Mills, (MD) 12 August 1880, (MG) J. P. McNail, Minister

Joseph Baker and Cytha Lester, (MD) 30 December 1880, (MG) J. P. McNail, Minister, (PM) Married at the residence of Daniel Lester

Alexander Brooks and Mary E. Gentry, (MD) 2 January 1881, (MG) J. P. McNail, Minister

Jesse Lester and Genora Russell, (MD) 11 May 1882, (MG) J. P. McNail, Minister

Thomas M. Walker and Lucy Mills, (MD) 28 September 1883, (MG) J. P. McNail, Minister

W. H. Russell and Artemissa E. Goggin, (MD) 13 December 1883, (MG) J. P. McNail, Minister

John Tedder and Genora Lester, (MD) 20 May 1884, (MG) J. P. McNail, Minister

J. R. Baker and Mary C. King, (MD) 13 November 1884, (MG) J. P. McNail, Minister, (PM) Married at the brides home

James Warren and Sary M. Wamble, (MD) 19 August 1876, (MG) W. K. Johnson, Minister

Eli M. Pogue and Rody J. Walles, (MD) 1 March 1877, (MG) W. K. Johnson, Minister, (PM) Married at the residence of Wm. Crafton

Francis M. Davidson and Martha E. Johnson, (MD) 28 December 1876, (MG) W. K. Johnson, Minister

George W. Counts and Rebeca Zearry, (MD) June 1877, (MG) W. K. Johnson, Minister

Hardy Chitwood and Ally Davis, (MD) 3 September 1877, (MG) W. K. Johnson, Minister

Caleb Spears and Artia Missie Chitwood, (MD) 12 December 1877, (MG) W. K. Johnson, Minister

Wiley S. Pogue and Charity Chitwood, (MD) 17 March 1878, (MG) W. K. Johnson, Minister

James A. Meed and Roda E. Conway, (MD) 11 April 1878, (MG) W. K. Johnson, Minister

Ephram Dillard and Ellen Spears, (MD) 15 August 1878, (MG) W. K. Johnson, Minister

Thomas Davis and Jane Chitwood, (MD) 22 December 1878, (MG) W. K. Johnson, Minister

George W. Jorden and Charlotte Cox, (MD) 15 January 1879, (MG) W. K. Johnson, Minister

Augustus Kitchell and Charlotta Ford, (MD) 23 March 1879, (MG) W. K.

Johnson, Minister
Seth Chitwood and Sarah Fanny Rutter, (MD) March 1880, (MG) W. K. Johnson, Minister
John Bowlin and Nancy Mooney, (MD) 10 January 1880, (MG) W. K. Johnson, Minister
James Warren and Rachel Wadkin, (MD) 5 July 1880, (MG) W. K. Johnson, Minister
J. M. Camden and Ellen Miller, (MD) 4 November 1880, (MG) W. K. Johnson, Minister
William G. Madden and Amy E. Piles, (MD) 23 April 1881, (MG) W. K. Johnson, Minister
R. M. Neill and Sarah Pritchett, (MD) 14 August 1881, (MG) W. K. Johnson, Minister
Hewey Chitwood and Laura Spear, (MD) 20 March 1884, (MG) W. K. Johnson, Minister
John Randolph and Sarah Weems, (MD) 17 August 1876, (MG) William R. Radford, Minister
Charles Hart and Polly Dillard, (MD) 28 September 1876, (MG) William R. Radford, Minister
M. Conway and Manada Counts, (MD) 14 September 1876, (MG) William R. Radford, Minister
Stephen Haulkum and Easter Radford, (MD) 19 October 1876, (MG) William R. Radford, Minister
Alexander Hardcassel and Mary Forgason, (MD) 22 March 1877, (MG) William R. Radford, Minister
William Callahan and Easter Slutcher, (MD) 4 February 1877, (MG) William R. Radford, Minister
James Eivans and Eliza Brudan, (MD) 21 May 1877, (MG) William R. Radford, Minister
Isach N. Gore and Eliza Jane Weems, (MD) 16 August 1877, (MG) William R. Radford, Minister
William Smith and Malinda Dillerd, (MD) 4 August 1878, (MG) William R. Radford, Minister
John Counts and Sarah Ann Womble, (MD) 22 March 1860, (CMTS) Reaffirmed after the fire
Isaac Fillmore and Laura T. Johnson, (MD) 25 June 1881, (MG) William R. Radford, Minister
Isaac N. Anderson and Eliza Jane Hill, (MD) December 1882, (MG) William R. Radford, Minister
W. S. Sutterfield and Mariah J. Polk, (MD) 25 December 1882, (MG) William R. Radford, Minister
Andrew J. Sullivan and Allena V. McCloud, (MD) 12 October 1882, (MG) William R. Radford, Minister, (PM) Married at Judge Johnson's

residence.
James E. Sutterfield and Martha E. Walker, (MD) 10 January 1883, (MG) William R. Radford, Minister
James Weems and Missouri Ann Angle, (MD) 23 August 1883, (MG) William R. Radford, Minister
S. J. Freeman and Nancy I. Polk, (MD) 27 July 1887, (MG) William R. Radford, Minister
Elvis Harrison and Mary E. Pratt, (MD) 20 October 1853, (MG) William Sartin, J. P.
Benjamin Chaney and Mary S. Worley, (MD) 4 February 1877, (MG) J. C. Goodson, Minister, (CMTS) Both of Wayne Co Mo.
William Pinkney and Lucinda Rich, (MD) 14 December 1876, (MG) J. C. Goodson, Minister
George Brown and Elvira Boggs, (MD) 28 February 1878, (MG) J. C. Goodson, Minister
John W. Vaughn and Vira L. Mills, (MD) 29 November 1890, (MG) J. C. Goodson, Minister
Adam Sherril and Mary Edams, (MD) 11 March 1877, (MG) William Huff, Minister
John C. Strickland and Matildy Jane Sherrill, (MD) 18 July 1880, (MG) William Huff, Minister
Lafayette F. Carty and Sarah Ann Copeland, (MD) 18 January 1857, (MG) Jas. Copeland, J. P.
Samuel Piles and J.S.F. Hackworth, (MD) 9 August 18??, (MG) J. S. Clark, Minister
Samuel Heddy and Betty Ann Allen, (MD) 27 November 1887, (MG) J. S. Clark, Minister
James M. King and Julia R. Eads, (MD) 10 April 1879, (MG) J. S. Clark, Minister
Genty Mills and Anderson Collman, (MD) September 1879, (MG) J. S. Clark, Minister
John E. Charlton and Dora C. Mann, (MD) 17 March 1888, (MG) J. S. Clark, Minister
M. P. Whitworth and Rebecca Piles, (MD) 14 August 1888, (MG) J. S. Clark, Minister
Edward Barnes and Sinthy E. Crownover, (MD) 5 December 1867, (MG) J. A. Allison, Minister
Joseph Barton and Sarah ????, (MD) 8 November 1877, (MG) William H. Crozier, Minister
Benjamin H. Hutchings and Ermana G. Jackson, (MD) 8 November 1877, (MG) R. C. Williams, J. P.
Henley N. Campbell and Elizabeth M. Munger, (MD) 20 December 1877, (MG) James Ross, Minister

Elijah D. Wadlow and Lucy Coil, (MD) 10 March 1876, (MG) James Ross, Minister

John C. Blankenship and Sarah Barton, (MD) 9 May 1843, (CMTS) Reaffirmed after the fire by J.A. Smith, J. P. August 1, 1878 record of A.P. Shriver.

R. F. Holloman and Mollie Buckner, (MD) 21 August 1881, (MG) James Ross, Minister,(CMTS) Both of Hogan in Iron Co.

Oliver A. Nahanm of Randolph Co., IL, and Miss John E. Cromer, of Perry Co., (MD) 22 July 1878, (MG) J. M. Rains, Minister

I. G. Roe and Mary Thurman, (MD) 2 November 1879, (MG) J. M. Rains, Minister

Jacob Marlor and Mary E. Boatright, (MD) 20 December 1881, (MG) J. M. Rains, Minister, (PM) Married at the bride's home.

Thomas D. Harrison and Charlotte Belle, (MD) 15 November 1878, (MG) B. F. McNail, Minister

William Kichel and Jane Miller, (MD) 12 December 1878, (MG) S. D. Biffle, Minister

John A. Troutman and Marietta G. Crossland, (MD) 25 December 1878, (MG) J. B. Heaton, Minister

Green L. Warren and Matilda E. Radford, (MD) 23 December 1878, (MG) Francis M. Warren, Minister

Allen Sutterfield and Mary C. Angle, (MD) 16 November 1878, (MG) Francis M. Warren, Minister

Nehimiah Balke and Sarah A. Warren, (MD) 23 December 1878, (MG) Francis M. Warren, Minister

John H. Alexander and Sarah H. Conway, (MD) 9 July 1879, (MG) Francis M. Warren, Minister

William R. Higgenbothen and Amanda Conway, (MD) 9 June 1887, (MG) Francis M. Warren, Minister

W. G. Gofourth and Cynthia Knuckles, (MD) 27 September 1887, (MG) Francis M. Warren, Minister

Charles Winterbottom and Ferby Hardcastle, (MD) 26 February 1888, (MG) Francis M. Warren, Minister

Burell Thomas and Isabell Williams, (MD) 6 September 1888, (MG) Francis M. Warren, Minister

Reason W. Neill and Catherine Mogue, (MD) 6 September 1879, (MG) George W. Jordan, Minister

Louis Conway and Malinda Pritchet, (MD) 31 January 1880, (MG) George W. Jordan, Minister

Samuel Herin and Caroline Har (?), (MD) 19 March 1885, (MG) George W. Jordan, Minister, (PM) Married at the residence of L. D. Knuckles

Zachariah Pogue and Sophia J. Winkleman, (MD) May 1885, (MG) George W. Jordan, Minister

C. P. Black and A. C. Madden, (MD) 20 March 1886, (MG) George W. Jordan, Minister

Phineas Cox and Margaret J. Maddin, (MD) 4 March 1886, (MG) George W. Jordan, Minister

Henderson Chitwood, Jr. and Eviline Edmonds, (MD) 18 May 1886, (MG) George W. Jordan, Minister

Jerome Sullivan and Delila C. Patterson, (MD) 19 January 1888, (MG) George W. Jordan, Minister

James T. Brooks and Lucy A. Brooks, (MD) 19 February 1888, (MG) George W. Jordan, Minister

Patrick Chronister and Cynthia C. Dawson, (MD) 5 January 1879, (MG) John Myers, J. P.

William B. Masters and Martha Brewer, (MD) August 1879, (MG) John Myers, J. P.

Emanuel Guffey of Reynolds Co. and Sarah J. Killen of Iron Co., (MD) 22 October 1880, (MG) John Myers, J. P.

James Cox and Elen Brooks, (MD) 1 January 1881, (MG) John Myers, J. P., (CMTS) Both of Iron Co.

William Lewis of Iron Co. and Polly A. Johnson, (MD) 2 January 1881, (MG) John Myers, J. P.

John S. Allison and Lucy E. Chronister, (MD) 2 February 1882, (MG) John Myers, J. P.

John A. Inman and Rachael Jane Guffey, (MD) 5 January 1882, (MG) John Myers, J. P.

W. D. Fancher and Nancy Ellen Guffey, (MD) 9 Apr. 1882, (MG) John Myers, J. P.

Thomas Griggs, of Shannon Co. and Sarah A. Williams, (MD) 19 December 1882, (MG) John Myers, J. P.

James L. Tilley and Amanda F. Cohn, (MD) 19 February 1885, (MG) John Myers, J. P.

L. B. Charlton and Levina Fe?, (MD) 6 May 1886, (MG) John Myers, J. P.

Thomas L. Brawley and Maberry Mills, (MD) 6 May 1886, (MG) John Myers, J. P.

W. N. Brewer and Artena Hackworth, (MD) 11 July 1886, (MG) John Myers, J. P.

John C. Torrey and Julia Mann, (MD) 18 July 1886, (MG) John Myers, J. P.

George C. Colyott and Martha Pullem, (MD) 16 September 1886, (MG) John Myers, J. P.

Isaac M. Johnson and Mary E. Brewer, (MD) November 1886, (MG) John Myers, J. P.

Green Brewer and Martha M. Wadlow, (MD) 9 December 1886, (MG) John Myers, J. P.

William T. Lee and Cynitha L. Brewer, (MD) 2 January 1887, (MG) John Myers, J. P.

William Smith and Allis Skaggs, (MD) 23 January 1887, (MG) John Myers, J. P.

William Silvy and Mary J. Justice, (MD) 6 February 1887, (MG) John Myers, J. P.

J. N.(?) Rutter and Nancy J. Mead, (MD) 17 March 1887, (MG) John Myers, J. P.

Jacob Stuart and Mary A. Brawley, (MD) July 1887, (MG) John Myers, J. P.

M. Brown and Sarah J. Mann, (MD) 6 November 1887, (MG) John Myers, J. P.

E. J. Johnson and Sarah E. Bone, (MD) 17 June 1888, (MG) John Myers, J. P.

R. H. Abrams and Naoma Lewis, (MD) 10 June 1888, (MG) John Myers, J. P.

Thomas B. Hendrinson and Sarah C. Cook, (MD) 2 December 1888, (MG) John Myers, J. P.

Johnathan Johnson and Pearlee Swafford, (MD) 20 October 1889, (MG) John Myers, J. P.

William H. Dunnigan and Annie Dunn, (MD) 16 February 1880, (MG) John Myers, J. P.

J. H. Brawley and Julia A. Stuart, (MD) 11 May 1890, (MG) John Myers, J. P.

Anderson Massie, of Shannon Co., and Artamissa Copeland, (MD) 23 February 1879, (MG) S. W. Munsell, Minister, M.E. Chruch

Alfred N. Massie, of Shannon Co., and Mary Elizabeth Allen, (MD) 15 January 1880, (MG) S. W. Munsell, Minister, M.E. Chruch

Harris S. Sinclair, of St. Francois Co., and Amanda A. Powell, of Shannon Co., (MD) 28 January 1879, (MG) F. R. Cole, J. P.

Perryman Johnston and Matilda Richmond, (MD) 21 March 1878, (MG) F. R. Cole, J. P.

Daniel Davison and M. Sarha Warren, (MD) 20 November 1879, (MG) F. R. Cole, J. P.

J. H. Haly and Nancy Coil, (MD) 24 April 1879, (MG) James M. Laws, J. P.

Woolson Robinett and M. Nancy Goggin, (MD) 10 July 1870, (MG) James M. Laws, J. P.

B. F. Dennison and Rebecca J. Stevens, (MD) 14 August 1879, (MG) James M. Laws, J. P.

J. A. Baker and Martha Hunter, (MD) 20 November 1879, (MG) James M. Laws, J. P.

George W. Rayfield and Callie Root, (MD) 24 December 1879, (MG)

Laws, J. P.
George W. Rayfield and Callie Root, (MD) 24 December 1879, (MG) James M. Laws, J. P.
John W. Medlen and Martha J. McMurry, (MD) 11 March 1880, (MG) James M. Laws, J. P.
John T. Goggin and Margaret N. Rayfield, (MD) 18 August 1880, (MG) James M. Laws, J. P.
James Faulkenberry and Martha Welch, (MD) 15 September 1880, (MG) James M. Laws, J. P.
J. J. Jamison and Mary A. Robinett, (MD) 4 November 1880, (MG) James M. Laws, J. P.
John S. Dobbins and Eliza J. George, (MD) 13 January 1881, (MG) James M. Laws, J. P., (BPRTS) John P. and Lucy George
John S. Hartman and Emily S. Carty, (MD) 14 April 1881, (MG) James M. Laws, J. P.
F. F. Gallaher and Mahala E. Goggins, (MD) 18 August 1881, (MG) James M. Laws, J. P.
William Reed and Martha P. Parks, (MD) 6 October 1881, (MG) James M. Laws, J. P.
Henry C. Bonny and Mary S. Brooks, (MD) 29 December 1881, (MG) James M. Laws, J. P.
William G. Wilson and Jennie E. Pratt, (MD) 16 March 1882, (MG) James M. Laws, J. P.
Edward F. McCabe and Anna M. Faulkenberry, (MD) 11 May 1882, (MG) James M. Laws, J. P.
James H. Pinley and Elizabeth A. Proffitt, (MD) 4 July 1882, (MG) James M. Laws, J. P.
Monroe Johnston and Ella Chappell, (MD) 11 May 1882, (MG) James M. Laws, J. P.
William H. Sutton and Margaret S.M. Francis, (MD) 4 June 1882, (MG) James M. Laws, J. P.
J. F. Wilson and Mollie J. Johnston, (MD) 3 August 1882, (MG) James M. Laws, J. P.
W. O. Goggin and Corilla Parks, (MD) 14 September 1882, (MG) James M. Laws, J. P.
Joseph Pearee and Sarah Walker, (MD) 16 February 1879, (MG) James Dodson, J. P.
George Stringer and Delphia Letha S. Adams, (MD) 14 September 1879, (MG) James Dodson, J. P.
John Martin and Edith Gant, (MD) 13 June 1880, (MG) James Dodson, J. P.
George W. Reese and Sarah E. Martin, (MD) 18 July 1880, (MG) James Dodson, J. P.

Loranzo I. Reese and Caldonia Tucker, (MD) 13 June 1880, (MG) James Dodson, J. P.
Alfred Bay and Jane Smith, (MD) 4 August 1880, (MG) James Dodson, J. P.
Andrew J. Tucker and Serena Catherine Gant, (MD) 27 February 1881, (MG) James Dodson, J. P.
Joseph Parker and Roxeyanor Ball, (MD) 25 August 1881, (MG) James Dodson, J. P.
Pleas Chamerlain and Mary Ann Adams, (MD) 21 August 1881, (MG) James Dodson, J. P.
George Brown and Mary Jane Ball, (MD) 29 September 1881, (MG) James Dodson, J. P.
Thomas Miner and Matilda Miner, (MD) 8 December 1881, (MG) James Dodson, J. P.
George W. Jaycox and Nancy J. Hasty, (MD) 20 July 1879, (MG) James Smith, Minister
John Cole and Marga I. Hasty, (MD) 9 May 1880, (MG) James Smith, Minister
Joseph S. Gaston and Anny Dorene Wilson, (MD) 13 November 1880, (MG) James Smith, Minister
Walter N. Parker and Nancy E. Pinkley, (MD) 23 September 1881, (MG) James Smith, Minister
Samuel King, of Iron Co., and Catherine Scaggs, (MD) 19 October 1879, (MG) Joel Clark, Minister, (PM) Married at Silas Scagg's home
Benjamin Seal and Mary J. Lewis, (MD) 17 November 1880, (MG) Joel Clark, Minister
Nimrod Brewer and Martha Mann, (MD) 28 January 1882, (MG) Joel Clark, Minister
William Boyd and Ida Buckner, (MD) 26 October 1882, (MG) Joel Clark, Minister, (PM) Married at the brides home
J. H. Camden and Sarah Newton, (MD) 2 February 1890, (MG) Joel Clark, Minister
James S. Dennison and Martha Ratliff, (MD) 20 December 1890, (MG) Joel Clark, Minister
John H. Mathews and Barley Asher, (MD) 17 October 1879, (MG) J. M. Lewis, J. P.
Joseph Black and Martha M. Black, (MD) 24 November 1880, (MG) J. M. Lewis, J. P.
Jacob Moses and Nancy Jane Bredwell, (MD) 8 April 1881, (MG) J. M. Lewis, J. P.
Henry Edmanson Thompson and Winney Johnson, (MD) April 1881, (MG) J. M. Lewis, J. P.
Jefferson Adams and Nancy Ann Yates, (MD) 8 April 1881, (MG) J. M.

Lewis, J. P.
Samuel Black and Anariah Smith, (MD) September 1882, (MG) J. M. Lewis, J. P.
John Maburry and Rebecca Ann Dearing, (MD) 1 January 1880, (MG) E. D. Brawley, Judge
William Albert and Eliza Barnes, (MD) 8 January 1880, (MG) E. D. Brawley, Judge
Taylor Maburry and Juley Ann Randolph, (MD) 11 April 1880, (MG) E. D. Brawley, Judge
John Brawley and Adiline Barnes, (MD) 22 October 1880, (MG) E. D. Brawley, Judge
George Fitzgerald and Elizabeth Barnes, (MD) 16 January 1881, (MG) E. D. Brawley, Judge
William Ratliff and Belinda Taylor, (MD) December 1880, (MG) E. D. Brawley, Judge
Franklin Sanders and Tattilitia Parks, (MD) 23 February 1881, (MG) E. D. Brawley, Judge
John B. Dearing, of Ripley Co., and Mary Ann Rook, (MD) 8 January 1882, (MG) E. D. Brawley, Judge, (PM) Married at E. D. Brawley home
John P. Myers and Annia Gilkerson, (MD) 1 January 1882, (MG) E. D. Brawley, Judge
Charles C. Ford and Sarah J. VanDyke, (MD) 21 September 1882, (MG) E. D. Brawley, Judge, (PM) Married at the bride's home.
W. J. Randolph and Sarah Black, (MD) 18 March 1888, (MG) E. D. Brawley, Judge
Goldsmith Keathley and Zorada Randolph, (MD) 20 March 1888, (MG) E. D. Brawley, Judge
James Ratliff and Martha J. Johnson, (MD) 8 April 1888, (MG) E. D. Brawley, Judge
William J. Randolph and Lusety Eveline Fry, (MD) 11 February 1890, (MG) E. D. Brawley, Judge
Martin S. Copeland and Mary A. Dickson, (MD) 27 November 1879, (MG) J. B. Rice, Minister
Henry Dawson, of Carter Co., and Manerva J. Barnes, (MD) 1 January 1878, (MG) Bailey Smith, J. P.
Edward N. Wilkins and Nancy Ann Smith, (MD) 22 December 1880, (MG) Bailey Smith, J. P.
John R. Ging and Catharine Marbary, (MD) 29 February 1880, (MG) Henry C. Wilkinson, Minister of Christian Church, (PM) Married at Spencer Eaton's home
William V. Wheeler and Martha J. Mann, (MD) 14 March 1880, (MG) Henry C. Wilkinson, Minister of Christian Church
Thomas A. Tucker and EmalineYoung, (MD) 24 December 1879, (MG)

W. H. Casteel, Minister, (PM) Married at Simon Smith's home
Henry Parker and Mary E. Troutman, (MD) 8 April 1880, (MG) W. H. Casteel, Minister
H. F. Shaw and Susan Gant, (MD) 21 January 1883, (MG) W. H. Casteel, Minister
John Parks and Margaret F. Miner, (MD) 14 March 1883, (MG) W. H. Casteel, Minister
F. E. Parks and Margaret E. Wilson, both of Dent Co., (MD) 29 October 1888, (MG) W. H. Casteel, Minister
John Bardsley and Susan Parker, (MD) 11 November 1888, (MG) W. H. Casteel, Minister
William H. Bay and Martha Jane Foster, (MD) 3 January 1889, (MG) W. H. Casteel, Minister
T. S. Dickson and Mary C. George, (MD) 10 January 1889, (MG) W. H. Casteel, Minister
Squire Barton and Sallie Lawson, (MD) 13 Apr. 1880, (MG) George W. Brown, J. P.
James T. Lewis and Mary Jane Black, (MD) 12 October 1882, (MG) George W. Brown, J. P, (PM) Married at the bride's home
W. F. Fitzgerald and F.M. Temple (Tempy), (MD) 23 July 1880, (MG) J. H. Roberson, J. P.
John C. Brawley and Lydia A. Brewer, (MD) 11 April 1884, (MG) J. H. Roberson, J. P.
Henry Harmon and Rachiel Pullman, (MD) 12 December 1880, (MG) James M. King, J. P.
James Middleton and Martha Elizabeth Keathley, (MD) 20 August 1882, (MG) James M. King, J. P.
Milton S. Harrison and Amanda J. Hunter, (MD) 11 November 1880, (MG) B. F. Bucher, J. P.
W. H. Powers and Sarah A. Parks, (MD) 15 June 1883, (MG) B. F. Bucher, J. P.
Sterling P. Wadlow and Rachel Coil, (MD) 6 September 1883, (MG) B. F. Bucher, J. P.
James B. Barnes and Mrs. Mary Parks, (MD) 11 October 1883, (MG) B. F. Bucher, J. P.
Samuel B. Miller and Dollie Estes, (MD) 15 November 1883, (MG) B. F. Bucher, J. P.
William Evans and Nancy Wadlow, (MD) 23 November 1883, (MG) B. F. Bucher, J. P.
F. H. G. Warren and Sarah H. Barnes, (MD) 28 February 1884, (MG) B. F. Bucher, J. P.
John T. Brooks and Lucy A. Brooks, (MD) 19 February 1888, (MG) B. F. Bucher, J. P.

Wiiliam Hart and Sarah Counts, (MD) 23 December 1880, (MG) W. A. Goforth, J. P.

Coleman Williams and Rebeccah E. Edmonds, (MD) 12 January 1881, (MG) W. A. Goforth, J. P.

Steven Scarlett and Sarah Pierce, (MD) ?, (PM) Married at Joseph Baker's home, (MG) E.B. Huff, J. P., (BPRTS) Joseph Baker.

Thomas B. Bundy and Lucy A. Mann, (MD) 13 September 1883, (MG) F. M. Bunyard, Minister

Benjamin Cheney and Nancy O'Dell, (MD) 27 November 1881, (MG) F. M. Bunyard, Minister, (PM) Married at the bride's home.

John E. Vandiver and Mrs Lucy Dunn, (MD) 17 June 1883, (MG) F. M. Bunyard, Minister, (PM) Married at William Carter's mill.

H. T. Sawyer and L. J. Brown, (MD) 9 August 1883, (MG) F. M. Bunyard, Minister

George W. McAlester and Sarah F. Brown, (MD) 5 August 1883, (MG) F. M. Bunyard, Minister

George C. McNeely, of Piedmont in Wayne Co., and Dora Heltibidal, (MD) 6 January 1884, (MG) F. M. Bunyard, Minister

Thomas S. Barnes and Ellana Chitwood, (MD) 21 March 1872, (MG) H. R. Dickson, J. P.

S. W. Maulsby and Mrs. Scaggs, (MD) 1 August 1881, (MG) John Suthy, no office (CMTS) Both of Washington Co.

Joseph P. McNail and Luticia O'Brien, of Iron Co., (MD) 9 March 1882, (MG) William J. Baker, Minister

Carol Welch and Nannie A. King, (MD) 22 February 1883, (MG) William J. Baker, Minister, (PM) Married at the bride's residence

George W. Lester and Lucy F. King, (MD) 18 February 1883, (MG) William J. Baker, Minister

John W. Pogue and Lizzie Vinson, (MD) 19 December 1883, (MG) William J. Baker, Minister

Nim Brewer and Isadore Stitth (?), (MD) 24 February 1884, (MG) William J. Baker, Minister

William E. Tedder and Nancy E. Bond, of Iron Co., (MD) 9 October 1884, (MG) Wm. J. Baker, Minister, (PM) Married at bride's home

James F. Johnson and Emily Brewer, (MD) 13 January 1885, (MG) William J. Baker, Minister

George W. Lester and Martha E. Lewis, (MD) 5 August 1886, (MG) William J. Baker, Minister

William J. Smith and Elizabeth King, (MD) 2 September 1886, (MG) William J. Baker, Minister

Thomas W. Russell and Margaret Black, (MD) 13 October 1886, (MG) William J. Baker, Minister

B. F. Scott and Nancy Asberry, (MD) 23 October 1882, (MG) Floyd

William J. Baker, Minister

B. F. Scott and Nancy Asberry, (MD) 23 October 1882, (MG) Floyd Knight, Minister, (PM) Married at the bride's home

W. T. Barnes and Martha Ellen Stout, (MD) 30 July 1882, (MG) Floyd Knight, Minister

Samuel W. Copeland and Hester Callahan, (MD) 18 November 1882, (MG) J. W. Slade, J. P.

J. F. January and Margaret Faulkenberry, (MD) December 1882, (MG) J. W. Slade, J. P.

T. J. Reed and Zoridia George, (MD) 17 May 1883, (MG) J. W. Slade, J. P.

A .J. Rayfield and Belle Goggin, (MD) 23 May 1883, (MG) J. W. Slade, J. P.

John W. Welch and Mollie Wilkins, (MD) 2 August 1883, (MG) J. W. Slade, J. P.

A. P. Walker and Martha J. Jennings, (MD) 30 August 1883, (MG) J. W. Slade, J. P.

S. D. Reynolds. of Benton Co., Arkansas and Lucy E. Pogue, (MD) 28 November 1883, (MG) J. W. Slade, J. P.

T. E. Edmonds and F. L. Davis, (MD) 10 July 1885, (MG) J. W. Slade, J. P.

J. S. Wadlow and Mary Liza Stegall, (MD) 23 October 1884, (MG) J. W. Slade, J. P., (PM) Married at the residence of J. H. George

James H. Davis and Teritha Helvy, (MD) 31 December 1882, (MG) F. H. Lane, Minister

George Chilton, colored, and Eliza Clark, colored, (MD) 25 February 1883, (MG) F. H. Lane, Minister

M. P. Henry and Mary Meshwert, (MD) 24 December 1882, (MG) John E. Gilmer, J. P.

James Larkin and M.E. Hunter, (MD) 18 October 1883, (MG) John E. Gilmer, J. P.

D. T. Williams and Roda Dillard, (MD) 24 November 1883, (MG) John E. Gilmer, J. P.

Hiram Hodges and Charlotte Dodson, (MD) 13 March 1884, (MG) John E. Gilmer, J. P.

Charles J. Irons and Nanie Howell, (MD) 29 May 1884, (MG) John E. Gilmer, J. P.

James F. Martin and Antha C. Dodson, (MD) 24 July 1884, (MG) John E. Gilmer, J. P.

Wm. O. Perry and Martha Wooten, (MD) 14 February 1884, (MG) John E. Gilmer, J. P.

Daniel Clinton and Cleary D. Hughes, (MD) 29 March 1883, (MG) Jas. Sutterfield, J. P.

Samuel Estep and Amanda Jane Tucker, (MD) 11 May 1884, (MG) James Sutterfield, J. P.

James Lee and Naoma J. Miner, (MD) 17 December 1884, (MG) James Sutterfield, J. P.,(PM) Married at the bride's home

S. P. Wadlow and Cynthis Wadlow, (MD) 29 May 1883, (MG) L. W. Allen, Minister

C. B. Brooks and Sarah E. Shrum, (MD) 23 August 1883, (MG) David H. Hartman, J. P.,(PM) Married at the residence of Jacob Shrum

H. C. Stevens and Angnes Goforth, (MD) 1 January 1884, (MG) David H. Hartman, J. P.

William B. Pile and E.E. Price, (MD) 4 October 1883, (MG) John A. Jenkins, J. P.

John Harrison, of Iron Co., and Lucinda S. Bell, (MD) 25 October 1883, (MG) John Webb, J. P.

Wm. P. Daniel and Margahie Sanders, (MD) 27 December 1883, (MG) John Webb, J. P.

Henry Johnson and Mary J. Johnston, (MD) 24 February 1884, (MG) John Webb, J. P.

William Carterand Alpha Black ,of Wayne Co., (MD) 3 January 1884, (MG) James M. Birdwell, Minister

Will S. Hines and Mary E. Duree, (MD) 29 December 1883, (MG) James M. Birdwell, Minister

B. Z. Gossett and Mrs. Mary C. Taylor, (MD) 21 September 1884, (MG) James A. Webb, J. P., (PM) Married at the residence of Wiley Price

James Henry Piles and Mrs. Anna Decker, (MD) 26 November 1884, (MG) James A. Webb, J. P., (PM) Married at the bride's home

Thomas E. Thompson and Flora Segastine, (MD) 28 December 1884, (MG) James A. Webb, J. P., (PM) Married at the residence of Joseph Collins

Richard P. Brown and Mexico Sander, (MD) 25 December 1884, (MG) James A. Webb,J. P., (PM) Married at the bride's home

John T. Campbell and Alice Newell, (MD) 1 January 1885, (MG) James A. Webb, J. P.,(PM) Married at the residence of John Potter

W. H. Freeze and Elizabeth Johnston, (MD) 1 August 1886, (MG) James A. Webb, J. P.

Milton Goggin and Maggie Love, (MD) 4 March 1885, (MG) T. R. Terry, J. P., (PM) Married at the residence of L. Love

C. J. Jackson and Margaret Vaughn, (MD) 22 February 1884, (MG) A. J. Parks, Minister

Richard McMillen and Jane Caulley, (MD) 27 July 1884, (MG) A. J. Parks, Minister

Joel D. Brawley and Mary E. Reed, (MD) 4 September 1884, (MG) A. J. Parks, Minister

John Vinson and Elvina Munger, (MD) 24 December 1884, (MG)
A. J. Parks, Minister
J. M. Wadlow and Anna B. Moyer, (MD) 8 January 1885, (MG) A. J.
Parks, Minister
A. J. Vaughn and Lillie Gouche, (MD) 15 January 1885, (MG) A. J.
Parks, Minister
Thomas W. Rogers and Mollie White, (MD) 29 January 1885, (MG)
A. J. Parks, Minister
J. H. Miller and Sinai Sutton, (MD) 17 September 1885, (MG) A. J. Parks,
Minister
Joel Barton and Katie Mullen, (MD) 15 April 1886, (MG) A. J. Parks,
Minister
Redman Black and Nancy Wadlow, (MD) 8 September 1886, (MG)
A. J. Parks, Minister
J. A. Bowles and Mary E. Buford, (MD) 4 November 1886, (MG) A. J.
Parks, Minister
M. S. Russell and Silla T. Radford, (MD) 1 January 1891, (MG) A. J.
Parks, Minister
Elijah Radford and Mary McGlothlin, (MD) 10 February 1891, (MG)
A. J. Parks, Minister
William A. Tucker and Mary E. Nash, (MD) 6 April 1884, (MG) Henry
McLarney, J. P.
Charles Ross and Sarah Nash, (MD) 19 June 1884, (MG) John Warsham,
Minister
James Helm, of Dent Co., and Emily Wilhite, (MD) 23 March 1890, (MG)
John Warsham, Minister
F. M. Willis and Margaret A. Barnes, (MD) 17 September 1884, (MG)
C. W. Clouse, J. P.
Thomas C. Speer and Malinda Chitwood, (MD) 24 January 1887, (MG)
C. W. Clouse, J. P.
William Ball and Martha Allen, (MD) 24 December 1884, (MG) Justin
Temple, J. P.
George R. Morris and Anna Fitzgerald, (MD) February 1885, (MG) Justin
Temple, J. P., (PM) Married at the residence of Mr. Dickson
B. McPolk and Mary Going, (MD) 24 September 1885, (MG) Justin
Temple, J. P.
J. A. Hawn of Farmington in St. Francois Co and Judia Moore, (MD) 16
December 1886, (MG) Justin Temple, J. P.
John R. Evans and Martha C. Brown, (MD) 11 January 1885, (MG) W.
B. Graham, Minister, (PM) Married at the bride's home
William J. Lee and Louisa G. Martin, (MD) 1 January 1885, (MG) James
Johnson, County Judge, (PM) Married at the bride's home
John M. Johnson and Mrs. Sarah A. Miner, (MD) 11 January 1885,

(MG) James Johnson, County Judge, (PM) Married at the residence of J. Amsden

Joseph L. Brawley and Lucretia Sanders, (MD) 21 August 1885, (MG) J. G. Clarkson, J. P. of Iron Co. Mo.

G. A. Farriss and Maria Dunn, of Iron Co., (MD) 1 April 1885, (MG) G. E. McNeely, J. P.

T. S. Burke, of Sabula,Iron Co. Mo. and Melvina A. Counts, (MD) 13 June 1885, (MG) A. J. Tucker, J. P.

B. Frank Rayfield and Margaret Smith, (MD) 21 June 1886, (MG) Thomas Parmer, J. P.

J. J. Simpson and Elizabeth Pyrtle, (MD) 12 July 1886, (MG) Thomas Parmer, J. P.

John A. Martin and Susan Parks, (MD) 6 June 1886, (MG) Martin Cox, Minister

Charles Lee and Josephine Rice, (MD) 2 October 1887, (MG) Martin Cox, Minister

Joseph W. Evans and Maggie S. Bonney, (MD) 19 October 1890, (MG) Martin Cox, Minister

John W. Brawley and Sarah Reed, (MD) 3 October 1886, (MG) W. L. Gower, Minister

T. J. Pogue and Manerva Myers, (MD) December 1890, (MG) W. L. Gower, Minister

Andrew Marconnet and Ellen Sheets, (MD) November 1886, (MG) L. W. Pickens, Minister

Samuel Cook and Francis L. Davis, (MD) 24 November 1886, (MG) S. D. Hopkins, Minister, (CMTS) Both Iron Co Mo

W. D. Hubble and Laura Conway, (MD) 2 January 1887, (MG) J. M. Ratliff, Minister

George Miner and Mary Parker, (MD) 1 December 1886, (MG) A. J. Lindsay, J. P.

John Leneberger and Elisa Rothlisberger, (MD) 31 December 1886, (MG) A. J. Lindsay, J. P.

J. W. Clinton, of Grantville, Iron Co., and Nancy Davidson, (MD) 3 July 1887, (MG) A. J. Lindsay, J. P.

Alfred Norris and Martha Alice Lane, (MD) 30 January 1887, (MG) M. H. Moss, J. P.

Joseph Fears and Elvira Harrison, (MD) 9 June 1887, (MG) D. H. Smith, J. P.

T. W. Harrison and Mary Barnes, (MD) 27 October 1887, (MG) D. H. Smith, J. P.

John Stout and Eliza Jane Atkins, (MD) 13 November 1887, (MG) D. H. Smith, J. P.

Joseph Brawley and Polly Brown, (MD) 10 July 1888, (MG) D. H. Smith,

R. C. Albert and Sarah C. Brown, (MD) 13 July 1888, (MG) D. H. Smith, J. P.

J. M. Helvy and Susan Faulkenberry, (MD) 28 July 1888, (MG) D. H. Smith, J. P.

William A. Hill and Elmira Helvy, (MD) 31 July 1888, (MG) D. H. Smith, J. P.

Eli Barber and Sarah Buford, (MD) 10 August 1888, (MG) D. H. Smith, J. P.

John E. Helvy and Iva Hill, (MD) 23 August 1888, (MG) D. H. Smith, J. P.

Thomas Parmer and Mary C. Hill, (MD) 30 November 1888, (MG) D. H. Smith, J. P.

W. A. M. Buford and Amanda E. Faulkenberry, (MD) January 1889, (MG) D. H. Smith, J. P.

Charles Brawley and Nancy Barnes, (MD) 28 November 1889, (MG) D. H. Smith, J. P.

L. H. Pyrtle and Lucy Buford, (MD) 18 September 1890, (MG) D. H. Smith, J. P.

John D. Hicks, of Marion, Oden Co., IL, and Ludie M. Fox, (MD) 21 December 1890, (MG) D. H. Smith, J. P.

J. B. Smith and Emma J. Perry, (MD) 23 February 1887, (MG) John L. Weible, J. P., (PM) Married at the residence of John R. Fitz

Alexander Black and Francis Parker, (MD) 22 December 1887, (MG) L. Weible, J. P.

Wm. Lawson and Reine Decker, (MD) 27 February 1887, (MG) John A. Mullikin, J. P.

William T. Vineyard and Alabama Merrill, (MD) 24 March 1887, (MG) John A. Mullikin, J. P.

Jackson Morris and Mary E. Hatridge, (MD) 28 April 1887, (MG) W. H. Hale, Minister

W. C. Darden and Alice Pennington, (MD) August 1887, (MG) W. M. Wart, Minister

W. A. Simpson, of Iron Co., and Martha E. Guilliams, (MD) 18 December 1887, (MG) W. M. Wart, Minister

Allen D. Mann and Julia Mackey, (MD) 6 September 1888, (MG) W. M. Wart, Minister

C. J. Wadlow and Maggie Orrick, (MD) 2 September 1888, (MG) W. M. Wart, Minister

O. D. Moore and Emma Barlow, (MD) 1 December 1889, (MG) W. M. Wart, Minister

Ed Mank and Susan Hackworth, (MD) 21 November 1889, (MG) W. M. Wart, Minister

Joshua Wood, of St. Francios Co. and M. J. Smith, (MD) 22 September 1887, (MG) David Cowan, Minister, (PM) Married at Bailey Smith's home.
Robert Johnston and Bell Parker, (MD) 1 January 1888, (MG) J. T. Hill, Minister
Thomas Clark and B.A. Kline, (MD) 2 January 1888, (MG) James Lay, Minister
R. W. Jordan and Lucy A. Davis, (MD) 11 October 1888, (MG) James Lay, Minister
James W. Barnes and Julia A. Johnson, (MD) 25 October 1888, (MG) James Lay, Minister
Alijah Sutton and Mary Botkins, (MD) 18 October 1888, (MG) James Lay, Minister
Cornelous Sutton and Sarah C. Byrd, (MD) 19 December 1889, (MG) James Lay, Minister
Samuel T. Chapman and Mary Hughes, (MD) 2 June 1888, (MG) F. M. Johnston, J. P.
Joseph Webb and Lucy Marton, (MD) 5 July 1888, (MG) J. R. Ledbetter, Minister
Walter L. Lathim and Isabella Imboden, of Iron Co., (MD) 26 March 1887, (MG) J. C. Williany, J. P.
George A. Farley and Louisa J. Light, (MD) 4 July 1888, (MG) William Pinkley, J. P.
Green B. Boyd and Mary C. Hendrix, (MD) 9 January 1889, (MG) R. G. Sloan, Minister
J. L. Jackson and Margaret J. Piles, (MD) 29 January 1890, (MG) R. G. Sloan, Minister
W. E. Speer and Rebecca Crownover, (MD) 20 March 1890, (MG) R. G. Sloan, Minister
William Lewis and Polly Ann Barton, (MD) 25 January 1889, (MG) R. F. Elder, Minister
T. B. Miner and Josephine Thompson, (MD) 2 October 1889, (MG) R. F. Elder, Minister
R. A. Hawkins and Belle Miner, (MD) 3 October 1889, (MG) R. F. Elder, Minister
Guy McHenry and Lucy Parks, (MD) 18 December 1889, (MG) T. F. Lightfoot, Minister
James F. Weeks and Cynthia S. Mills, (MD) 31 October 1889, (MG) J. F. January, J. P.
George W. Black and Nancy Lumpkin, (MD) 26 March 1890, (MG) J. F. January, J. P.
Henry W. Lee and Minnie Mills, (MD) 1 May 1890, (MG) J. F. January, J. P.

W. A. Baker and Isabelle Wadlow, (MD) 18 June 1890, (MG) J. F. January, J. P.
John W. Hendrix and Louisa Carty, (MD) 18 December 1890, (MG) J. F. January, J. P.
John Light and Lutrecia McNail, (MD) 9 January 1890, (MG) W. J. Baker, J. P.
James Inmom and Ada Pritchet, (MD) 1 July 1890, (MG) A. P. Dace, Minister
John T. Webb and Low Pennington, (MD) 3 April 1890, (MG) W. H. Paschall, J. P.
Charles F. Helvy and Ella May Mulligan, (MD) 16 October 1890, (MG) W. H. Paschall, J. P.
David Deem and Melissa Middleton, (MD) 9 March 1890, (MG) J. C. Farris, J. P.
Nelson Barton and Sarah E. Smith, (MD) 4 March 1890, (MG) L. P. Whitney, J. P.
Green Brewer and Hepsie L. Castile of Iron Co., (MD) 1 June 1890, (MG) J. B. Hampton, J. P.
J. G. Carty and Lizzie Goggin, (MD) 5 February 1891, (MG) J. G. Hartman, J. P.
Moses C. Brooks and Margaret J. McDonald, (MD) 12 March 1891, (MG) W. J. Hunter, J. P.
Daneil Milford Lay and Mary Counts, (MD) 19 March 1891, (MG) W. J. Hunter, J. P.
William J. Cavesy and Drucilla F. Galian, (MD) 12 November 1874
Thomas F. Wadlow and Lucy M. Parks, (MD) 5 August 1878
James Kitchell and Eliza Fox, (MD) 27 October 1878
Jackson Hensin (?) and Sallie Goforth of Shannon Co. (?), (MD) ? February 1882
Shelby Carty and Sarah Lucetta Chance, (MD) ? October 1883
John William Middleton, of Wayne Co. and Nancy N. Keethly, (MD) 13 January 1884
Charles B. Larkin and Belle Hunter, (MD) 13 March 1884
William H. Lay and Mollie E. Bailey, (MD) 2 March 1884
Thomas J. Pogue and Mary Jane Ratliff, (MD) 30 October 1884, (PM) Married at John Ratliff's home
R. V. Sumpter and Mary J. Goggin, (MD) 17 February 1886, (PM) Married at the Goggin residence
M. D. L. Lewis and Margaret J. Barton, (MD) 25 February 1886
John Kuntz, Jr. and Algiline Davidson, (MD) 11 March 1886
Patton Radford and Rebecca McMullens, (MD) 9 March 1887
B. F. Gore and Scioto Jones, (MD) 25 March 1887
C. M. Santhuff and Roisa Piles, (MD) 27 November 1887

G. T. Lewis and Harriet J. Haywood, (MD) 23 July 1888
C. C. Bone and Mary J. Hope, (MD) 2 September 1888
John Ellis and E. J. Camden, (MD) 4 September 1888
Henry T. Chitwood and Fannie Coleman, (MD) 16 January 1890
George W. Blankinship and Rosa J. Johnson, (MD) 26 February 1891

Coleman Cemetery, Babler State Park, St. Louis County, Missouri.

Name	Birth	Death
John P. Coleman	May 28, 1848	Mar. 3, 1897
Robert Goodwin Coleman	Sep. 18, 1843	May 12, 1904
Eugene Coleman	May 31, 1859	Feb. 8, 1905
Mary ???ris Coleman(*)	Oct. 14, 1848	Oct. 31, 1888

*Head stone damaged, wife of Robert G. Coleman, Jr.

Harris Coleman	1888	1950
??? Kennett	Apr. 19, 1903	

Cass County, Missouri, March 31, 1885, Election of Township Officers, Pleasant Hill Precinct, Pleasant Hill Township.

Judges: W. R. Tayler, C. M. Baird, R. C. Williamson, T. J. Buchanan. C. O. Race, J.P.

Clerks: Duncan Hickman, C. I. Parker, Amos Carter, I. L. Wood.

Voters: M. H. Good, P. D. Gorden, R. N. Bush, W. H. Parker, C. S. Bush, W. L. Jarrott, Thos. Hair, T. H. Cloud, Wm. Koskey, John J. Barnes, Henry Codrell, B. Zick, John Fidler, I. J. Norris, J. C. Pelsor, B. L. Reed, T. H. Gregg, L. D. Shaw, A. G. Cosby, J. T. Boswell, W. W. Mathews, J. H. Roof, W. W. Kenedy, A. M. Hervey, Abe Simmons, H. Pyburn, F. W. Little, Sr., J. W. Chambers, B. D. Stephens, Aron Davis, Jas. L. Cook, J. H. Skillman, W. E. Carter, B. M. Best, John Ittle, J. R. Hickman, J. A. Shuttleworth, J. W. Sneed, J. F. Bennett, J. K. Anderson, J. L. Sullivan, D. A. Mers, Wm. Haley, Frank Cordell, R. H. Skillman, J. W. Walker, O. L. Beasley, J. A. Logan, Fred Carle, Scott Wilson, B. Bradey, Chas. Vickinberg, J. R. Rhea, T. Evans, O. Clark, Sam Herndon, W. O. Miller, J. M. Duncan, R. K. Maiden, Arch Johnson, Green Wood, John Miller, T. J. Turpin, J. H. Dobbins, T. O'Connell, Jr., D. Troup, B. F. Lacy, H. T. Moore, Jeff Green, F. P. Neyman, Philip Thornton, Jas. Thornton, Noah Ragsdale, S. B. Neyman, Fred Edmonson, G. Griffeth, G. C. Broadhead, S. Simpson, Sr., L. W. Frazier, L. D. Foree, J. C. Hon, J. Watkins, F. A. Beeler, John Cornman, Jas. O'Connell, C. H. Joy, Geo. Rheem, G. W. Holliwaw (?), M. J. Lynch, Chas. Calliway, A. L. Reed, W. A. Fleming, J. Hess, W. G. Evans, J. Benington, J. Shade, R. Irvin, J. M. Momve, Jessie McAninch, J. S. Underwood, C. G. Briscoe, J. W. Briscoe,

Merifield, J. Specht, Geo. Winn, Nelson Brown, M. Chipley, J. G. Alexander, George Pence, Bird White, Wm. Gardiner, H. M. Hogjitt, G. H. Green, A. W. Young, W.C. VanHoy, Mark Barber, P. Ostimyer, W. D. Myers, H. T. Skillman, H. Scott, E. W. Parker, E. Davis, J. Downey, Geo. Gosch, J. G. Sparks, J. B. Stacy, J. Schader, W. B. Pitts, W. H. H. Gustion, Jas. Linsley, S. P. Fleming, Dave I. Fleming, W. H. Meyers, John Merifield, H. H. Barker, S. E. Brown, Wm. Jones, P. Hemsley, G. M. Hill, H. J. Casey, J. Armstrong, A. D. Harbison, J. D. Tuttle, Robt. Scott, Jeff Moton, Wm. Montgomery, J. Calliway, Chas. Moore, S. Fowler, Wm. Vanhultz, L. Z. Fenton, W. E. Whitsett, J. H. Van Arsdell, Abe Smith, T. J. Troupe, J. Halet, W. H. Powd, M. J. McArthur, E. B. Stalnaker, M. Smith, Wm. McKee, F. Donnelly, ??? Fenton, T. H. Marshall, H. L. Freeman, T. H. Callahan, J. C. Westfall, J. S. Forbs, T. J. Foster, L. E. Winfield, Joseph Schader, Chas. Neyman, Pat. Mahan. Chas. Rheem, Lee Bruton, A. H. Shiveley, E. H. Charlton, C. B. Pole, W. R. Thompson, B. F. Preston, J. L. Smith, J. R. Lowe, J. T. Smith, G. T. Bailey, Ben Duncan, Jas, Plummer, Smith Freeeman, D. G. Landes, C. L. Mayo, J. B. Williams, Theo Stanley, J. J. Mahony, J. L. Jones, R. W. Gillet, Ralph Green, John Thornton, G. W. Trombo, J. B. Wilson, R. Chance, R. Thomas, W. H. Gardiner, Geo. Freeman, John Criteser, L. H. Larkin, A. H. Page, J. S. Wailson. F. Rhodes, A. S. Trotter, Clay Fleming. Thomas Easman, A. D. Prater, F. Johnson, Jas. Riley, B. F. McDonnel, John Carlisle, Tyler Thompson, Thomas Quigley, John Bow, C. C. Dawson, E. R. Wherrett, Chris Schuler, J. R. Bridgewater, C. O. Race, E. W. Hockidy, A. G. Spears, W. E. Pearce, A. R. Wherrett, S. A. McPherron, S. McAninch, H. T. Smith, W. W. Prater, Joseph Henlyey, Wm. Smoot, Thomas Carol, A. M. Chaney, F. Lynn, J. T. Simpson, J. Maurer, Chas. Bickle, M. Gardiner, F. P. Smith, W. F. Heyden, W. P. Kazee, Wm. Rhea, J. P. Ogden, G. H. Short, John Prater, E. W. Smith, T. G. Vandevanter, Wm. Olson, M. Huston, J. D. Moffat, R. M. Smith, R. R. Stripe, W. T. Lampkin, P. Bitz, G. M. Kellogg, S. Simpson, Jr., A. Adams, W. A. Wilson, Leslie Clark, W. F. Thornton, J. I. Thomas, J. Britton, Smith Duncan, S. L. Christ, Jas. Nichelson, W. Brannock, N. Davis, R. W. VanHoy, J. E. McKesson, Welsey Neal, E. H. Nelson, Wm. H. Martin, L. J. Tyler, Wm. Kissic, J. C. White, Frank Merrifield, F. W. Robinson, Chas. Windfield, D. A. Marshall, J. A. Prater, Steph. Alexander, B. Sneed. John Rostin, Perry Humsley, Sr., G. Lamont, J. McFadden, Jack Riley, J. W. McAninch, Mike Droyer, H. C. Ostrander, E. H. Yarnald, S. B. Wilson, S. A. Henley, J. H. Frakes, J. J. Kelley, John L. Powell, H. C. White, John Agy, M. Thompson, W. Hemsley, C. B. Bledsoe, Wm. Clay, J. P. Lynch, J. H. Stripe, G. I. Shepherd, Jas. Boswell, C. Herring, W. C. Smith, Simon Head, J. W. Smith, J. L. Warden, Sylvester Powell, J. T. Russell, W. L. Ainsworth, D. H. Harbison, Sherman Keen, J. Finely, Chas. Henderson,

Head, J. W. Smith, J. L. Warden, Sylvester Powell, J. T. Russell, W. L. Ainsworth, D. H. Harbison, Sherman Keen, J. Finely, Chas. Henderson, Cook Nelson, G. W. Petree, Owen Wilson, J. B. Cabness, Robt. Brown, W. S. Bowden, N. Miller, John Hoofer, J. L. Barnes, G. W. Stephenson, W. Pickthorn, W. H. Dinges, Jas. Cameron, Robt. Davis, P. Reed, W. G. Virgin, J. W. Virgin, S. Young, D. F. Virgin, C. S. McArthur, E. B. Smith, G. H. Stalen, W. P. Wherrett, W. M. Bernard, Harry Garigan, Richard Pearce, Robt. Auldridge, Fred. Laub, W. A. Buckner, John Bour, Frank Moore, A. Allen, J. L. Preston, C. E. Wilson, G. A. Clay, Herman Whitsel, Jas. Carney, W. W. Winfrey, B. C. Smith, J. A. Ainsworth, F. D. Mers, S. T. Ward, Jas. McGrath, Jas. Howard, Geo. Cook, Richard Clay, J. O. P. Sherlock, J. B. Hon, Joseph Boyd, Allen Overton, S. Long, Paul Handy, J. Loback, Abe Hess, G. B. Thomas. T. F. Simons, G. H. Gibbons, Henry Cleay, W. S. Shepherd, G. Dooley, R. Dotsey, H. Scott, Beverly Hockaday, W. Cunningham, A. G. Richardson, C. O. Chilton, J. H. Lofland, E. R. Mathews, Jerry Taylon, Dan Dwyer, Jas. Allen, Willis Gates, Tho. Fitzgerald, H. H. Ison, Wm. Davidson, W. Shortridge, Tho. Napier, J. K. Burnes, G. M. Bolinger, G. Parker, W. P. Parker, J. F. Kelley, J. Frazier, W. R. Taylor, T. J. Buchanan, F. P. Stalnaker, I. L. Wood, C. N. Baird, F. A. Gardiner, Amos Carter, J. Roebuck, E. B. Hart, Robt. T. Elmore, A. D. Harbinson, A. Mathews, Tho. Reed, Wm. Bledsoe, W. Duglas, J. H. Dallas, C. W. Dasher, H. B. Hook, Nelson Thompson, Joseph Denton, D. Helmer, E. N. McFarland, W. S. Symington, W. I. Bowing, H. G. Ainsworth, Thos. J. Lynch, John Brown, M. F. Parker, Dustin Adams, O, Cooper, Z. Leonard, H. G. Burgess, Wm. Vickery, W. J. Vansickle, A. D. Paul, A. M. Dunn, R. T. Brown, D. P. Dunn, Chas. Trotter, Wils Mers, Wm. Chashiner, Wm. Byers, R. Burnes, J. (?) D. Myers, P. N. McMurtry, Wm. Davis, J. M. Gillet, Chas. Hunter, E. R. Gill, D. F. Trotter, J. L. Dunn, G. A. Ostrander, S. Heyden, E. S. Sax, D. Taylor, G. N. Dun, R. B. Bernaw, J. A. Dunn, W. H. Whittey, W. A. Farmer, J. H. Stone, J. L. Scott, Chas. Rolley, Harvey Russel, A. Harrison, Isaac Linton, J. Calihan, S. H. Bohall, G. Rodgers, F. Lipfret, J. Murry, Cass. Rodgers, Wm. Buttermore, L. Crotty, J. C. Pearce, C. Cashines, W. H. Myers, J. L. Clements, G. M. Neff, John Simpson, R. Shelton, W. H. Bohartm W. A. McArthur, Ben Watkinson, Levy Honn, G. H. Caughren, Thomas Foster, Sam Bronough, W. H. Patterson, W. M. Powell, Levy Powell, John Boardman, A. Carret, Brown Reed, E. T. Sim-mons, E. A. Gowdy, Crit. Whaley, R. Van Hoy, Sam Wilkinson, J. F. McAfee, Geo. Williams, F. B. Henley, J. A. Watkinson, J. M. (?) Cook, J. J. Watkinson, R. N. Sebree, Andy Anderson, A. Hubbard, Wm. Merret, John Sebree, S. S. Sebree, S. Boyer, T. C. Best, G. T. Rowe, Tom Cheatham, Westley Penics, John Holliway, J. C. Knorpp, David Black, W. S. Slown, John Schader, T. A. Grant B. F. Fenton, G. Overton, J. K. P. Scott, R. Sneed, L.

Fristo, H. Berry, Wm. Snyder, Milton Alexander, Wm. Bryan, John Olson, A. B. Prosser, Will Williams, Dan Merideth.

Andrew County, Missouri, Testimonials for Nichols' Sanatorium, 1935.

Iowa

Name	City
Mr. W. B. Adams	Blanchard
Mr. J. M. Addison	Afton
Mr. G. R. Akey	Gravity
Mr. L. Albin	Stanton
Mr. William Allan	Baxter
Mrs. Flora L. Alleman	Boone
Gilbert L. Allgood	Rose Hill
Mrs. H. J. Allyn	Lewis
Albert L. Anderson	Ringsted
Miss Allie Anderson	Calmar
Mrs. Archie Anderson	Shellrock
Mrs. E. Anderson	Dunbar
Mrs. F. W. Anderson	Coon Rapids
Mrs. John T. Anderson	Meltonville
Mr. J. W. Anderson	Manson
Mrs. Oscar Anderson	Creston
Mrs. R. R. Anderson	New Market
Mr. W. H. Anderson	Eddyville
Oscar Andrew	Blanchard
Mrs. Ida Anema	Rock Valley
Mr. Bert G. Armstrong	Marshalltown
John S. Armstrong	Springville
Morris Arnold	Garden Grove
George E. Arthur	Raymond
Mr. J. H. Arthur	Bedford
Mr. O. T. Ashenhurst	Tingley
Mrs. O. T. Ashenhurst	Tingley
Mrs. S. E. Ashmore	Hepburn
Dick H. Assing	Pomeroy
Mrs. S. H. Assing	Manson
Mr. A. C. Bacan	Manson
Mr. J. M. Bacon	Hopkinton
Mrs. Daniel Baker	Spirit Lake
Mr. E. M. Baker	Gravity
Mr. Mills Baker	Otranto Station
Mrs. Minne Baker	Clarinda

Name	City
Mr. W. W. Baldwin	Algonda
Mr. C. L. Bales	Indianola
Wilton Ball	Cromwell
Mr. C. M. Barber	Rodman
Mr. E. E. Bardsley	Clear Lake
Joe M. Barker	Keosauqua
Mr. N. A. Barker	Williamsburg
Mrs. H. W. Barnes	Cedar Rapids
Mr. J. T. Barrett	Perceival
Mrs. Sarah Bartels	Sioux Center
Mr. L. F. Bartholome	Moville
Mrs. Villa Bartlett	Garden Grove
Mr. C. W. Barton	Gravity
Mrs. Albert F. Behnke	Whittemore
Joseph Beiser	Algona
George E. Bell	West Bend
Mr. O. R. Benson	Creston
Mrs. Mathilda Bergstrom	Manson
Mr. R. L. Berner	Clear Lake
Mr. G. H. Besco	Blockton
Mr. J. B. Biedenbach	Mechanicsville
Mr. F. L. Biggerstaff	Malvern
Mr. A. W. Bishop	Knoxville
Mr. T. G. Bishop	Mason City
John Blaha	Iowa City
Mrs. William Blair	Clarinda
Mr. W. L. Blasey	Manson
Mrs. Sarah Blatt	Des Moines
Peter Blenderman	Anthon
Mr. F. G. Blessman	Clearfield
Mr. E. Grant Blick	Washington
Mrs. Frank Blonigen	Osage
Sam Blumer	Creston
Mr. G. B. Bly	Swan
Orval Bodger	Des Moines
Mrs. H. G. Bohn	Fenton
Peter Bohlen	Alexander
Mr. I. C. Bollman	Luana
Mrs. Clara E. Boltinghouse	Lenox
Mrs. Orintha E. Booe	Nodaway
George Booth	Bagley
Mr. W. A. Boots	Morley

Name	City
David Borop	Dawson
Martin H. Borrusch	Bedford
Mr. E. E. Bosley	Clarinda
John C. Bracy	Belle Plaine
Carl H. Brandt	Hubbard
Mrs. Carl Breckenfelder	Masonville
Mr. L. E. Bridges	Coulter
Mrs. J. H. Brinkmann	Estherville
Mrs. F. T. Bridwell	Villisca
Tom A. Briscoe	Keokuk
Mrs. C. E. Brott	Indianola
Mrs. A. H. Brown	Clearfield
Mr. B. F. Brown	Prescott
Clarence L. Brown	Boone
George Brown	Logan
Soloman Brown	Iowa City
Charles T. Bruce	Rockwell
Mrs. M. T. Bruce	Indianola
Mrs. Ann Bruner	Conway
Mrs. Sarah Brush	Cedar Rapids
Mrs. Mary L. Bryan	Lineville
Mr. M. T. Bundy	Cedar Rapids
Mrs. E. T. Bryan	Estherville
Everett Bunker	Lorimer
Mrs. M. G. Burch	Braddyville
Mrs. Minnie Burch	Lake City
Thomas Burke	Riceville
Mr. W. R. Burns	Mason City
Mr. J. P. Burrus	Prole
Mr. R. E. Busby	Clearfield
Mr. G. A. Bushnell	Sioux City
Jesse R. Butcher	Onawa
Mr. P. D. Butler	Fort Dodge
Mr. W. T. Butler	Creston
Mr. V. Byers	Lake Park
Mr. W. F. Butman	Mount Edna
Mrs. C. J. Bywater	Riceville
Mr. C. L. Cahail	Guthrie Center
Mrs. R. H. Calvert	Arion
Mr. J. C. Campbell	Spencer
Mr. M. Campbell	Westfield
Mrs. Myrtle Carder	Osceola

Name	City
Mrs. A. Victor Carlson	Albert City
Edwin Carlson	Essex
Mrs. Mary A. Carr	Honey Creek
Mr. J. P. Carroll	Diagonal
Mr. O. L. Carson	Clearfield
Mrs. O. L. Carson	Clearfield
Mr. C. W. Carter	Lytton
Mrs. Day Carter	Tingley
Stewart Cavner	Clarinda
Mrs. E. R. Cecil	Creston
Harvey Chance	Washington
Frank Chandler	Gravity
Theodore Chestock	Tama
Mrs. John Chilote	Beacon
Mrs. Cora Chinn	Marshalltown
Mrs. W. S. Chinn	Sioux City
Mrs. Chris Christensen	Council Bluffs
Mrs. Elmo Clapp	Riceville
Mr. R. E. Clark	Clear Lake
Mrs. A. B. Clarke	Boone
Mrs. Jesse Clayton	Clearfield
Fred Coakley	West Chester
Mrs. H. C. Coates	East Cedar Rapids
Benton Cobb	Bedford
Mrs. W. H. Cochrane	Corning
Mr. M. V. Cole	Woodward
Mr. S. F. Cole	Pella
Abner Colee	Fort Dodge
Mrs. A. Colee	Fort Dodge
Mrs. J. R. Colvin	Yale
Jasper Conard	St. Charles
Mrs. Jasper	St. Charles
Mr. H. Congdon	Clarinda
Mrs. Bessie Conrad	Adair
Mr. M. S. Conrad	Malvern
Mr. W. A. Cook	Mount Ayr
Mr. H. C. Cooper	Webster City
Joseph Cooper	Clearfield
Mr. A. L. Cornwell	Perry
Mr. R. C. Couch	Casey
Mrs. Anna Courtnet	Algona
Mrs. Bessie Courtright	Sioux City

Name	City
Mrs. W. M. Cowman	Perey
Mr. J. M. Cox	Northboro
Louis Cox	Dubuque
Thomas H. Coyoe	Marshatown
John B. Crawford	Des Moines
Mr. P. E. Crawmer	Malvern
Mr. C. E. Creamer	Batavia
Jerry Cronin	New Virginia
Mrs. J. W. Croskey	Tama
Samuel Cross	Baxter
Mr. T. C. Crosser	Eldora
Mr. W. F. B. Crouse	Strahan
Mrs. W. F. B. Crouse	Strahan
John Culbreth	Cedar Rapids
Mr. F. W. Cunningham	Creston
Elmer E. Curry	Guthrie Center
Mrs. L. T. Danielson	Keokuk
Mr. I. M. Danskin	Belle Plaine
Miss Zilpha Davenport	Leon
George R. Davis	Emerson
Mr. M. T. Davis	Malvern
Will A. Davis	Oakland
Mr. E. C. Decker	Sioux City
Mr. J. M. Decker	Little Cedar
Mrs. John Decker	Little Cedar
Mrs. Mary DeFord	Columbus Junction
Mrs. Edward Degen	Sioux Center
Mrs. Dena Denekas	George
James C. Denhart	Diagonal
Orin Denning	McGregor
Mrs. W. H. Denton	Sioux City
Mrs. H. E. Deters	Ackley
Mrs. Anna M. Detlefsen	Schleswig
Peter DeVries	Sheldon
Dr. F. T. DeWitt	Doon
Mrs. Clara M. Dickey	Lamoni
Mrs. Melissa Diller	Washington
Mrs. Henry Dix	North Buena Vista
Francis Dobson	Ellston
Lawrence Doege	Titonka
Mr. J. F. Dowdall	Guthrie Center
Mrs. Mary F. Downing	Orient

Name	City
Franklin S. Downs	West Union
Stephen T. Doyle	Davenport
Mrs. John Drews	Farmersburg
Al Diskill	Davis City
Mr. D. L. Driver	Algona
Mr. W. H. Dudley	Lake City
Miss May Duncan	New Market
Philip Dunn	Sioux City
Mr. W. Z. Dutton	Clear Lake
Roy Dyer	Fort Madison
Mr. R. F. Eck	Richland
Mrs. Oscar Eden	Newton
Mr. J. J. Eddy	Davenport
William H. Edgar	Mapleton
Mr. C. N. Edmonds	Clarinda
Charles L. Edwards	Boone
Edward Ehlert	Sumner
Mrs. Ernest Ehrig	Gladbrook
Louis J. Eickelberg	Janesville
Mrs. E. B. Elliott	Grinnell
Joe Emerson	Olin
Mrs. J. S. Emerson	Peru
Mrs. A. E. Erickson	Ogden
Mrs. Emil Erickson	Sioux City
Charles I. Evans	Searsboro
Mrs. G. W. Evans	Clarinda
Mrs. R. L. Fairman	Council Bluffs
Mrs. Mae Faust	St. Charles
Anderson Fenimore	Peru
Mr. J. W. Ferguson	Plover
Julius Ferstl	Algona
Lars M. Finnestead	Fenton
Mrs. C. H. Fishburn	Crawfordsville
Dave Fisher	Livermore
Mrs. C. B. Fisher	Thayer
Mr. R. L. Flora	Davis City
Charles Fletcher	Clarinda
Mr. T. J. Forbes	Redding
Charles A. Foote	Corning
Mrs. Margaret A. Ford	Creston
S. Edward Fortsch	Cedar Falls
Mr. S. H. Fosmire	Clearfield

Name	City
Mr. T. J. Foughty	Ventura
Mr. M. D. Fox	Odebolt
Virgil D. Foy	Griswold
Mrs. A. R. Francis	Kent
Mrs. Ernest Frank	Truro
Mrs. S. G. Frantz	Blairstown
Mrs. Charles Frederick	Strawberry Point
Mrs. J. W. Freeman	Council Bluffs
Henry Friday	Sigourney
Mrs. Charles Frush	Jesup
Mrs. W. J. Friese	Grundy Center
Mrs. George Fry	Barnes City
Mr. F. B. Fryer	Villisca
Josephus Fuller	Bedford
Mrs. George Fults	Clarinda
Mrs. S. G. Furnas	Ottumwa
Ben Gacke	Alvord
Frank M. Gallant	Sioux City
Mr. J. I. Galt	Meltonville
Mr. E. L. Gamble	Mechanicsville
Mr. C. M. Gardner	Osceola
Mr. G. C. Gardner	Osceola
Mrs. J. H. Garfield	Early
Miss Grace Garner	Leon
Mrs. Peter Garvin	Muscatine
Mrs. Sarah E. Gates	Menlo
Miss Carrie M. Gerberling	West Burlington
Henry Gibbs	Strawberry Point
Mrs. Henrietta Gillet	Corning
Mr. C. E. Gish	Kirkman
Mr. F. K. Gleason	Mechanicsville
Mr. J. D. Goble	Clearfield
John Goeddertz	Algona
Ed F. Goeke	Postville
Mr. F. A. Goeke	Waukon
Mrs. A. Goeschel	Turkey River
Mr. M. Gokey	Hampton
Thomas Goodall	Shenandoah
Mr. T. L. Goeldner	Webster
Mrs. I. G. Gordon	Creston
George Gorsuch	Shannon City
Mr. R. M. Gourley	Villisca

Name	City
Peter Govern	Titonka
Mrs. Frank Gowing	Essex
Mr. J. G. Graul	Clinton
Earl E. Gray	Blockton
Mrs. Charles Greazel	Iowa City
Mr. E. S. Green	Woden
Mrs. Peter Greenfield	Batavia
Mr. W. H. Greenwood	Tabor
Mrs. Rose Gregory	Lake Park
Mr. J. J. Griffith	Redding
Fred Gronau	Kiron
Mrs. E. Groth	Postville
Wester Gruchow	Spencer
John M. Guinan	Sioux City
Louis P. Gunderson	Fort Dodge
Mrs. Albert H. Guse	Sanborn
Barney Hagemmann	Atkinson
Lloyd Hagensick	St. Olaf
Mrs. Eva Haile	Birmingham
Charles F. Haines	Iowa Falls
Mr. C. E. Hall	Centerville
Mr. C. W. Hall	Hubbard
Mrs. Charles Hall	Hubbard
Mr. D. A. Hall	Sioux City
Mrs. Sarah J. Hall	Benton
Arthur Halsey	Greenfield
Thomas G. Hamilton	Creston
Mrs. Charles C. Hand	Osceola
Mrs. Frank Hannah	Blanchard
Ed Hansen	Sloan
Hugo J. Harberg	Clayton
Mr. E. P. Hardee	Shambaugh
Joe Hardee	Nodaway
Frank Harmon	New Sharon
Frank Harms	Harris
Hans Harmsen	Garwin
Walter S. Harris	New Madrid
Wash Harris	West Bend
Mrs. C. E. Hart	Indianola
Mr. A. O. Hartwig	Meservey
Mrs. C. E. Harvey	Creston
George Hauser	New Hampton

Name	City
Mrs. J. Hauser	Melbourne
Mrs. B. L. Havdahl	Hornick
Mr. E. G. Haydon	Des Moines
Mrs. Charley Haynes	Shenandoah
Harry I. Heath	Mount Sterling
Mrs. Samuel Heather	Van Wert
Mrs. J. S. Hebron	Barnes City
Mr. S. Heggem	Slater
Mrs. Clara Heidemann	Manchester
Mrs. John Heinmiller	Riceville
Mr. G. A. Heitland	Latimer
Miss Maggie Helphrey	Newton
John Hemesath, Sr.	Ossian
Mr. F. E. Henderson	Arnolds Park
Mrs. Mary E. Henderson	Hawarden
Mrs. Emma Henrich	Sac City
Fred Hendricks	Allison
Mrs. Mary E. Henry	Des Moines
Mr. M. W. Henry	Strawberry Point
Mrs. W. M. Henry	Hamburg
Mr. F. J. Henser	Rockwell City
Mr. J. P. Heser	Charles City
Mrs. George Hevener	Vinton
Mr. E. J. Hewitt	Livermore
Bert Hewitt	New Hampton
David Hiatt	Sidney
James F. Hibbs	Seymour
Miss Mary Hicks	Gowrie
Mrs. Tille Hicks	Early
Mrs. W. A. Hildreth	Estherville
Mrs. Alice Hilliard	Des Moines
Myron Hines	Tipton
Mr. A. C. Hinman	Belmond
Jacob Hipsley	New Market
Mr. C. A. Hirschler	Donnellson
Mrs. Clara E. Hockenbery	Moville
Mrs. John Hodgson	Clarksville
Julius Hoeper	Waverly
Mrs. Carl R. Hoff	Ames
Miss Bernadeen Hoffman	Shannon City
Frank Hoffman	Blencoe
Mrs. C. J. Hofmaster	Williamsburg

Name	City
Mr. J. F. Hohl	Eddyville
Gust Hokenson	Odebolt
Mrs. Gust Hokenson	Spencer
Mr. Earl Holsapple	Cedar Rapids
William Holroyd	Albion
Mrs. Frances Holub	Traer
Mrs. R. H. Hook	Corydon
Mrs. V. J. Hooley	Richards
Oscar Hooper	Early
Mrs. Henry Hoover care of Frank G. Anderson	Mt. Etna
Earl D. Hopkins	Vinton
Mrs. Aaron Horn	Elkhart
Miss Callie Horn	Prairie City
Mr. H. O. Horn	Solon
John G. Horn	Boyden
Mrs. J. W. Horn	Hull
Mr. E. B. Horstmeyer	McClelland
Mrs. T. D. Hosman	Bedford
George W. Hough	Des Moines
Mr. R. A. Howard	Saint Charles
Mr. W. B. Huff	Wapello
Mr. E. A. Hughart	Cromwell
Mrs. R. P. Hughes	Eldora
Mrs. Richard Hughes, Jr.	Newton
Mr. W. J. Hughes	Sumner
Mrs. W. J. Hughes	Sumner
William Humphreys	Oakley
Mr. G. C. Humston	Washington
Mrs. A. S. Hutcheson	Kent
Mrs. Hugh Ingram	Clarinda
George S. Iverson	Legrand
Byron Jackson	Lorimor
Mr. G. E. Jenison	Belmond
Mr. C. L. Jernegan	Hampton
Andrew E. Johnson	Essex
Mrs. Dave Johnson	Rock Valley
Ed Johnson	Oseceola
James Johnson	Eddyville
Joe E. Johnson	Klemme
Mr. F. H. Johnston	Columbus City
George W. Johnston	Kent

Name	City
Amos R. Jones	Knoxville
Mrs. D. A. Jones	River Sioux
Mrs. Harriet A. Jones	Des Moines
Walter E. Jones	Red Oak
Mrs. A. E. Jordan	Leon
Mrs. Susie Joegenson	Clinton
Garrett Jurrens	Charles City
Mr. P. H. Kafer	Mt. Vernon
Mr. C. F. Kallenberger	Wapello
Pete Kaltenheuser	Mitchellville
Mrs. S. E. Kane	Anamosa
Mrs. Fred Karg	Muscatine
Mr. R. H. Kaster	Centerville
Mrs. Anna Kauble	Altelstan
Mr. T. M. Keeran	Red Oak
Mr. U. G. Keesy	Gladbrook
Mr. W. F. Kelleher	Lansing
Orien Keller	Davis City
Mr. W. S. Keller	Marshalltown
Mr. C. W. Kelly	Onawa
Mr. B. F. Kelso	New Market
Ival W. Kenan	Ogden
Mr. P. H. Kennedy	Nodaway
Mrs. J. F. Kensett, Sr.	Keokuk
Mr. C. H. Kern	Muscatine
George Kern	Columbus City
William Kernen	Nodaway
Mrs. Anna Kerr	Harlan
Mr. L. M. Kerr	Harlan
Joseph H. Kessels	Muscatine
Mr. W. R. Kester	Buckeye
Mrs. August Ketelsen	Walnut
Miss Jean Kettle	Blockton
Will S. Keyes	Boone
Mrs. George Killian, Jr.	Sigourney
Mr. W. C. Kimball	Shellrock
Mr. G. E. Kingsbury	Sumner
Mrs. W. M. Kinney	Lohrville
Mrs. Lennie Kinser	Promise City
Mrs. M. Kinser	Des Moines
Mrs. W. A. Kinser	Creston
Mrs. Amelia Kirchoff	Lewis

Name	City
Mr. D. M. Kite	Walnut
Mrs. Otto Kjosa	Farmsburg
Mrs. M. J. Klein	Ossian
Mr. H. H. Kinefelter	Grundy Center
Mrs. H. L. Kling	Newton
Mr. A. J. Klingeman	Monona
Mrs. R. Klinger	Donnellson
Mr. J. A. Knepper	Marengo
Mr. C. A. Kness	Harris
Mrs. Ann O. Knudsvig	Ossian
Herman Koch	Standwood
John Kottke	Fredericksburg
Adolph G. Kracht	Baxter
Mr. F. W. Kreitlow	Galt
Mr. J. L. Krieger	Donnellson
Mr. U. D. Kruse	Little Rock
John Lahs	Delphos
Ray Lambley	Conway
Mrs. Catherine Lamken	Gladbrook
Mr. C. H. Lark	Ogden
Mrs. F. G. Larrabee	Dundee
Alfred Larson	Albert City
Mrs. Dale Laub	Braddyville
Mr. C. W. Laughery	Guthrie Center
Mrs. Emeline Lawrence	Braddyville
Mrs. E. E. LeBeau	Victor
Mrs. Florence Leaming	Des Moines
George H. LeCornu	Muscatine
Mrs. A. H. Lee	Sioux City
Henry Lee	Delta
Mr. W. J. Lee	Van Wert
Mrs. L. F. Leighton	Belknap
Charles Lentz	Le Mars
Scott Leonard	Clearfield
Charley Leppert	Richland
Mrs. Walter Lettington	Indianola
Mr. Ole Levorson	Osage
Mrs. H. C. Lewis	Council Bluffs
Mrs. Taylor Lewis	Osceola
Mr. W. T. Libbey	Winterset
Mrs. W. T. Libbey	Winterset
Jacob C. Liechty	Polk City

Name	City
Albert Linton	Turin
Mrs. W. R. Lippincott	Indianola
Mr. W. S. Listen	Colfax
Mrs. Frank Little	Little Sioux
Mr. Wils Little	College Springs
Carl Loesche	Muscatine
Mr. W. R. Long	Williamsburg
Mrs. Hazxel Lookabill	Malvern
Mrs. Herman Lorenz	Des Moines
James D. Loudon	Creston
Mr. C. O. Love	Winthrop
Mrs. Mary J. Lowden	Winterset
Howard Lowman	Algona
Mr. L. J. Lowman	Algona
William Lowrance	Leon
Mr. Leavitt Luce	Shenandoah
Mr. J. A. Luhr	College Springs
George Lyddon	Clearfield
Mrs. C. E. Lyon	Ames
Miss Esther Machlan	Weldon
Mr. C. V. Magneson	Stanton
Mr. A. L. Mahan	Guthrie Center
Mrs. Elie Mahaffey	Letts
Fred Mallett	Gutherie Center
Mr. G. D. Marsh	Strawberry Point
Mr. R. L. Martin	Pleasanton
Mrs. Martin Martinsen	Farragut
Mr. C. W. Mather	Bussey
John W. Mathis	Bondurant
Mrs. A. C. Matson	Randall
Alexander Matt	Guttenberg
Mrs. Harriett Maxwell	New Market
James C. May	Barnum
John H. May	Kanawha
Mrs. J. M. Mayall	Clarinda
Mr. E. R. Mayhew	Watkins
Mrs. J. A. Meadows	Creston
Mrs. Ivan Means	Lorimor
Melvin A. Means	Creston
Mr. J. R. Meekins	Radeliffe
Thomas Meester	Parkersburg
Mr. C. J. Meiners	Manson

Name	City
Mrs. J. W. Meloy	Sioux City
Mr. W. F. Melvin	Bedford
Mr. J. W. Meneely	Fairfield
Mrs. Anna Meredith	Muscatine
Harry Merrimen	Dallas
Henry Meyer	Perry
Mr. J. F. Meyer	Sidney
Philip Michel	Sigourney
Mrs. T. W. Millea (sic)	Fort Dodge
Mr. C. H. Miller	Moscow
Mr. E. M. Miller	Ottumwa
George G. Miller	Council Bluffs
Mrs. H. C. Miller	Bennett
Mr. J. C. Miller	Livermore
John Miller	Riceville
Mr. L. W. Miller	Malvern
Mrs. Merritt Miller	Hawarden
Mr. W. C. Miller	College Springs
Mr. E. J. Mitchell	Graettinger
Roy Mills	Grant
Mr. J. W. Mitchell	Armstrong
Mrs. Oliver J. Mitchell	Council Bluffs
Mr. C. W. Monn	Cedar Rapids
Mr. Truls Monson	Buffalo Center
Mrs. Anna Montague	Blanchard
Mrs. Opal Montgomery	Des Moines
Mr. J. D. Moodie	Emmetsburg
Mr. W. J. Mooney	Sac City
Mrs. C. C. Moore	MacIntire
Mr. E. E. Moore	Cinncinnati
Mrs. F. S. Moore	Leon
Frank Moran	Clinton
Mr. B. D. Morgan	Kellerton
Mrs. Wm. B. Morrison	Eldon
Mr. J. E. Mote	Carlisle
Mrs. A. I. Moyer	Oelwein
Mrs. Elizabeth Mulhollen	Des Moines
Charles E. Mull	Jefferson
John J. Murphy	Bettendorf
William Murphy	Fort Dodge
Frank T. Myers	Guthrie Center
Mr. F. S. Myers	Martelle

Name	City
Mrs. S. R. McAninch	Hawarden
Mrs. Myrtle McBeth	Richland
Mr. A. R. McCart	Avoca
Mrs. Joe McCauley	Avoca
Mr. C. E. McClain	New Virginia
Mr. W. H. McClelland	Rodman
Guy McCloud	Creston
Mrs. Newt McConnaha	Muscatine
Mrs. Elizie M. McCrill	Blencoe
Mr. J. W. McCullough	College Springs
Mrs. Kate McCumber	Eldora
Mr. W. F. McFarland	Bancroft
Mr. P. J. McGuire	Clear Lake
Mrs. Octavia McKay	Corning
Mrs. James McLane	Strawberry Point
Mr. H. E. McLaughlin	Milford
Mrs. E. I. McLeod	Coin
Mr. J. Q. McMahon	West Liberty
Mrs. Belle McManis	Shannon City
Mrs. L. O. McNeill	Swea City
Mr. W. L. McNiel	Batavia
Mr. A. J. McNichols	Oskaloosa
Mr. W. J. McPherren	Stanton
Mr. T. H. McShane	Blencoe
James McTgert (sic)	Strawberry Point
Mrs. Alice E. Neal	Cedar rapids
Mr. E. C. Nichols	Manly
George P. Nichols	West Liberty
Mrs. Lulu Nickell	Lineville
Ernest Nielsen	Geneva
Mrs. Lillie M. Mielsen	Harlan
Henry Nieuwendorp, Sr.	Sheldon
Mrs. Margaret Nine	New Virginia
Mrs. Mae A. Nolta	Marshalltown
Mrs. M. F. Norcutt	Nodaway
Mr. R. O. Norton	Boone
Evan Noyes	Monadamin
Mrs. Mary Nuessle	Leeds
Mrs. John Oberthien	Watkins
Mr. N. N. O'Dell	Gravity
Eugene N. Ogbin	Plainfield
Mr. S. A. Olden	Hardy

Name	City
Goodman Olson	Kelley
John J. O'Neil	Elma
Dr. O. T. Onstott	Gladbrook
Niels Overgaard	Cedar Falls
Mr. W. J. Oviatt	Villisea
Mr. C. A. Pace	Diagonal
Mr. C. M. Pantier	Elma
Mrs. Frank Parcell	Fair Field
Frank Parizek	Solon
Mrs. S. E. Park	Indianola
Mr. A. C. Parker	Derby
Pete O. Parker	Leon
Thomas A. C. Parker	Bedford
Mrs. L. A. Parks	Conway
Mrs. Frederick C. Parrish	Cedar Rapids
Mr. J. H. Patrick	Boone
Arthur Paterson	Orient
F. E. Payne (? male/female)	Wall Lake
Mrs. Margaret Pearson	Sioux City
Joseph Pech	Clinton
Allen Pence	Grand River
Mr. E. A. Pendergraft	Clarinda
Mrs. G. H. Perkins	Indianola
Edwin Perry	Colfax
Mrs. George Pestotmik	Boone
Mr. N. S. Peterman	Toledo
Charles Petersen	Lorimor
Mrs. Ellen Peterson	Union
Henry Peterson	Kingsley
Lars Peterson	St. Ansgar
Mr. A. I. Pettit	Keosauqua
William Phelan	Des Moines
Mr. E. A. Phillips	Fairfield
Leonard Phillips	Armstrong
Mrs. S. J. Phipps	Farragut
Mrs. Charles B. Pierce	Iowa Falls
John A. Pierce	Woodward
Mr. J. M. Pierce	Bartlett
Raymond Pipho	Waverly
Frank Pitman	New Market
Clarence C. Planalp	Baxter
William Pipho	Sumner

Name	City
Albert Plueger	Ireton
Mr. W. A. Poore	Kellerton
Mr. S. J. Porter	Storm Lake
Mrs. James Potts	Lenox
Anthon Poulsen	Boone
Mr. G.E. Prentis	Leon
Mr. S. H. Preston	Mount Etna
Owen Price	Emerson
Harley L. Pyle	Carroll
Mr. R. Query	Nodaway
John Quinn	Tama
Mrs. W. G. Randall	Marshalltown
Mrs. Lewis Rayburn	Honey Creek
Mrs. S. E. Raynor	New Market
John Redden	Ruthven
Mr. C. S. Reece	Derby
Mrs. T. M. Reed	Braddyville
Mr. B. M. Reeves	Clarinda
Mrs. Charles Reimer	Elkport
Guy W. Reid	Eldora
Chris Reimers	Boyden
Mrs. Henry Reitz	Donnellson
Mr. D. B. Rynolds	Glenwood
Mr. T. V. Reynolds	Thayer
Mrs. Thomas Rhoades	Shenadoah
Mrs. W. F. Richard	Pisgah
Mrs. Mary Richards	Hudson
Mrs. Josephine Richardson	Le Mars
Mr. W. R. Richardson	Gravity
Geo. Franklin Rickett	Marshalltown
Mr. J. T. Rickey	Winfield
Mr. S. P. Rocketts	Percival
Mr. J. E. Rittenhouse	Muscatine
Mrs. C. C. Roberts	Guthrie Center
Mrs. G. C. Roberts	Centerville
James E. Roberts	Perry
Mrs. L. Roberts	Sac City
Mr. E. B. Robinson	Dallas Center
Mrs. A. Rockefeller	Keokuk
William Roepke, Sr.	Oelwein
Mrs. Ara E. Rogers	Anthon
Mr. C. J. Roman	Sioux City

Name	City
Mrs. John H. Romine	Wellman
Mrs. G. I. Roorda	Pella
Robert Roosa	Dows
Harry Rossander	Stanton
Mr. E. J. Rossiter	Tabor
Mr. G. C. Rossler	Solon
Mrs. George C. Rossler	Solon
Mr. J. F. Rossow	Lohrville
Mrs. Jessie E. Roush	Valley Junction
Mr. D. E. Routh	Clearfield
Mrs. Lulu Rowley	Bussey
Mr. W. Grant Rubey	Shenandoah
Mrs. William Rummel	Clarence
Mrs. Clyde Rupert	Clearfield
Col. Farris Russell	Creston
Mr. D. J. Ryan	Leonx
Mrs. J. H. Ryan	Leon
Mr. J. L. Ryan	Murray
Mrs. G. J. Ryken	New Sharon
Walter E. Sabin	Wallingford
Mrs. W. H. Sabin	Mallard
Mr. H. E. Safford	Maquoketa
Grant Sample	Muscatine
Albert C. Sandhagen	Dundee
Mr. E. H. Sands	Belmond
Mrs. John Sandusky	Newton
Mrs. J. A. Saville	Redding
Mr. J. E. Sawhill	Truro
Mrs. Charles Schamel	Lohrville
Charles Schmidt	Watkins
William Schmoll	Clearlake
Otto Schoeneman	Sheldon
George Schoon	Fonda
Henry P. Schramm	Early
Mrs. W. C. Schrier	Indianola
Rev. G. Schroeder	Belle Plaine
Henry Schultz	Blairstown
George W. Scroggie	Blockton
Mrs. George W. Scoggie	Blockton
John Scully	Hiteman
Mrs. J. D. Seamster	Shenandoah
Mr. B. T. Sears	Decatur

Name	City
Mr. E. K. Sears	Perry
Mrs. Antonia Sedlacek	Solon
Mrs. C. B. See	Grinnell
Mr. W. H. See	Peru
Mr. J. C. Shafer	Kinross
Mrs. Martha E. Shafer	Redding
John W. Shaffer	Murray
Mrs. Sadie Shaffer	Anamosa
William A. Shaner	Eldora
Charles W. Shank	Red Oak
Jay Shanstrom	Fairfield
Mr. W. O. Sharpe	Clarinda
Frank M. Shearer	Des Moines
Mrs. Amos Sheets	Cambria
William Sheetz	Muscatine
Mr. L. P. Sheldon	Osage
Albert Shell	Boone
Mr. M. S. Shepherd	Cedar Rapids
Clark Sherman	Postville
Ira Shields	Kellogg
Mrs. W. S. Shinn	Eddyville
Mrs. George Sibert	Waterloo
Maurice Silver	Elma
Mrs. Clara E. Slasor	Elma
Mr. A. D. Smith	Aurora
Mrs. A. D. Smith	Aurora
Mrs. A. D. Smith (sic)	Glidden
Mr. E. A. Smith	Ackworth
Earl N. Smith	Marshalltown
Mrs. George W. Smith	Le Mars
Mrs. H. H. Smith	Monona
Mrs. H. W. Smith	Braddyville
Mr. J. N. Smith	Kellerton
John Smith	Dundee
Mrs. Josephine O. Smith	Ireton
Lewis M. Smith	Washington
Mrs. R. B. Smith	Sidney
Mr. R. J. Smith	Ireton
Mrs. Robert Smith	Glidden
Mr. W. J. Smith	Sharpsburg
Mr. S. B. Smith	Mapleton
Joseph Smrcek (sic)	Traer

Name	City
Mrs. Clara B. Smull	Plainfield
Mrs. Joe Snider	Waterloo
Mr. M. L. Snider	Richland
Uriah Snider	Winterset
Mr. L. G. Snively	New Market
Mrs. Nellie Songer	Webster City
James Sorensen	Turin
Mrs. Nita Soults	Oskaloosa
Mr. W. C. Sparks	Boone
Mrs. Mary Specht	Lamont
Mr. D. L. Spiker	Anita
James Spirek	Fort Dodge
Mrs. Daisy Spooner	Valley Junction
Mrs. Richard Stamper	Creston
Mrs. Addie Stanley	Creston
Mr. A. E. Starrett	Newton
George M. Stauffer	Gladbrook
Mrs. Levi Stutsman	Kalona
Mr. G. W. Stambaugh	Corwith
John Stapefeldt	Marengo
Mr. F. A.. Staton	Tabor
Nick Starck	Muscatine
Mr. F. L. Starweather	Boyden
Henry Stecker	Titonka
John Stenberg	Slater
Mrs. Martha Stenberg	Slater
Henry Stenson	McCallsburg
Mrs. Mary Stephens	Des Moines
Mrs. H. W. Stephenson	Cromwell
Mrs. J. A. Stevenson	Atlantic
Mr. O. L. Stevenson	Clearfield
James M. Stewart	Colfax
Miss Winfred Stewart	North Liberty
Mrs. A. H. Stock	Dumont
William Stockham	Hamburg
Col. F. L. Story	Olin
Mrs. Amelia Striemer	New Hampton
William H. Stout	Boone
Mr. G. J. Struthers	West Bend
Mrs. L. S. Suits	Malvern
James A. Surber	Des Moines
Mr. B. Sutherland	Decatur

Name	City
Mr. W. G. Swaim (sic)	Webb
Mr. A. C. Swain	Union
Mrs. E. L. Sweeney	Monroe
Miss Clarice Swinehart	Keokuk
Ed. J. Taha	Corning
Mr. Ell. Taylor	Deep River
Mrs. N. C. Taylor	Blencoe
Daniel Teeters	New Marlet
Mrs. J. J. Temple	Boone
Mr. Amiel Tesman	Wilton Junction
Mrs. William S. Tharp	Casey
Mr. H. H. Thies	Elma
Thomas Thiesen	Gladbrook
Mrs. Charles Thompson	Chelsea
Elmer R. Thompson	Kingsley
Frank L. Thompson	Belle Plaine
Mr. J. G. Thompson	Boone
Mrs. Sadie Thorn	Afton
Clarence Thornton	Clo
Mrs. Martha Tickner	Lamont
Mrs. Myrtle Tillman	Creston
Charlie Tilton	Carlisle
Mr. M. L. Tilton	Walnut
Mr. J. W. Tinsley	Des Moines
Mr. Len Tipton	Armstrong
Mr. J. F. Townley	Sioux City
Mrs. Idella Trout	Eldora
Mr. W. A. True	Richland
Mrs. M. M. Tucker	Pandora
Mr. H. L. Tullis	Leon
Miss Blanche Turgeon	Sidney
Mr. A. Turner	Fairfield
Mrs. D. B. Twinam	Crawfordsville
Mrs. Salestine Uhlenhake	Ossiam
Anton W. Ulch	Iowa City
Charles E. Urmy	Cedar Rapids
Mr. E. H. Urry	Graettinger
Mr. A. D. Valentine	Gravity
Mrs. L. L. Valliere	Cedar Rapids
Mrs. John G. Van Den Berg	Rock Valley
Mrs. Alice Vanderford	Indianola
Mr. C. C. Van Houten	Battle Creek

Name	City
Mr. J. D. Van Reenen	Bedford
Mrs. Maude Vanston	Des Moines
Mrs. Susie Vaughn	Benton
Mr. Lara Veland	Clater
David Vetter	Grant
Robert Votteler	Fenton
Frank Wade	Sidney
Mrs. Lena W. Wade	English
Robert Wade	Carlisle
Mrs. O. E. Waldo	Polk City
Mr. C. A. Walker	Northwood
Mr. F. L. Wallace	North English
Mr. G. W. Wallace	North English
Alfred Ward	Center Point
Mr. C. O. Ward	Murray
Mrs. Lora Ward	Centerville
Mr. C. G. Webb	Afton
Mrs. G. C. Webster	Blanchard
Mrs. Mary Glass Weger	Strawberry Point
Mrs. George Wehland	Walnut
William Wehrman	Melbourne
Mrs. Margaret Weingarth	Bedford
George D. Weintz	Sioux City
Mrs. James O. Weitgenent	Creston
Mrs. C. H. Weltzin	Raymond
Mr. J. M. Weltzin	Porte City
William Wessling	Marengo
Mr. F. W. Whan	Tipton
Mrs. Ben White	New Market
Mr. W. B. White	Olin
Mr. W. H. White	Keokuk
Mr. W. J. White	Oelwein
Mrs. S. S. Whitfield	Ames
Mrs. Arthur Wilcox	Akron
Mrs. H. D. Wilkey	State Center
Mrs. A. A. Williams	Bedford
Mrs. E. R. Williams	Hepburn
Miss Lillie C. E. Williams	Boone
Mrs. W. G. Williams	Williamsburg
Mr. F. K. Willloughby	Rockwell City
Mrs. F. E. Wilson	Lenox

Name	City
Mr. W. F. Wilson	Arispe
Mrs. Edna Winchell	Sioux City
Mr. J. F. Winter	Sumner
Mrs. John Witt	Remsen
Mrs. W. R. Wolfe	Fenton
Mr. C. T. Woodard	Mason City
Mrs. A. A. Woods	Creston
Mrs. Hal Woodward	Atlantic
Lewis B. Woolridge	Correctionville
Mrs. C. E. Work	Boyden
Mrs. David Wray	North Liberty
Mrs. Alfred Wright	Ackworth
Mr. J. A. Wullbrandt	Des Moines
Leonard Yaple	Braddyville
Mr. J. J. Yoder	Wellman
James E. Young	Charles
Mrs. A. L. Youngers	Hospers
Mrs. Eliza V. Zeck	Des Moines
Sandford Zeigler	Fairfield
Mr. W. C. Zickefoose	Des Moines
Mr. B. F. Zollner	Muscatine

Carter County Missouri, Aldrich Valley Cemetery, 5 Miles Off Hwy 60 In Aldrich Valley.

Name	Birth	Death
Loyd Bales	Apr. 2, 1910	Apr. 18, 1957
Robert Gene Bales	May 29, 1945	May 28, 1976
son of Loyd and Lucille Bales		
William R. Bales	May 17, 1943	Apr. 16, 1969
son of Loyd and Lucille Bales		
Browley Bales	---	---
Elisha Campbell	---	---
James William Campbell (Age: 90Y 9M 19D)		Jun. 23, 1974
Ralph Crouch	Mar. 11, 1917	Jun. 10, 1959
Zora Gore Crouch	Jun. 12, 1939	
Dicia Ann Dorris	Oct. 15, 1870	Jun. 6, 1946
Thomas C. Dorris	Apr. 4, 1867	Jul. 8, 1932
James P. Farris	---	Mar. 8, 1924
Mattie Johnson Felling	1861	1945
Samuel Ogden Furness	Nov. 18, 1862	Feb. 19, 1920

Name	Birth	Death
Sidney Wineford Gore	1930	1933
Sherman Gresham	Nov. 8, 1916	Mar. 3, 1917
Woodrow G. Gresham	Jun. 27, 1918	Mar. 27, 1922
Josephine Gresham	May 3, 1922	Apr. 11, 1932
Anna Harris	Jul. 3, 1863	May 30, 1936
Lurita Harris	Sep. 11, 1872	May 14, 1910
F. M. Harris	May 30, 1906	Apr. 24, 1925
Christopher Harris	Jul. 17, 1901	Nov. 3, 1951
Ruth Ellen Harris	Mar. 11, 1906	Aug. 11, 1939
Frank B. Harris	1896	1959
Henry Harris	1872	1961
Nancy Harris	May 4, 1910	Sep. 12, 1912
Daughter Of F.M. & Lurita		
Tolman Harris	May 19, 1907	Mar. 3, 1976
Mary Stewart Haynes	Sep. 15, 1861	Jul. 2, 1952
Enoch S. Johnson	Apr. 4, 1883	Jul. 7, 1960
Richard "Dick" Johnson	1852	1894
L. Ray Kester	Sep. 25, 1892	Sep. 4, 1954
Garnett Kester	Jun. 25, 1899	Mar. 18, 1968
Baby Daisy Moore	---	---
Baby Loyd C. Moore	---	---
Henry O. Moore	Mar. 22, 1875	Jun. 5, 1959
Mrs. Mageline Moore	Nov. 29, 1891	Nov. 2, 1935
Clara Renda Poe	Mar. 15, 1904	Jan. 8, 1926
Della Harris Price	Nov. 21, 1904	Jan. 13, 1987
Timon Price	Feb. 9, 1903	Aug. 9, 1979
Ruth Ethel Harris		May 13, 1903
Hanner T. Scears	1876	1952
Josephine Scears	Oct. 15, 1886	Dec. 15, 1915
W.A. Scears	Nov. 13, 1852	Dec. 17, 1947
Alpha Van Dyke	Nov. 26, 1896	Mar. 16, 1919
Esker Edward Woodard	Dec. 11, 1888	Sep. 27, 1955
Son Of Andy and Minnie		
Edith Worlow	Aug. 4, 1925	Feb. 18, 1964

Platte County, Missouri, Index to the Official Land Record Copy

Name	Section	Page
Joseph C. Abbott	29	17
Joseph C. Abbot	30	17
James Adams	04	10
Thomas Adams	32	16
William Adams	09	03

Name	Section	Page
Jacob Adamson	11	16
Larkin Adamson	11	16
Levi L. Adamson	11	16
John D. Alderson	22	17
John Aldridge	28	12
Nelson D. Alexander	01	18
Bethel Allen	28	16
Isaac Allen	17	16
Jesse R. Allen	07	15
Moses Allen	24	12
Robert Allen	05	13
Samuel Allen	19	16
Soloman Allen	30	16
Thomas Allen	19	16
William B. Almond	20	15
Alfred A. Ambers	31	04
Charles Anders	04	18
James Anders	04	18
Andrew W. Anderson	20	11
David Anderson	26	11
George W. Anderson	14	16
James W. Anderson	06	04
James W. Anderson	07	04
John R. Anderson	08	05
Rebecca Anderson	30	15
Daniel Andrews	14	04
Elias M. Andrews	17	04
Elias M. Andrews	19	04
James Andrews	04	17
William W. Andrews	20	04
Mary Anno	28	17
Isaac Archer	09	12
John Artman	05	04
David Ashby	25	08
Newton Ashby	26	04
William Asher	17	03
James Ashworth	23	12
James Ashworth	27	15
Starling Ashworth	35	15
William Ashworth	35	15
Jeremiah Atkins	15	16
William A. Austin	14	15

Name	Section	Page
Zabina Babock	05	05
Isham Baber	03	12
John Baber	36	08
Jordan Baber	12	11
Randal G. Baber	17	12
Thomas Baber	03	12
Daniel B. Bailey	04	18
John P. Bailey	05	18
Martin T. Bailey	05	18
Alexander Baker	13	07
John W. Baker	17	15
Larkin Barker	18	10
Larkin Barker	27	11
Lawson Barker	13	16
Martin Baldwin	12	12
Caleb Baley	05	06
Preston Ballard	06	02
Baldwin Bane	12	08
John Bane	11	08
William R. Bane	17	07
William Banta	29	14
Henry Barker	31	07
Henry Barnes	01	15
James Barnes	01	15
John Barnes	11	04
Thomas Barnes	09	17
Nancy Bates	13	12
Washington C. Bates	24	12
William H. Bates	21	11
Christopher Bauman	05	01
Peter Bauman	05	01
James baxter	05	08
Benjamin Bean	12	18
Benjamin Bean, Jr.	11	18
LeRoy Bean	11	18
Phantly R. Bean	18	17
Thomas Beasly	24	04
Stephen Bedwell	09	03
Stephen Bedwell	02	17
Godfrey Beaumont	33	17
Jno. Beckham	35	12

Name	Section	Page
John Beery	13	11
Nicholas Beery	09	10
James Begle	02	13
Alexnader Belcher	09	05
David R. Bell	34	17
John H. Bell	31	10
Lewis H. Bell	03	16
Thomas H. Bell	25	04
William Bell	23	04
William Bell	18	14
William Bell	23	15
William Bell	24	15
William H. Bell	03	16
William H. Bell	22	17
William H. Bell	23	17
William H. Bell	28	17
Nicholas Benner	10	13
Claton Bennett	32	08
Mary Bennett	29	08
Thomas Bennett, Jr.	05	02
James H. Berry	32	06
James H. Berry	35	07
Sidney G. Berry	32	06
William G. Berry	30	06
William Best	04	17
Samuel Betts	18	14
Joseph H. Biggs	32	17
Byrd Billings	11	17
John Bingham	02	17
Charles W. Bingley	22	05
Charles C. Birch	05	01
Charles C. Birch	34	10
Thomas E. Birch	02	07
Henry Bittleman	31	03
James Blackwell	01	05
James Blakely	14	12
Joseph Blakely	24	12
Thomas Blankenship	08	10
Ezekiel Blanton	19	07
Isaac Blanton	11	12
Joel Blanton	11	12
John Blanton	31	07

Name	Section	Page
Washington L. Blanton	26	08
Christopher H. Block	32	14
Arnold D. Blythe	10	13
Arnold D. Blythe	14	13
George W. Boardman	07	08
George W. Boardman	01	09
George W. Boardman	25	15
Henry Bolinger	06	01
John M. Bollinger	06	01
Joshua Bollinger	06	01
William L. Bonnell	20	16
Lucy Boon	13	18
Abner Boozarth	32	07
Leslie C. Bostick	36	16
John Boulware	29	12
John Boulware	30	12
Henry B. Bouton	06	01
John Bowen	01	04
Henry I. Bowers	04	10
Samuel C. Bowers	05	10
Delaney Bowlin	13	08
John Bowlin	14	08
William Bowlin	14	08
Abraham Bowman	09	05
George Bowman	33	08
Henry Bowman	17	05
Henry Bowman	08	05
Jacob Bowman	33	08
John W. Bowman	09	05
Joseph Bowman	08	05
Michael B. Bowman	08	08
Samuel Bowman	05	05
Samuel Bowman	32	08
Thomas Bowman	33	08
Henry Boydston	01	15
Henry Boydston	02	15
Jacob Boydston	35	07
William Boydston	17	11
Samuel Bradbury	07	01
Samuel C. Braden	23	12
Henry Bradley	15	17
Thomas K. Bradley	14	11

Name	Section	Page
Charles Bradshaw	26	17
Barzillai Brady	14	17
Benjamin Brady	22	17
Janes Brasfield	25	11
John Bretz	34	16
Walter L. Brightwell	20	07
Henry Brill	11	13
Elijah W. Brink	29	04
Henry Broadhurst	20	03
Jacob Broadhurst	20	03
John F. Broadhurst	29	03
James A. Brock	31	15
Perry G. Brock	05	07
Henry Brooks	29	15
John M. Brooks	29	15
Samuel J. Brooks	07	06
Adam Brown	12	04
Anchiser Brown	14	05
Andrew H. Brown	28	06
Archibald Brown	18	03
Christopher P. Brown	10	03
Colden C. Brown	19	03
Elam Brown	29	16
Francis Brown	22	04
Gray B. Brown	36	04
Gray B. Brown	26	08
Hiram Brown	13	04
Hugh Brown	18	11
James Brown	13	12
James H. Brown	20	03
James R. Brown	36	04
John E. Brown	05	02
John W. Brown	06	03
Josiah Brown	19	03
Micajah Brown	18	03
Milton Brown	35	12
Obadiah Brown, Jr.	13	07
Rowland Brown	03	05
Samuel A. Brown	18	07
Samuel N. Brown	14	04
Samuel Brown, Sr.	19	03
Sarshel C. Brown	07	03

Name	Section	Page
Townsar F. Brown	13	04
William Brown, Jr.	13	04
Willian Brown, Sr.	13	04
George W. Browning	24	09
John Brunts	27	11
John L. Brunts	35	11
Anderson Bruton	02	04
David Anderson, Jr.	11	04
Andrew Cieson	04	02
David Anderson, Jr.	36	07
David Anderson, Sr.	01	04
David Anderson	11	04
Milton I. Bryan	06	17
John Bryant	08	07
John Bryant	09	07
William K. Bryant	01	07
John R. Buchanan	28	12
Martin Buff	24	08
Martin Buff	25	08
Addison L. Bullock	28	03
John H. Bunemann	30	03
John Burge	29	16
John Burgen	33	10
Cornelius Burgess	13	16
John Burgess	01	16
Philip J. Burgess	19	16
Henry F. Burke	27	17
Allen J. Burks	05	13
Fielding Burnes	20	15
Lewis Burnes	28	08
Lewis Burnes	29	08
William D. Burnes	31	06
James Burnes	17	15
James Burnes	20	15
William G. Burns	08	13
Joseph Busby	01	09
Archibald Buster	17	08
Jacob Butcher	11	15
James Butler	18	10
James Butler	30	14
William Butler	20	14
Enos Butrick	34	03

Name	Section	Page
Jackson Butts	22	17
William Byrd	09	10
James Byrd	20	07
Michael Byrd	21	07
John C. Bywaters	04	11
John C. Bywaters	09	11
John C. Bywaters	33	15
Charles L. Cain	17	16
Eli D. Cain	14	04
Jesse Cain	17	16
John B. Cain	10	07
Robert Cain	15	07
Robert Cain	30	07
William R. Cain	15	17
Barton W. Calvert	04	12
Jeremiah Calvert	07	12
Lewis Calvert	04	12
Smith Calvert	09	12
Point Camden	32	22
Andrew Campbell	32	07
George W. Campbell	09	04
John S. Campbell	33	03
Temperance Campbell	09	04
Thomas H. Campbell	05	02
Thomas H. Campbell	31	04
Cephas Cane	12	13
Joseph T. Cannon	06	10
Francis J. Carpenter	27	07
Jonathan Carpenter	26	07
Jonathan Carpenter	34	07
James Carr	04	03
David Carson	22	08
James Carson	31	15
Thomas P. Carter	24	07
Daniel Cary	15	07
Thomas Catlett	28	03
James Cave	03	04
John B. Cavin	13	11
Joseph Cearnes	29	17
Allen Chance	08	03
Allen Chance	09	03
Allen Chance	14	17

Name	Section	Page
Arnold Chance	12	09
William Chance	31	16
Elizabeth Chandler	02	05
John Chandler	35	08
William H. Chapman	31	14
James Childress	07	16
Lewis B. Chinn	17	10
Adam Christison	18	07
John W. Christy	11	05
Alfred M. Clark	10	03
Gabriel P. Clark	18	16
Maclomn Clark	36	13
Charles Clarke	32	07
Edward Clarke	06	04
James M. Clay	21	14
Johnson Clay	24	16
Thomas H. Clay	21	14
William Clay	23	16
Joseph Claybrook	30	16
Lewis Clemens	06	16
Mathias Cline	05	15
Isaac Clinkenbeard	17	16
Isaac Clinken beard	18	16
George Coakley	25	04
John J. Coakley	25	04
Clinton Cockrill	34	12
Fielding Cockrill	34	12
John R. Cole	05	03
William Cole	07	07
William Cole	01	08
James Coleman	08	17
Abraham Collett	26	16
Elijah W. Colley	08	06
James Collins	28	07
John Collins	28	11
Zenas Collins	03	07
Henry Collit	25	05
William Conaway	04	03
William Conaway	21	03
Francis Conlin	05	08
Leander Conwell	24	11
Richard Conwell	14	11

Name	Section	Page
Adam Cook	07	14
Thomas Cook	21	17
Joseph F. Coons	24	08
George W. Cooper	24	16
Greenberry Cooper	24	16
Henry Cooper	21	12
John Y. Cooper	15	12
Patrick Cooper	18	07
Robert Y. Cooper	14	12
Thomas Cooper	01	12
William Cooper	07	04
Wylie Cooper	22	12
David Corbin	04	01
Thomas Corcrane	12	09
Reuben M. Cother	31	16
Isham Cox	29	16
Jacob Cox	05	12
Jacob Cox	32	16
James Cox	06	03
John Cox	32	06
John B. Cox	08	03
John B. Cox	09	03
Joseph Cox	20	16
Joseph Cox	03	13
Joseph Cox	10	13
Thomas Cox	09	13
William Cox	32	16
William Cox	34	17
David Cracraft	33	16
Washington Craft	15	18
Adams Crites	04	01
William M. Croach	25	07
Adam Crouse	07	15
George W. Crowbarger	26	12
Aaron Cunningham	19	10
John Cunningham	07	14
John Cunningham	08	14
Moses Cunningham	08	14
Madison Dale	26	17
Thomas A. Dale	07	06
Michael Daniels	29	04
David R. Davidson	17	16

Name	Section	Page
Joseph Davidson	01	16
Caswill Davis	28	06
Hampton Davis	20	06
John Davis	13	12
Joseph Davis, Sr.	15	17
Merrick Davis	24	08
William Dawson	28	10
Abner Dean	09	16
Francis Dean	33	04
Francis Dean	10	16
Isaac B. Dean	10	16
John Dean	09	16
John B. Dean	03	16
Mary Denver	15	08
Thomas Denver	15	08
John L. Derriberry	31	10
John C. Diester	31	03
Daniel Dix	07	17
Joseph Dixon	10	13
David Dodson	07	14
Nancy Dodson	08	14
Thomas L. Doggett	08	06
William F. Dollins	04	14
Garrett Dorland	22	16
James Dorland	23	16
Josiah Dorris	19	15
Presly Dorris	06	15
Thomas M. Dorris	02	06
George P. Dorriss (sic)	36	12
James Dougherty	19	17
John Dougherty	22	18
John Doughtery	25	18
William H. M. Doughtery	04	10
Robert Douglass	18	10
Evan Downey	18	17
John H. Downing	08	16
Samuwl Downey	04	13
Michael Doyle	19	08
Michael Doyle	24	16
Jackson Drais	10	15
James Drais	10	15
Madison J. Drais	25	16

Name	Section	Page
Robert Drennon	34	06
John W. Drew	15	03
Washington Drew	27	06
Joseph Drum	06	01
Joseph Drurn	29	03
John Dunagan	36	05
Thomas Drury	36	13
Joseph Dunagan	36	05
Davis Duncan	13	13
Edward P. Duncan	07	15
Elizabeth Duncan	05	12
George B. Duncan	08	07
Nelson Duncan	09	08
Perry A. Duncan	13	15
Perry A. Duncan	23	15
Philemon Duncan	17	03
Robert Duncan	23	15
Dury O. Duncan	22	15
James Duunigan	14	05
James Dunlap	30	16
Preston Dunlap	04	10
Preston Dunlap	05	10
Daniel Durbin	07	12
James H. Durham	08	11
Adam B. Durning	36	04
Waller H. Durrett	08	12
George W. Dye	13	13
James Dyer	17	12
Thomas J. Dyer	19	12
Thomas J. Dyer	17	17
Washington Dyer	21	17
Isaac Eads	34	11
Jesse Eads	32	11
Jesse Eads	33	11
Soloman Eads	19	06
Francis Early	30	12
Thomas I. Eastburn	20	17
John Eaton	06	07
John Edmundson	08	15
Joseph Edwards	10	05
Mathew Ehrsier	12	18
Jacob Eiler	05	10

Name	Section	Page
Elizabeth Elder	29	06
John Eldridge	21	15
Robert P. S. Elley	21	12
Robert C. Ellfritt	29	17
Robert C. Ellfritt	33	17
Robert C. Ellfritt	26	18
Alpheus Ellington	30	14
Pleasant W. Ellington	05	14
Pleasant W. Ellington	27	14
Pleasant W. Ellington	28	14
Pleasant W. Ellington	33	14
Pleasant W. Ellington	34	14
William Ellington	22	14
William Ellington	33	14
James C. Elliott	21	03
John Elliott	01	13
William Elliott	28	06
Zachariah Elliott	27	03
Doctor Ellis	13	05
John Ellis	22	04
Peter H. Ellsworth	23	11
James M. Embry	08	01
James M. Embry	01	02
John English	18	12
Willie N. English	08	16
James M. Estill	05	14
James M. Estill	06	14
David Evans	02	08
Robert T. Evans	25	16
Thomas H. Evans	19	15
William Evans	02	08
William H. Ewings	31	09
Richard Eyler	20	16
??? Farley	28	20
??? Farley	33	20
Charles A. Farley	01	18
Charles A. Farley	22	18
Josiah Farley	28	08
Robert Farley	34	08
Jeremiah Farmer	31	14
Oxsum Farmer	27	11
Alva Farnsworth	06	06

Name	Section	Page
George W. Farris	08	04
Isaac Farris	21	07
Abraham Faubion	19	14
Isaiah Faubion	06	01
Jacob Faubion	08	06
James Faubion	06	01
Abraham Ferguson	14	11
Absalom S. Fickle	04	04
Aurna Fickle	09	04
Ambrose Field	30	16
Nathaniel Finch	15	13
Samuel Findley	25	08
Rochard C. Finley (sic)	04	07
Benjamin F. Flack	17	15
Elijah Flanary	21	11
Thomas Flanary	02	07
James Flannery, Jr. (sic)	34	11
Joseph Fanning	36	11
John Flemans	26	07
John Flemans	35	07
Robert W. Fleming	25	11
John W. Forbes	33	15
Jonathan J. Forbes	27	15
James W. Forbion	32	03
James Ford	12	11
Samuel Ford	11	04
William Ford	17	03
William Ford	21	03
John M. Forrest	21	16
John M. Forrest	22	16
Ambrose Foster	33	11
Andrew Foster	07	10
James Fox	19	07
William Fox	25	07
William Fox	36	07
William A. Fox	17	07
William M. Fox	12	04
Elisha Francis	36	17
C. M. Frazier	18	08
Brokenberry G. Frazier	18	08
Ephraim L. Frazier	01	18
Jeremiah Frazier	13	09

Name	Section	Page
John Freeland	28	15
William Freeman	13	07
Franklin Fresh	17	06
James Fry	36	05
John S. Fry	01	12
Royal S. Fugatt	18	14
Hugh Fulton	12	12
John M. Fulton	24	18
William Fulton	12	12
Samuel M. Gaines	24	07
Richard B. Gains	19	11
George Galbert	31	16
Barnabas Gamble	34	15
William M. Gamble	01	15
Samuel Gann	02	05
Samuel Gann	11	05
William M. Gardiner	23	08
Joel Garges	20	04
Andrew Gartin	28	03
Jacob Gayer	18	12
John Gentry	01	08
Mary G. Gentry	08	10
Isaac W. Gibson	32	11
James M. Gibson	31	09
Oliver H. P. Gibson	33	04
William Gibson	01	08
William Gibson	31	11
Williamson P. Gibson	34	10
Philip E. Gill	25	17
Andrew J. Gilliam	05	15
Jesse Gilliam	06	15
Daniel Gillis	36	05
Moses Ginnings	17	14
William W. H. Gist	07	13
Harman Glasscock	08	11
George W. Goodlander	29	12
Peter Goodman	18	15
Arad J. Goodyear	06	01
Arad J. Goodyear	01	02
Arad J. Goodyear	12	02
Arad J. Goodyear	30	04
Arad J. Goodyear	34	04

Name	Section	Page
James C. Gordon	13	11
Randal M. Gordon	06	07
Thomas C. Gordon	10	08
William R. Gordon	03	08
Henry C. Gragg	28	06
James H. Gragg	06	14
Alvey Graves	28	17
Elizabeth Graves	11	18
Shelby Graves	20	17
Anthony Gray	01	11
Richard C. C. Gray	30	04
George W. Grayson	29	14
George W. Grayson	13	15
Elisha Green	20	08
Elisha Green	30	08
Jeremiah J. Green	33	04
Nancy Green	02	11
Ager Gregg	22	04
David Gregg	09	04
Jacob Gregg	03	04
Davis C. Gregory	07	14
James H. Gribble	33	07
John H. Gribble	33	07
James Griffith	13	04
Joseph Griffith	14	04
John Groff	12	09
Philip Groh	33	03
John Groom	35	07
Robert Grooms	06	08
Joel Grover	11	07
Edgecomb Guilliams	19	11
David Guinn	07	14
Thomas Guinn	34	17
Jacob L. Cgurwell	22	16
William Gutherie	31	16
William Gutherie	32	16
Rebeca Gwin	10	16
Thornton Gwinn (sic)	12	15
Emsley Hackett	01	16
Henry Hackman	29	03
John Hague	13	12
James P. Hallford	28	11

Name	Section	Page
John Hallford	28	11
Henry D. Hamblin	29	14
Thomas Hamilton	27	11
Thomas Hamilton	27	12
Jacon Hamm	11	13
Ezekiel L. Hampton	21	06
Daniel Hancock	25	05
Major T. Hancock	27	06
James P. Harland	09	14
John Harmond	18	08
Charles Harnes	32	08
Elisha Harrington	02	05
Elisha Harrington	36	08
Miles Harrington	05	11
Thomas Harrington	01	12
Benjamin F. Harris	05	02
Benjamin F. Harris	32	04
James Harris	04	16
John Harris	15	05
John C. Harris	24	17
Moses Harris	08	16
Norman Harris	08	03
Samuel T. J. Harris	07	12
Warren Harris	07	03
James Hartley	14	05
Henry Hartman	31	03
Catherine Hatfield	24	11
David Haun	10	13
Zimry Hawn	32	04
Alexander Hawner	10	01
John G. Haydon	01	07
James Haynes	33	06
Jacob Hays	23	12
John M. Hays	36	16
Samuel McC. Hays	23	12
Washington M. Hays	25	05
James H. Heard	10	04
John Hearpst	23	18
James Heath	35	08
Giles Henderson	09	11
John Henderson	35	12
John H. Henderson	02	11

Name	Section	Page
Joseph Henderson	09	11
Perman Henderson	03	11
Perman Henderson	34	15
Thomas Henderson	21	02
John Hendricks	11	07
James B. Henley	12	02
Horace B. Hernden (sic)	33	16
Frazer D. Herndon	09	12
John Herndon	15	12
Simeon B. Herndon	22	12
John Herron	02	13
John Herron	03	13
Isaac C. Hiatt	11	17
James Hiatt	10	17
Jesse I. Hiatt	03	17
John Hickey	29	12
Jacob Higgins	03	04
Jacob Higgins	10	04
Philemon Higgins	02	04
Jesse Highfield	22	15
Addison L. Hill	18	15
Archibald Hill	12	11
Jonathan Hinshaw	04	04
Charles Hodges	10	16
Evander T. Hodges	27	16
Welcane Hodges	08	16
Henry B. Hokit	29	03
Benjamon Holland	03	15
Jacob D. Holland	10	15
John C. Holland	10	15
Nathaniel Holland	25	15
Robert W. Holland	11	15
Thomas L. Holland	02	15
James S. Holman	04	11
R. Holt	15	12
Isabella Holt	22	12
William Holton	30	10
John Honey	08	01
Abraham Hooper	26	04
Jacob Hooper	30	03
Jacob Hoover	06	03
Jacob Hoover	31	06

Name	Section	Page
George W. Hopkins	30	06
Adams Hornback	17	10
James M. Hornbuckle	02	18
Isaac House	10	07
Franklin R. Houston	28	16
John Houts	05	02
John Houts	32	04
John Houts	25	05
John Houts	36	05
Enoch Howard	11	07
John Howard	03	17
Richard E. Howard	02	18
James C. Hoy	22	04
James C. Hoy	25	04
Jones Hoy	23	04
Samuel B. Hoy	33	07
William Hoy	03	04
William F. Hubbard	30	06
George R. Hudson	04	18
George R. Hudson	09	18
Simon P. Hudson	28	03
William D. Hudson	32	04
William Huff	18	12
Graham L. Hughes	03	10
Margaret Hughes	21	10
Matthew Hughes	28	07
Sarah Hughes	17	11
Bela M. Hughs	29	17
Johnson C. Hughs	22	07
Leander Hughs	17	07
Leander Hughs	28	07
Matthew M. Hughs	22	07
Rhoda S. Hughs	18	17
Samuel R. Hughs	21	07
William S. Hughs	07	11
James Hull	18	11
William Humphreys	03	08
Charles Hundley	07	16
Sarah Hungerford	23	16
David Hunt	04	07
David Hunt	33	11
Silvester Hunt	30	11

Name	Section	Page
George Hunter	07	10
John Huntington	07	07
Hileman Hurlburt	33	11
Daniel W. Hurst	02	16
David W. Hutson	09	18
Isaac Hutson	08	18
Isaac Hutson	10	18
Isaac Hutson	11	18
??? Iatan	19	24
Henry Iler	21	16
Calvin Irby	06	14
David S. Irwin	12	07
Smith Isaac	21	11
Alfred Jack	26	15
Alfred Jack	34	15
Lamanza C. Jack	19	15
Lamanza C. Jack	26	15
William A. Jack	27	15
William A. Jack	30	15
Elias Jacks	15	04
Elias Jacks	19	04
Elias Jacks	21	04
Richard Jacks	25	04
Thomas Jacks	18	03
David Jackson	35	16
James Jackson, Jr.	02	12
John Jackson	03	07
Wallace Jackson	35	16
David James	21	15
Felix Jarrett	23	08
Achilles Jasper	10	11
Brookin Jeffers	26	11
William Jefferson	31	12
Hiram Jeter	05	11
Andrew Johnson	24	04
Andrew Johnson	10	12
Archibald Johnson	19	06
Archibald Johnson	14	07
Barbara Johnson	18	15
Benedict Johnson	15	18
Benjamin Johnson	02	16
David Johnson	24	04

Name	Section	Page
Edward Johnson	02	16
James D. Johnson	18	15
Lewis Johnson	02	16
Robert D. Johnson	06	07
Stephen Johnson	30	11
Thomas Johnson	24	04
James Johnston	09	07
James H. Johnston	36	12
Jeremiah Johnston	02	05
John Johnston	02	05
Albert G. Jones	21	16
Daniel Jones	20	07
George Jones	06	01
George W. Jones	21	07
Lewis Jones	24	08
Nathaniel Jones	25	17
Rodham Jones	29	06
Thomas Jones	28	11
William S. Jones	35	08
Zachariah Jones	22	11
James A. Justice	18	17
Henry Kane	14	08
George Kay	20	11
George Kay	25	12
John Kay	15	11
John Kay	19	11
John Kay	29	11
John C. Kay	02	12
Nancy Kay	01	12
Miles Keeton	04	03
George H. Keller	03	13
Henry B. Keller	26	17
John Keller	06	11
Thomas J. Keller	36	16
William M. Keller	11	13
William R. Kelley	35	12
Alex Kelly	35	08
John Kelly	05	05
John Kelly	06	05
John Kennedy	22	11
Caleb Kerr	01	16
William Kerr	33	14

Name	Section	Page
Francis Kessler	03	03
James C. Key	19	08
Thomas A. Key	19	08
William Key	15	17
Robert Kidd	07	08
Alvis Kimsey	07	04
Benjamin Kimsey	32	07
James Kincaid	32	15
James H. Kincaid	33	15
William M. Kincaid	29	15
William M. Kincaid	32	15
Daniel King	29	07
James King, Jr.	35	07
James King, Sr.	29	07
Louisa King	21	06
Thomas G. King	36	08
James Kinsey	36	08
Thomas Kinsey	22	08
Thomas Kinsey	23	08
Alexander Kirk	04	07
Alfred Kirkpartick	34	17
Weston Kitchen	06	12
James Knight	15	08
James Kukendall	10	17
Matthew W. Kyle	17	17
Jonathan M. Lacy	21	11
Elleanor Lafferty	25	11
William P. Lamb	15	08
Elizabeth Lampson	19	16
Benjamin L. Lampson	15	06
Benjamin L. Lampson	21	06
Benjamin L. Lampson	22	06
James Lancaster	02	12
Thomas Lane	29	12
Joseoh Langley	01	09
Coalby Lanham	10	11
Thompson B. Lanham	03	11
James Lanier	14	16
Eli Lank	13	07
John Lansburg	14	08
John Larkin	08	07
John Larkin	01	08

Name	Section	Page
David Lason	32	11
Thomas Lauter	09	08
John Laverty	06	08
John Lawerence	06	17
Andrew Lawson	24	17
James H. Layton	07	16
James Leachman	35	17
Thoornton Lee	28	17
William J. Lee	21	12
Archibald F. Leonard	34	11
Solomon L. Leonard	31	11
Daniel P. Lewis	18	07
David Lwis	23	08
Edmund Lewis	07	07
Ezekiel Lewis	27	08
Ezekiel Lewis	34	08
Hugh Lewis	10	17
Isaac F. Lewis	10	16
Jesse Lewis	07	07
Jesse Lewis	18	08
John Lewis	08	07
John Lewis	15	17
Nathaniel Lewis	14	08
Sloan Lewis	02	08
Squire T. Lewis	28	16
William Lewis	31	06
William Lewis	17	07
William Lewis	22	08
William Lewis	27	08
William Lewis	28	16
John Ligget	20	14
Daniel Lindsley	15	08
David Lindsley	22	08
James C. Lindlsley	34	16
John Lineas	18	17
Isreal Link	18	06
Daniel Linn	04	13
Granville Linville	12	17
John Linville	07	16
Richard Linville	04	16
Marcus Lipscomb	35	17
William Litle (sic)	01	05

Name	Section	Page
Calvin M. Little	26	07
Martin Logue	32	15
Levi Lollar	10	17
Benjamin S. Long	22	03
James H. Long	09	03
James H. Long	28	03
John Long	21	15
Levi Long	30	15
Souther W. Long	31	12
George W. Love	05	01
George W. Love	09	01
Jackson Lovelady	23	17
James Lovelady	09	17
Moses Lovelady	20	12
Polly Lovelady	20	12
Sheltin D. Lowe	34	17
Samuel Lowman	15	10
Samuel Lowman	21	10
Samuel Lowman	22	10
William Loy	06	16
Henry Loyd	12	11
Endicott W. Ludlow	09	03
Philip Lundbeck	26	18
John Lynch	02	04
Joseph R. Lynch	01	04
Joseph R. Lynch	36	07
Daniel Lynn	31	04
Hines C. Linn	05	02
Hines C. Linn	25	05
Nathaniel Lynn	31	04
William Lytle	11	05
John McAdow	04	17
Samuel McAdow	17	17
William McAlexander	04	04
Samuel McCall	06	14
William J. McCarthy (sic)	24	13
James McCarty	09	05
John McCarty	31	11
William McCarty	31	11
John McClain	08	08
John McCletchey	28	04
Burke McComas	34	08

Name	Section	Page
Burke McComas	35	08
George McComas	14	05
Hiram McComas	10	05
Moses McComas	15	05
Sanders W. McComas	15	05
James McCord	24	09
Ansen McCorkle or McCracken	35	08
John McCown	23	11
William McCoy	07	17
William McCrary	01	08
Samuel C. McCron	07	08
John McDaniel	20	17
John McDaniel	32	17
Donald M. McDonald	14	11
Donald M. McDoanld	15	11
Simon McDonald	18	16
Huston McFarland	36	17
Thomas McGachager	32	04
William McGee	23	15
Hugh McGown	12	07
Callaway McGreggor	31	10
James McGuire	21	04
Melvin McKee	26	08
Melvin McKee	03	17
Melvin McKee	05	17
Melvin McKee	01	18
Peter McKee	04	08
John McKinney	09	11
Jacob McKissick	04	17
Francis McLain	27	16
Hiram McLain	27	16
James McLain	26	16
John T. McLain, Jr.	35	16
John T. McLain, Sr.	26	16
Thomas McLain	03	12
Thomas McLain	35	16
William McLain	26	16
Allen McLane	30	11
Richard McMaham	12	18
Lawrence W. McManus	11	04
Samuel W. McManus	11	04

Name	Section	Page
Charles McMillen	18	10
Edward McPherson	15	12
Thomas McQuean	12	08
David McWilliams	27	03
James H. McWilliams	26	04
William M. Macey	04	05
Henry Mack	33	03
David P. Magill	17	06
George Malon	20	11
William Malott	03	04
John S. Malott	04	07
John S. Malott	05	07
Charles A. Mann	32	10
Thomas B. Markham	08	13
Thomas B. Markham	29	17
William Markwell	33	12
Sarah Marr	08	05
John S. Marsh	06	07
Frederick Marshall	14	08
Frederick Marshall	25	12
James W. Marshall	15	05
James W. Marshall	22	05
Thomas Marshall	05	06
Ulster Marshall	33	06
Anderson Martin	13	09
Benjamin Martin	12	08
Brightberry Martin	10	05
David W. Martin	05	17
Elsberry Martin	03	05
Franklin Martin	02	05
Franklin Martin	26	12
George Martin	02	17
Greenberry Martin	04	05
Greenberry Martin	24	05
Greenberry Martin	25	05
Hardin D. Martin	25	12
Hardin D. Martin	26	12
James M. Martin	09	14
John Martin	29	16
Joseph Martin	31	07
Zadock Martin	36	12
Albert Mason	01	05

Name	Section	Page
Albert Mason	11	05
Albert Mason	12	05
Albert Mason	13	05
Hilliard Mason	23	17
Robert F. Mason	28	08
William S. Mason	15	05
William R. Massie	17	12
Catherine Masten	35	11
Mathias Masten	35	11
Mathias Masten	36	11
Levi Masters	30	11
William Masterson	07	10
Thomas Matlott	18	11
David Matney	21	04
Michael Maupin	27	12
Isreal May	33	14
Samuel May	26	12
Samuel May	12	16
Silas May	02	17
Ware S. May	14	07
William D. Maynard	34	17
Nathan Mayner	17	06
James I. Mays	36	15
Russell Means	35	11
Hall Medlin	19	10
Jarret Medlin	03	07
Levi Medlin	29	11
Richard Meek	12	13
Thomas Melton	06	04
Abraham Miller	22	07
Andrew Miller	01	17
David A. Miller	07	11
Elliott J. Miller	14	05
James Miller	04	01
James I. Miller	12	17
Jesse Miller	11	05
John Miller	01	17
John Miller	15	17
Lewis Miller	01	13
Richard Miller	01	17
Samuel Miller	06	12
William Miller	36	07

Name	Section	Page
William Miller	34	16
Robert Milligan	12	08
David Mitchell	23	17
Jonathan Mitchell	11	08
Robert B. Mitchell	33	15
Thomas W. Mitchell	08	12
James Mize	05	04
James Mizee (sic)	21	04
Lewis Mizee	33	04
James Mobley	07	07
Erwin Montgomery	05	04
William L. Montgomery	10	07
Andrew J. Moody	31	04
Isaac Moody	18	14
Thomas B. Moody	32	04
Benjamin D. Moore	01	05
Eli Moore	12	17
James Moore	04	07
James Moore	11	13
Jesse Moore	19	14
William Moore	18	03
William C. Moore	12	12
Chesley Moreland	22	15
Elijah Morgan	04	08
Ruby Morgan	01	11
Thompson Morgan	30	03
Jesse Morin	25	12
Jesse Morin	36	12
Charles Morris	19	06
James B. Morris	27	08
John N. Morrow	24	05
Samuel C. Morrow	08	08
William Mosby	22	03
Aaron Moshier	08	10
Eli Moshier	08	10
Jokam	08	10
Jacob Motz	35	11
Joseph Mower	05	12
Charles D. Mulkey	11	08
Benjamin Munkers	10	12
William R. Munkers	11	12
John Munse	26	11

Name	Section	Page
John Munse	35	11
George H. Murch	02	18
George Murphy	10	11
George Murphy	11	11
Jacob Mutphy	28	14
Peyton Murphy	11	11
William L. Murphy	18	17
Hiram Myers	24	05
William Nane	04	11
Alfred G. Naylor	10	04
Alfred G. Naylor	30	04
Alfred G. Naylor	31	04
Andrew J. Naylor	30	04
Daniel Neel	15	13
Gabriel Nelson	09	16
Joel Nelson	03	12
Henry Nethertoon	01	07
Henry Netherton	12	07
Nathan Newby	23	17
William Newcomb	14	05
David Newman	18	14
Peyton Newman	28	14
William Newman	18	14
William Newman	21	14
William A. Newman	06	12
Christopher C. Nichols	02	15
James Nichols	02	15
Thomas G. Noel	27	07
William Noel	04	12
William Noffinger	14	18
James Noland	24	17
John Noland	17	04
Joshua Noland	20	04
Obed Noland	07	14
Obed Noland	17	04
Isaac Norman	19	11
Abner Norris	30	15
Hosea Norris	09	17
Ira Norris	25	12
William J. Norris	18	12
William J. Norris	29	12
John Norvell	28	15

Name	Section	Page
Henry D. Olden	26	15
William Oldeworth	07	17
Leonidas Oldham	17	11
Samuel Oldham	07	03
John Olinger	10	05
John Oliver	02	08
Jepha Osborne	27	16
Aaron Osbourne	15	16
Peter Overly	18	16
Jackson H. Owen	03	08
James H. Owen	32	15
James L. Owen	32	15
John R. Owen	34	12
Moseley N. Owen	27	12
Henry Owens	09	10
John Owens	03	10
John Owens	10	10
John Owens	15	10
Mason H. Owsley	06	11
James Pace	01	13
John Pace	01	13
Orvilla Pack	19	14
John Packwood	10	12
John Palmer	20	17
George S. Park	06	01
George S. Park	01	02
George S. Park	21	04
George S. Park	30	04
George S. Park	35	04
George S. Park	36	04
George S. Park	24	05
George S. Park	25	05
Simpson Park	19	07
Nathaniel Parker	30	16
Walter S. Parker	27	07
Evin Parrott	08	15
Isaac Parsons	35	04
Gordon Pate	22	16
Enoch Patrick	12	16
Robert Patton	21	12
John Pauley	01	17
William M. Paxton	18	06

Name	Section	Page
William M. Paxton	01	07
William M. Paxton	13	07
William M. Paxton	35	12
Alfred Peanick	01	02
Andrew Peery	14	16
Jesse Peery	04	17
William Peery	13	16
Merriman Pemberton	19	07
Alfred Penick (sic)	05	01
John Penick	04	01
Edward T. Perkins	26	08
Aytchman (?) L. Perrin	17	15
Aytchman (?) L. Perrin	24	16
Ephraim Perry	20	17
William Peters	12	16
John Pettibone	19	10
Joseph Pettigrew	05	17
James Pettijohn	05	16
Thomas Phelps	08	15
Stephen B. Phillips	07	11
John S. Pickett	31	11
Hilary Pickoral	06	12
Green B. Pitcher	08	11
Leroy M. Pitman	25	16
Hillory Pitts	25	09
Jacob Pitts	19	08
Jacob Pitts	25	09
John Popplewell	04	05
Enoch Porter	03	05
Enoch Porter	35	08
Hezekiah Porter	12	16
Thomas H. Porter	26	08
William Porter	36	08
Bentley Potter	19	06
Wilson Potter, Sr.	20	06
Coleby P. Powell	30	03
Elijah P. Powell	27	08
Luke Powell	04	14
Mary Powell	12	05
Sinclair Powell	14	07
Andrew B. Powers	12	13
Andrew B. Powers	13	13

Name	Section	Page
David W. Powers	25	09
William Prater	08	17
Fantly R. Price	31	07
James Price	28	03
Joseph Prigmore	09	13
Windle Proepstel	03	01
Leonard C. Prunty	07	06
Charles F. Putney	18	15
Benjamin Quinlan	35	17
John Rainey	08	06
John Rainey	17	06
William Rallston	12	17
William C. Rallston	26	15
Adam Rambo	13	18
Adam Rambo	14	18
David J. D. Ramey	23	07
James T. Ramey	18	06
Lewis C. Ramey	07	06
George R. Ramsey	26	17
Elihu H. Randolph	34	17
Jacob Rasdale	27	12
Elizabeth Ratliff	15	08
Elizabeth Ray	09	17
James Ray	19	15
Alexander P. Read	34	15
William W. Readman	15	03
William W. Readman	20	06
Isaiah Reynolds	33	08
Henry Rhada	05	15
John S. Rice	06	15
Vanrauselaer R. Rice	33	08
Jefferson Riddle	27	08
James B. Riggs	29	16
James B. Riggs	30	16
Amos Riley	19	12
Thomas Ring	17	11
Thomas Ring	20	11
Abraham Risk	27	??
Abraham Risk	28	??
Elkanah Risk	27	17
James I. Risk	35	17
John Ritner	21	10

Name	Section	Page
Harvey Ritter	11	05
Harvey Ritter	14	05
Benjamin F. Roberson	15	16
George Roberts	06	01
George Roberts	01	02
George Roberts	12	02
Hardy Roberts	22	04
John Roberts	13	17
Mary Roberts	03	15
Nathan Roberts	18	06
Charles Robertson	05	03
Hugh Robertson	10	18
Hugh Robertson	14	18
Hugh Robertson	15	18
Hugh Robertson	23	12
John E. Roberson	28	12
Alexs M. Robinson	21	10
Robert Robinson	11	05
William Robinson	14	15
William Robinson	20	17
Anderson Rogers	12	04
James W. Rogers	07	03
John Rogers	01	04
John Rogers	02	04
Lewis J. Rogers	06	03
Peter Rogers	20	03
Russell Rogers	12	04
William Rogers	28	06
Samuel N. Rorer	26	08
Jeremiah Rose	08	15
Thomas Rose	06	15
Robert Ross	03	17
John Roten	15	04
James M. Rothwell	33	03
James M. Rothwell	34	03
Herbert Rouleau	08	03
Andrew Roy	07	02
Lewis Roy	06	02
Lewis Roy	23	05
Lewis Roy	26	05
Matthew Rule	14	07
Jonathan Runyon	22	11

Name	Section	Page
David Rupe	32	10
James Rupe	04	11
James Rupe	05	11
William Rupe	05	11
William Rupe	06	11
Alexander Russells	12	05
Henry J. Rust	11	18
Noah St. John	11	15
William St. John	15	15
Veliroy Sample	29	07
John Sanford	08	12
Peter Sapp	13	17
John M. Savage	36	17
George W. Saxton	19	12
Thomas Scanlin	05	08
John G. Schultz	19	17
Anderson H. Scott	01	02
John C. Scott	14	17
Lewis Scott	32	14
Nathaniel Scott	17	16
William C. Scott	13	17
Alfred Seward	28	17
Daniel Shackleford	32	10
Daniel Shackleford	25	11
Robert T. Shanklin	03	06
William R. Shanklin	21	06
James G. Shannon	24	12
Joseph Shannon	14	17
Russell W. Shannon	21	04
Levi Sharp	06	16
William Sharpton	24	11
Nicholas Shaver	09	10
Coleman G. Shaw	01	13
Fielding L. Shaw	08	04
Francis Shaw	30	12
Jefferson R. Shaw	08	11
Robert Shaw	02	13
Solomon Shell	20	16
Eli Shepard	03	11
Amanda M. Shepherd	09	06
Elijah Shepherd	19	06
Elijah Shepherd	24	07

Name	Section	Page
Lycurgus Shepherd	30	07
Michael Shetterly	13	17
George Shortridge	28	16
John T. Shortridge	21	16
John T. Shortridge	25	16
William P. Shortridge	20	16
Nathaniel M. Shrick	24	12
John G. Shults	12	18
John G. Shults	13	18
Aquilla Shy	13	17
Frederick Siebold	25	13
Hardin P. Simmons	24	12
Mary A. Simmons	03	16
William Simmons	11	13
James Simpson	01	05
James Simpson	23	08
James Simpson	24	08
Preston Simpson	35	08
Thomas K. Simpson	24	08
William Simpson	06	04
William A. Singleton	27	15
Stanley Sisson	19	11
Stanley Sisson	20	11
Michael Skaggs	03	07
Christopher Skillman	29	17
Christopher Skillman	32	17
Phineas Skinner	02	05
Phineas Skinner	04	05
Phineas Skinner	10	05
Phineas Skinner	23	05
Phineas Skinner	02	11
Phineas Skinner	15	11
Phineas Skinner	04	18
Daniel S. Slaughter	19	06
William Sloan	04	07
Jacob Smelser	27	04
John Smelser	28	04
Adam Smith	03	01
Adam H. Smith	20	07
Asa Smith, Jr.	31	12
Benjamin F. Smith	11	08
Charles R. Smith	19	10

Name	Section	Page
Doctor Smith	07	10
Fountain Smith	30	12
George Smith	17	10
Henry B. Smith	06	01
James Smith	20	14
James W. Smith	06	08
John Smith	09	08
John Smith	24	13
John Smith	09	15
John Smith	02	18
Moses M. Smith	07	08
Thomas Smith	34	08
William Smith	14	05
William C. Smith	09	15
William G. Smith	09	08
Benjamin Smither	32	14
Margaret Smock	19	12
Alexander Smyth	28	14
Philip Smyth	01	09
George P. Southard	09	08
Joseph R. Speed	06	06
Andrew J. Spencer	05	01
Elijah Spencer	29	11
Elijah Spratt	20	12
Jeremiah H. Spratt	22	12
George Springer	33	07
Gurshum Springer	33	07
Byrd Spurlock	14	11
John P. Srite	20	06
Isaac W. Staats	33	16
Enoch F. Stagg	21	17
William C. Stagg	27	17
Dodson Standiford	17	14
Benjamin Stanton	11	12
Bluford Stanton	14	12
Terry Stapp	28	15
Jonas Statler	01	02
Drury Stayton	24	07
Oliver W. Steele	09	17
Albert Stephens	35	16
Joseph Stephens	06	14
Joseph P. Stewart	23	16

Name	Section	Page
Robert Stewart	10	04
Simeon L. Stewart	28	12
William Stewart	30	12
Conrad Stiggers	08	05
George Stiggers	05	05
Joseph F. Still	11	07
Samuel Still	23	04
Dixon Stillwell	02	13
John Stokes	04	03
Thomas A. Stokes	05	03
Nicholas Stoller	30	12
Joshua Stone	28	15
Noah Stewhum	35	12
Constat Strode	05	06
George Strouse	23	07
Martin Stucker	24	18
Henry Suggs	20	11
James H. Surritt	14	08
James H. Surritt	15	08
James H. Surritt	22	08
William Sutton	05	02
George W. Swain	11	16
Walter B. Swain	04	16
James Swaney	26	11
John Swaney	26	11
Obed Swearingen	09	16
Samuwl Swinney	12	12
Jacob Swope	09	14
Thomas W. Swope	04	14
Thomas Swoard	19	17
Thomas H. Talbott	25	17
John M. Tate	14	12
William O. Tate	09	07
Lydia Tebbs	23	07
Lydia Tebbs	24	07
David Templeton	07	11
John B. Terry	24	17
Solomon Teherow	17	15
Daniel Thatcher	29	10
Lutcher C. Thatcher	24	05
Daniel C. Thomas	02	12
Henry Thomas	27	04

Name	Section	Page
Andrew Thompson	05	17
Benjamin F. Thompson	27	08
Greenville Thompson	31	15
James L. Thompson	34	16
John P. Thompson	32	17
Thomas J. Thompson	24	18
Benjamin Thornburg	24	17
John Thorp	23	04
Squire B. Thorp	26	04
Thomas Thorp	23	04
Zacariah Thorp	32	14
Abner Tickle	15	16
Reuben D. Tilley	08	12
John W. Tilton	08	17
James H. Timberlake	11	05
John Timberlake	12	05
Samuel Tincher	31	15
Jonathan Tipton	23	08
Elza Todd	04	08
Jarrett Todd	05	08
John W. Todd	04	02
Jonathan Todd	33	12
Joseph Todd, Jr.	33	12
Joseph Todd, Sr.	32	12
Robert Todd	32	12
William Todd	33	12
John Toffelmire	22	15
Mary Tolsen	24	04
David Toms	12	16
Nathan Toms	08	17
William Tougate	22	18
William Tougate	23	18
William Tougate	27	18
Terry Trapp	17	14
William P. Trapp	30	15
James Treacy	08	08
William T. Treadyway	33	03
Andrew Tribble	34	12
Dudley Tribble	09	08
Dudley Tribble	10	08
John Tribble	10	08
Silas Tribble	03	08

Name	Section	Page
Francis Troop	22	11
Elizabeth Truitt	03	18
Jacob Trumbo	31	07
Joseph B. Tuder	30	07
Squire W. Tuder	21	04
Thomas Tuder	25	08
Tubman Tull	10	18
Charles Turner	30	14
Graham Turner	10	08
Joel H. Turner	14	07
Thomas Turner	15	07
William Turner	21	17
Charles Underhill	24	13
Henry Underhill	13	13
Asa Vallandingham	13	09
John Vance	29	04
Medders Vanderpool	04	16
John Vanneman	20	12
Abraham Vaughn	12	11
David Vaughn	15	15
David Vaughn	21	15
Lydia Vaughn	13	11
Martin Vaughn	01	08
Samuel Venard	22	11
Jesse Vineyard	17	12
John W. Vineyard	05	12
John W. Vineyard	09	12
Eli Vinson	22	08
James Vivian	21	03
William Wait	35	17
??? Waldron	15	26
Andrew J. Walker	33	16
John Walker	30	09
William H. Walker	26	08
Francis J. Wallace	07	01
James Wallace	30	08
James Wallace	31	08
Mathias T. Wallace	20	14
Thomas L. Wallce	04	18
Absalom H. Waller	29	06
Elbert Waller	21	03
Hiram Waller	29	06

Name	Section	Page
T. Waller	03	13
John Walls	12	07
Thompson Ward	13	18
Thompson Ward	15	18
Theodore F. Warner	36	17
John Watkins	25	04
John Watkins	03	06
John Watkins	04	06
John Watkins	10	08
John Watkins	28	08
John B. Weaver	23	05
Elihu Weesner	19	11
John Welsch	19	03
Adam Weller	02	13
Alexander Wells	19	10
Charles Wells	28	12
Dudley Wells	07	12
Horeb Wells	02	13
Jefferson Wells	30	07
John B. Wells	12	13
John B. Wells	13	13
John C. West	31	04
John Whisman	22	16
James White	14	17
James White	15	17
John A. White	23	12
Levi White	05	14
Preston Whitlock	32	10
Robert Whitlock	08	04
Winneford Whitlock	32	10
Elijah Whitten	08	15
Frederick Wilcox	14	18
Frederick Wilcox	15	18
Eleazer Wilhite	31	16
Hall L. Wilkerson	20	12
John Wilkerson	20	12
Thomas J. Wilkerson	21	14
Ezekiel S. Wilkinson	31	15
Darling Williams	30	06
Edward Williams	33	06
Evan Williams	21	11
James Williams	03	08

Name	Section	Page
John Williams	02	16
Samuel I. Williams	18	17
Thomas H. Williams	20	11
William T. Williams	17	03
James Willoughby	02	07
Archibald B. Wills	05	06
George Wills	36	11
Esther Wilson	14	16
John Wilson	05	07
John Wilson	34	11
Josiah Wilson	23	05
Samuel Wilson	33	06
Simon H. Wilson	23	16
Vincent Wilson	09	05
William Wilson	21	06
John H. Winston	08	04
John H. Winston	11	05
John H. Winston	13	05
John H. Winston	14	05
John H. Winston	27	07
Joseph Winston	35	04
Letitia D. Winston	11	05
Letitia D. Winston	26	07
Letitia D, Winston	27	07
Richard P. Wood	02	07
Adam C. Woods	08	03
Archibald Woods	04	14
Cattirain Woods	09	06
Sarah Woods	10	06
William C. Woods	05	03
William C. Woods	03	03
Elizahbeth Yancy	03	16
Abel Yates	30	07
Joshua Yates	20	07
Solomon Yates	28	07
William Yates	33	07
Lazarus Yocam	08	08
Simon B. Yocam	08	08
George W. Yocum	07	12
Jesse Yocum	20	12
William Yocum	18	08
William Yohe	08	08

Name	Section	Page
Christian Young	26	05
David Young	08	08
James Young	19	14
John Young	31	11
John Young	09	17
Richard B. Young	08	14
Zacariah A. Young	08	14
Abraham Zavriskey	04	05
Isaac W. Zand, Jr.	04	01
Isaac W. Zand, Jr.	07	01

Jackson County, Missouri, Kansas City Police Officers Killed in the line of Duty, 1881 - 1949.

Name	Date
Martin Hynes	1881
Patrick Jones	1882
John Martin	1892
John E. Jacobson	1897
Joseph A. Zannella	1901
Frank McNamara	1902
Joseph Keenan	1903
Alexander R. McKinney	1903
Stephen O. Flanagan	1903
Frank C. McGinnis	1904
William P. Mulvihill	1905
John Dwyer	1906
Albert O. Dolbow	1908
Michael P. Mullane	1908
Joseph Raimo	1911
Homer Darling	1911
Robert L. Marshall	1912
Homer Riggle	1913
Andrew Lynch	1913
William F. Koger	1913
Bernard McKernan	1913
Samuel K. Holmes	1914
William Hauserman	1915
Glenn Marshall	1916
William A. Spangler	1916
John Houlehan	1916
Harris W. West	1917
Arthur M. Dorsett	1917

Name	Date
Michael Y. Sayeg	1918
Frank Mansfield	1918
Harry J. Keating	1918
Isaac Fenno	1919
Frederick F. Tierney	1919
Ula A. McMahan	1920
William H. Scobee	1920
James H. Horn	1920
Frank S. Archer	1920
Willard C. Bayne	1921
Carl J. Bickett	1921
James N. Brink	1921
Gerald L. Fackert	1921
Richard P. McDonald	1922
Hershel M. Wyatt	1923
William C. Zinn	1923
Willard L. Ferguson	1923
Wright D. Bryant	1923
Thomas J. Wilson	1923
Dennis J. Whalen	1924
Barney Jasper	1924
George E. Lawson, Jr.	1924
Emmett C. Barnes	1924
Jack P. Wilcox	1924
Albert B. Cummings	1925
John V. Kincaide	1926
John W. Leiter	1926
James H. Smith	1928
Ralph Hinds	1929
George R. Johnson	1929
Charles H. Dingham, Jr.	1929
Oliver P. Carpenter	1932
Richard E. Fitzgerald	1933
Leroy Van Meter	1933
William J. Grooms	1933
Frank E. Hermanson	1933
Morris Bigus	1933
Ric O. Bjorkback	1933
John Ruffolo	1934
William E. Wood	1934
Grant V. Schroder	1934
Frank P. Franano	1935

Name	Date
Frank Stevens	1936
William T. Cavanaugh	1936
Lawerence K. Morrison	1937
Thomas McAuliffe	1937
Henry S. Shipe	1938
Ralph R. Miller	1941
Arthur J. Morris	1942
Melvon L. Huff	1945
James H. Owens	1947
Floyd N. Montgomery	1948
Charles H. Perrine	1948
William S. Wells	1948
Charles W. Neaves	1948
Sandy W. Washington	1948
R. D. Edmunds	1949

Grundy County, Missouri. Register of Births, 1864-1870.

Sarah Virginia Wynn: (RD) Feb. 24, 1864; (B) Sep. 27, 1863; (PRTS) Pembroke L. Wynn, farmer, and Malinda H. Garvin.

Joseph William Metcalf: (RD) Sep. 4, 1864; (B) Sep. 5, 1844; (PRTS) Daniel Metcalf, lawyer, and Mary A. Crews.

Kate Wyatt: (RD) Sep. 22, 1865, (B) Sep. 30, 1865, (PRTS) Benj. F. Wyatt, farmer, and Corlisa Reynolds.

Louisa Ellen McColl: (RD) Jul. 2, 1866, (B) Dec. 18, 1860, (PRTS) Noah McColl and Elizabeth F. Simmons.

Norah Adaline McColl: (RD) Jul. 2, 1866, (B) Dec. 14, 1862, (PRTS) Noah McColl and Elzabeth F. Simmons.

John Wesley Smith: (RD) Sep. 8, 1866, (B) May 28, 1853, (PRTS) James M. Smith, carpenter, and Nida Delila (?).

Sarah Catherine Smith: (RD) Sep. 8, 1866, (B) Mar. 20, 1855, (PRTS) James M. Smith, carpenter, and Nida Delila (?).

Mary A. Smith: (RD) Sep. 8, 1866, (B) Oct. 15, 1856, (PRTS) James M. Smith, carpenter, and Nida Delila (?).

Sylvester N. Smith: (RD) Sep. 8, 1866, (B) Jan. 26, 1858, (PRTS) James M. Smith, carpenter, and Nida Delila (?).

James W. S. Smith: (RD) Sep. 8, 1866, (B) Mar. 21, 1862, (PRTS) James M. Smith, carpenter, and Nida Delila (?).

Martha Ann Estes: (RD) Oct. 5, 1866, (B) Apr. 2, 1854, (PRTS) Green B. Estes, farmer, and Mary C. Atkinson.

John Welsey Estes: (RD) Oct. 5, 1866, (B) Oct., 27, 1868, (PRTS) Green B. Estes, farmer, and Mary C. Atkinson.

Abram C. Estes: (RD) Oct. 5, 1866, (B) Oct. 27, 1856, (PRTS) Green

B. Estes, farmer, and Mary C. Atkinson.

George Washington Estes: (RD) Oct. 5, 1866, (PRTS) Green B. Estes, farmer, and Mary C. Atkinson.

Greenberry Estes: (RD) Oct. 5, 1866, (B) Nov. 27, 1861, (PRTS) Green B. Estes, farmer, and Mary C. Atkinson.

Rosecrans Lemmons: (RD) Dec. 6, 1866, (B) Feb. 24, 1863, (PRTS) John Lemmons and Sarah F. Turner.

William A. Sparks: (RD) Dec. 6, 1866, (B) Sep. 22, 1858, (PRTS) Addison Sparks and Mary E. Widner.

Parthena A. Sparks: (RD) Dec. 6, 1866, (B) Dec. 3, 1859, (PRTS) Addison Sparks and Mary E. Widner.

Sarah J. Sparks: (RD) Dec. 6, 1866, (B) Dec. 25, 1861, (PRTS) Addison Sparks and Mary E. Widner.

Arrilla A. Sparks: (RD) Dec. 6, 1866, (B) Nov. 13, 1864, (PRTS) Addison Sparks and Mary E. Widner.

Francis Marion Smith: (RD) Dec. 6, 1866, (B) Dec. 13, 1859, (CMTS) Male, (PRTS) Edward H. Smith and Ruth Cluster.

Daniel Edward Smith: (RD) Dec. 6, 1866, (B) Feb. 13, 1862, (PRTS) Edward H. Smith and Ruth Cluster.

Elizabeth Jane Dillion: (RD) Dec. 6, 1866, (B) Sep. 9, 1857, (PRTS) Joseph A. K. Dillon and Sarah Priest.

Mary Frances Dillon: (RD) Dec. 6, 1866, (B) Feb. 7, 1859, (PRTS) Joseph A. K. Dillon and Sarah Priest.

William Metcalf: (RD) Feb. 2, 1867, (B) Dec. 31, 1866, (PRTS) Daniel Metcalf, lawyer, and Mary A. Crews.

William W. Smith: (RD) Mar. 12, 1867, (B) Jun. 15, 1852, (PRTS) Richard S. Smith.

James M. Smith: (RD) Mar. 12, 1867, (B) Feb. 12, 1855, (PRTS) Richard S. Smith.

George W. Smith: (RD) Mar. 12, 1867, (B) Mar. 12, 1853, (PRTS) Owen C. Smith and Martha M. (?).

Jonathan Smith: (RD) Mar. 12, 1867, (B) May 4, 1857, (PRTS) Owen C. Smith and Martha M. (?).

Martha Smith: (RD) Mar. 12, 1867, (B) Dec. 8, 1860, (PRTS) Owen C. Smith and Martha M. (?)

Leonora E. Stanly: (RD) Aug. 6, 1867, (B) Apr. 2, 1857, (PRTS) Joseph Stanly and Matilda J. Stanly.

Mary Ann Sheils: (RD) Aug. 12, 1867, (B) Feb. 25, 1855, (PRTS) Silas Sheils and Elizabeth Ann Holloway.

Sarah Emeline Sheils: (RD) Aug. 12, 1867, (B) Sep. 25, 1858, (PRTS) Silas Sheils and Elizabeth Ann Holloway.

William Henry Sheils: (RD) Aug. 12, 1867, (B) Dec. 20, 1860, (PRTS) Silas Sheils and Elizabeth Ann Holloway.

Harriet Alexander: (RD) Sep. 5, 1867, (B) Jan. 18, 1855, (PRTS) Wesley E. Alexander, farmer, and Sarah Tull.
Albert Alexander: (RD) Sep. 5, 1867, (B) Jan. 10, 1857, (PRTS) Wesley E. Alexander, farmer, and Sarah Tull.
Olive Alexander: (RD) Sep. 5, 1867. (B) Feb. 5, 1859, (PRTS) Wesley E. Alexander, farmer, and Sarah Tull.
Wesley C. Alexander: (RD) Sep. 5, 1867, (B) Sep. 18, 1861, (PRTS) Wesley E. Alexander, farmer, and Sarah Tull.
Perry Schooler: (RD) Oct. 31, 1867, (B) Sep. 18, 1852, (PRTS) Abram Schooler and Rachel Jane King.
Francis Marion Schooler: (RD) Oct. 31, 1867, (B) Jan. 15, 1854, (PRTS) Abram Schooler and Rachel Jane King.
Viola A. Schooler: (RD) Oct. 31, 1867, (B) Oct. 27, 1860, (PRTS) Abram Schooler and Rachel Jane King.
Abraham Schooler: (RD) Oct. 31, 1867, (B) Apr. 21, 1862, (PRTS) Abram Schooler and Rachel Jane King.
Malzena Elizabeth Colclasure: (RD) Dec. 6, 1866, (B) May 27, 1858, (PRTS) Noah Colclasure, farmer and Sarah Holloway.
Mary Rosetta Colclasure: (RD) Dec, 6, 1866, (B) Aug, 5, 1860, (PRTS) Noah Colclasure, farmer and Sarah Holloway.
James C. Branson: (RD) Dec. 10, 1866, (B) Jun. 26, 1861, (PRTS) William W. Branson, farmer, and Mary L. Foster.
Catherine J. Branson: (RD) Dec. 10, 1866, (B) Apr. 18, 1863, (PRTS) William W.Branson, farmer, and Mary L. Foster.
James M. Young: (RD) Dec. 19, 1866, (B) Sep. 3, 1859, (PRTS) Wiley Young and Mary J. Nichols.
Wiley S. Young: (RD) Dec. 19, 1866, (B) May 25, 1862, (PRTS) Wiley Young and Mary J. Nichols.
Mary Ellen Ansell: (RD) Jul. 29, 1869, (B) Dec. 20, 1858, (PRTS) Wriland Ansell, farmer, and Rebecca J. Wane (?).
Jacob Henry Ansell: (RD) Jul. 29, 1869, (B) Sep. 18, 1863, (PRTS) Wriland Ansell, farmer, and Rebecca J. Wane (?).
Eliza C. Chrisman: (RD) Feb. 18, 1867, (B) Jan. 6, 1862, (PRTS) Samuel Chrisman, farmer, and Mary J. Holloway.
Samuel T. Chrisman: (RD) Feb. 18, 1867, (B) Jan. 6, 1862, (PRTS) Samuel Chrisman, farmer, and Mary J. Holloway.
John L. Brassfield: (RD) Mar. 12, 1867, (B) Mar. 31, 1852, (PRTS) Aaron Brassfield, farmer, and Nancy E. Kirk.
Ansel D. Brassfield: (RD) Mar. 12, 1867, (B) Sep. 15, 1853, (PRTS) Aaron Brassfield, farmer, and Nancy E. Kirk.
William W. Brassfield: (RD) Mar. 12, 1867, (B) Mar. 7, 1855, (PRTS) Aaron Brassfield, farmer, and Nancy E. Kirk.
Richard J. Brassfield: (RD) Mar. 12, 1867, (B) Jul. 11, 1857, (PRTS)

Aaron Brassfield, farmer, and Nancy E. Kirk.
Jackson Brassfield: (RD) Mar. 12, 1867, (B) Aug. 8, 1858, (PRTS) Aaron Brassfield, farmer, and Nancy E. Kirk.
Aaron T. Brassfield: (RD) Mar. 12, 1867, (B) Jan. 5, 1868, (PRTS) Aaron Brassfield, farmer, and Nancy E. Kirk.
Ephraim Crank: (RD) Mar. 12, 1867, (B) Nov. 6, 1850, (PRTS) Felix G. Crank, farmer, and Sarah (?)
Lucretia J. Crank: (RD) Mar. 12, 1867, (B) Mar. 2, 1852, (PRTS) Felix G. Crank, farmer, and Sarah (?)
Mary A. Crank: (RD) Mar. 12, 1867. (B) Oct. 9, 1858, (PRTS) Felix G. Crank, farmer, and Sarah (?)
Scilly C. Thomas: (RD) Apr. 16, 1867, (B) Apr. 24, 1856, (CMTS) Female, (PRTS) Jared F. Thomas and Martha J. Collins.
William P. Thomas: (RD) Apr. 16, 1867, (B) Dec. 30, 1858, (PRTS) Jared F. Thomas and Martha J. Collins.
Henrietta Beller (?): (RD) Apr. 17, 1867, (B) Nov. 30, 1866, (PRTS) James W. Beller (?), druggiest and Louisa Wall.
Alice Hathaway: (RD) May 18, 1867, (B) Jan. 16, 1860, (PRTS) Seth H. Hathaway and Emily A. Cannon.
Nancy Margaret Humphreys: (RD) May 23, 1867, (B) Oct. 28, 1861, (PRTS) John W. Humphreys and Elizabeth J. Tabor.
Mary H. Davis: (RD) Jun. 5, 1867, (B) Jun. 29, 1861, (PRTS) Jethro O. Davis and Julia Brown Robinson.
James Clement Davis: (RD) Jun. 5, 1867, (B) Mar. 16, 1863, (PRTS) Jethro O. Davis and Julia Brown Robinson.
Jethro O. Davis: (RD) Jun. 5, 1867, (B) Jan. 29, 1865, (PRTS) Jethro O. Davis and Julia Brown Robinson.
William L. Baker: (RD) Jun. 12, 1867, (B) Jan. 26, 1864, (PRTS) James Baker and Rachel M. Gentry.
Catherine Union Keith: (RD) Jun. 12, 1867, (B) Oct. 7, 1861, (PRTS) Andrew W. Keith and Nancy C. (?)
William D. Keith: (RD) Jun. 12, 1867, (B) Sep. 11, 1857, (PRTS) Andrew W. Keith and Nancy C. (?)
John B. Keith: (RD) Jun. 12, 1867, (B) Mar. 10, 1859, (PRTS) Andrew W. Keith and Nancy C. (?)
John L. Wilson: (RD) Jun. 12, 1867, (B) Apr. 13, 1851, (PRTS) Nathan Wilson.
David H. Wilson: (RD) Jun. 12, 1867, (B) Jul. 18, 1855, (PRTS) Nathan Wilson.
Jarsel (?) W. Wilson: (RD) Jun. 12, 1867, (B) Oct. 10, 1858, (CMTS) Male, (PRTS) Nathan Wilson.
Sarah C. Wilson: (RD) Jun. 12, 1867, (B) May 28, 1861, (PRTS) Nathan Wilson.

Mary E. Minshull: (RD) Jun. 23, 1867, (B) Jun. 22, 1857, (PRTS) Richard Minshull and Sarah Schertzen.

Rees M. Minshull: (RD) Jun. 23, 1867, (B) Apr. 11, 1859, (PRTS) Richard Minshull and Sarah Schertzen.

Malinda A. Minshull: (RD) Jun. 23, 1867, (B) Jan. 15, 1861, (PRTS) Richard Minshull and Sarah Schertzen.

Richard Vandyke: (RD) Jun. 28, 1867, (B) Dec. 7, 1854, (PRTS) John Vandyke and Senia White.

Roland W. Odom: (RD) Oct. 31, 1867, (B) Oct. 25, 1850, (PRTS) Willis G. Odom and Cynthia (?).

Cythnia Ann Odom: (RD) Oct. 31, 1867, (B) Feb, 4, 1852, (PRTS) Willis G. Odom and Cynthia (?).

Willis M. Odom: (RD) Oct. 31, 1867, (B) Jun. 23, 1854, (PRTS) Willis G. Odom and Cynthia (?).

George W. Odom: (RD) Oct. 31, 1867, (B) Apr. 25, 1856, (PRTS) Willis G. Odom and Cynthia (?).

Martha L. Odom: (RD) Oct. 31, 1867, (B) Apr. 27, 1859, (PRTS) Willis G. Odom and Cynthia (?).

Lafayette F. S. Odom: (RD) Oct. 31, 1867, (B) Mar. 1, 1862, (PRTS) Willis G. Odom and Cynthia (?).

Rebecca Jane Bryan: (RD) Nov. 12, 1867, (B) Nov. 7, 1853, (PRTS) Lewis Bryan, farmer.

James Lewis Bryan: (RD) Nov. 12, 1867, (B) Jan. 31, 1855, (PRTS) Lewis Bryan, farmer.

Dianna Melissa Bryan: (RD) Nov. 12, 1867, (B) Aug. 9, 1857, (PRTS) Lewis Bryan, farmer.

Nancy F. Bryan: (RD) Nov. 12, 1867, (B) Aug. 8, 1859, (PRTS) Lewis Bryan, farmer.

Alice Caroline Bryan: (RD) Nov. 12, 1867, (B) Jan, 29, 1861, (PRTS) Lewis Bryan, farmer.

Evaline Baker: (RD) Jul. 3, 1867, (B) Jan. 7, 1852, (PRTS) Andrew Baker, farmer, and Amanda Owens.

Horace Baker: (RD) Jul. 3, 1867, (B) Nov. 18, 1860, (PRTS) Andrew Baker, farmer, and Amanda Owens.

Joseph W. Brown: (RD) Jul. 4, 1867, (B) Jan. 7, 1859, (PRTS) Alfred Brown, farmer, and Mary E. Gilham.

Madora E. Brown: (RD) Jul. 4, 1867, (B) Nov. 11, 1860, (PRTS) Alfred Brown, farmer, and Mary E. Gilham.

Arminda J. Brown: (RD) Jul. 4, 1867, (B) May 12, 1862, (PRTS) Alfred Brown, farmer, and Mary E. Gilham.

America E. Talbert: (RD) Jul. 29, 1867, (B) Feb. 2, 1859, (PRTS) James Talbert and Ann Talbert.

Fannie A. Talbert: (RD) Jul. 29, 1867, (B) Dec. 8, 1861, (PRTS) James

Talbert and Ann Talbert.
James T. Talbert: (RD) Jul. 29, 1867, (B) Sep. 25, 1865, (PRTS) James Talbert and Ann Talbert.
James G. Keith: (RD) Jan. 13, 1868. (B) Nov. 11, 1863, (PRTS) Stephen H. Keith and Mary Scott.
Sarah Jane King: (RD) Jan. 13, 1868, (B) Sep. 18, 1851, (PRTS) Thomas King and Lavisa Ellis.
Mary A. King: (RD) Jan. 13, 1868, (B) Jul. 21, 1855, (PRTS) Thomas King and Lavisa Ellis.
Wesley E. King: (RD) Jan. 13, 1868, (B) Jul. 1, 1861, (PRTS) Thomas King and Lavisa Ellis.
Lewis Licken: (RD) Jan. 24, 1868, (B) May 20, 1847, (PRTS) George Licken and Phebe Ann Craymon (?).
Euphema Licken: (RD) Jan. 24, 1868, (B) Jun. 1, 1849, (PRTS) George Licken and Phebe Ann Craymon (?).
John W. F. Hughes: (RD) Jul. 7, 1868, (B) Jan. 11, 1847, (PRTS) James Hughes and H. (?) Eliza McLay (?).
Rachel A. Hughes: (RD) Jul. 7, 1868, (B) Dec. 18, 1848, (PRTS) James Hughes and H. (?) Eliza McLay (?).
Mary Jane Hughes: (RD) Jul. 7, 1868, (B) Apr. 12, 1850, (PRTS) James Hughes and H. (?) Eliza McLay (?).
Hannah E. Hughes: (RD) Jul. 7, 1868, (B) Apr. 12, 1857, (PRTS) James Hughes and H. (?) Eliza McLay (?).
James F. Hughes: (RD) Jul. 7, 1868, (B) Dec. 29, 1851, (PRTS) James Hughes and H. (?) Eliza McLay (?).
Joseph O. Hughes: (RD) Jul. 7, 1868, (B) Mar. 26, 1859, (PRTS) James Hughes and H. (?) Eliza McLay (?).
Harriet A. Hughes: (RD) Jul. 7, 1868, (B) Jun. 11, 1861, (PRTS) James Hughes and H. (?) Eliza McLay (?).
Ann E. Snedeger: (RD) Oct. 19, 1868, (B) Nov. 13, 1860, (PRTS) Enoch Snedeger and Mary A. Brown.
James T. Snedeger: (RD) Oct. 19, 1868, (B) Aug. 13, 1862, (PRTS) Enoch Snedeger and Mary A. Brown.
Abraham L. Dye: (RD) Dec. 1, 1868, (B) Jun. 27, 1861, (PRTS) Andrew Dye and Nancy Works.
Lucinda Chrisman: (RD) Feb. 7, 1870, (B) Nov. 9, 1854, (PRTS) Jacob Chrisman and Elizabeth Ishmail.
David Chrisman: (RD) Feb. 7, 1870, (B) Aug. 25, 1858, (PRTS) Jacob Chrisman and Elizabeth Ishmail.
John Syd Smith: (RD) Mar. 21, 1870, (B) Oct. 25, 1862, (PRTS) John Smith.
Timothy J. W. Rees: (RD) Jun. 18, 1870, (B) Jun. 26, 1860, (PRTS) Martin Rees and Margaret J. Ward.

Samuel M. Emhoff: (RD) Dec. 2, 1870, (B) Dec. 2, 1856, (PRTS) Andrew Emhoff and Nancy A. Jenkins.
Flora E. Emhoff: (RD) Dec. 2, 1870, (B) Apr. 1, 1858, (PRTS) Andrew Emhoff and Nancy A. Jenkins.
Laura (?) E. Emhoff: (RD) Dec. 2, 1870, (B) Oct. 12, 1861, (PRTS) Andrew Emhoff and Nancy A. Jenkins.
Sophronia A. Bales: (RD) Dec. 29, 1870, (B) Nov. 29, 1861, (PRTS) George M. Bales and Nancy J. Thompson.
John L. Inman: (RD) Mar. 28, 1871, (B) Aug. 19, 1868, (PRTS) Wm. Inman and George Ann Lucas
Ann Eliza Inman: (RD) Mar. 28, 1871, (B) Apr. 7, 1870, (PRTS) William Inman and George Ann Lucas.
Henry S. Collins: (RD) May 3, 1871, (B) Nov. 20, 1857, (PRTS) John C. Collins and Elizabeth A. (?)
Mary J. Collins: (RD) May 3, 1871, (B) Apr. 5, 1861, (PRTS) John C. Collins and Elizabeth A. (?)
John E. Collins: (RD) May 3, 1871, (B) Jan. 30, 1859, (PRTS) John C. Collins and Elizabeth A. (?)

Taney County, Missouri, Wolf Cemetery, Section 17, Township 22N, Range 17W

Name	Birth	Death
Mary T. Brewer	Apr. 25, 1895	Apr. 19, 1965
Thomas G. Brewer	Apr. 1, 1891	---
Ora Hankins Price	Jan. 3, 1872	Dec. 24, 1951
Elmo Blankenship	Mar. 11, 1911	Dec. 17, 1858
Clara Sowards	Aug. 7, 1877	---
O. R. B. Sowards	Jan. 27, 1878	May 16, 1956
Jerry Glen Ridinger	Aug. 8, 1957	Aug. 10, 1957
Donald Clark	1938	1959
Roy Oliver Bonner	Oct. 7, 1940	Nov. 27, 1961
Leavie Clemons	Nov. 22, 1890	Jan. 2, 1954
Ben Clemons	Jun. 2, 1885	---
Harley Ray Hunter	Nov. 26, 1935	Jul. 28, 1954
Elizabeth Blanton	Feb. 25, 1863	Aug. 20, 1954
Clara A. Hodges	1888	1964
Frank G. Hodges	1884	---
Algia Blankenship	Nov. 23, 1909	---
Almas L. Clark	Jan. 16, 1866	Jan. 27, 1948
Orpha F. Pride	1915	---
Carmel C. Pride	1911	1962
Rome Blankenship	Feb. 25, 1931	Jun. 21, 1952
Fred P. Thompson	May 19, 1865	Feb. 3, 1918

Name	Birth	Death
Mary A. Thompson	Nov. 29, 1869	Jan. 28, 1950
Hobert F. Fowler	Jan. 25, 1912	Jan. 24, 1959
Lucy F. Baughman	Jul. 4, 1901	---
Truett L. Baughman	Nov. 3, 1901	Jan. 31, 1959
Anita Louise Baughman	May 27, 1957	Jul. 2, 1958
Lillie M. Copelin	Nov. 15, 1875	Aug. 17, 1961
Elias E. Copelin	Mar. 17, 1873	Mar. 16, 1951
Norma B. Copelin	Jun. 22, 1906	Apr. 25, 1951
Finley R. Copelin	Sep. 30, 1903	---
Elzora Merideth	Feb. 23, 1884	---
John S. Merideth	Oct. 13, 1875	Feb. 8, 1961
Audrey F. Merideth	May 11, 1914	---
Leonard K. Merideth	Nov. 11, 1909	Apr. 4, 1962
Elijah E. Blankenship	Feb. 21, 1901	May 30, 1964
York Wolf	Apr. 5, 1919	Oct. 7, 1954
Clara Effie Wolf	Apr. 12, 1890	Mar. 31, 1943
Joseph G. Wolf	Feb. 27, 1899	Oct. 12, 1940
Elmer C. Wolf	Dec. 14, 1883	Nov. 2, 1949
Max Donald Blankenship	May 29, 1937	Oct. 2, 1952
Lou Blankenship	Aug. 3, 1887	Aug. 23, 1958
Ed Blankenship	Jan. 27, 1887	---
J. R. Blankenship	Jan. 6, 1919	Aug. 29, 1958
Small Nave	Sep. 30, 1892	Jul. 18, 1959
Mack Nave	1900	1959
Nina Nave	1905	---
Una Fowler	Feb. 26, 1912	---
Floyd Fowler	Feb. 9, 1906	Jul. 5, 1956
Lillie M. Ridinger	Mar. 13, 1897	---
James E. Lord	May 15, 1942	Sep. 5, 1959
Harve Thornton	Feb. 21, 1880	Sep. 9, 1946
Jack Blanton	1863	1950
Jessie Rozell	Apr. 15, 1895	---
Toney Rozell	Oct. 25, 1895	Sep. 29, 1958
Austa A. Rozell	Jul. 15, 1906	Feb. 16, 1951
John T. Rozell	Sep. 28, 1901	---
Mary A. Linkous	1874	1956
George W. Linkous	1877	1956
Ota Aldridge	Mar. 6, 1880	Dec. 14, 1952
William Aldridge	Mar. 14, 1871	Mar. 3, 1959
John Durbin Trimble	Oct. 31, 1907	Jul. 4, 1964
General D. Filling	Apr. 29, 1891	Aug. 11, 1961
??? Blanton	1883	1961

Name	Birth	Death
Martha Ingram	Jun. 9, 1914	---
Cleveland Ingram	Aug. 4, 1905	Jan. 18, 1956
Hazel McCall	Jun. 25, 1916	---
Cecil McCall	Apr. 23, 1914	Jan. 30, 1961
Hobert F. Fowler	Jan. 25, 1912	Jan. 24, 1959
Low Fowler	Jan. 13, 1886	---
John Fowler	Jan. 17, 1877	Jul. 1, 1951

Carter County, Missouri, Marriage Book 1 1860 - 1881.
Solomon Crites and Matilda Leach, (MD) 21 Feb. 1861.
E.W. Crittenden and Mary M. Stalcup, (MD) 14 Mar. 1861.
John Hardin and Mary Raymeri, (MD) 14 Feb 1861.
James Skiles and Billie A. Taylor, (MD) 19 Apr. 1861.
Josephus Moore and Elisabeth Woods, (MD) 12 June 1861.
Jessee R. Blackwell and Ellen Salina Lutta(?), (MD) 16 June 1861.
John Jones and Emily Snider, (MD) 19 Aug. 1861.
Thomas A. Kinard and Sarah Jane Hawkins, (MD) 30 June 1861.
F. Marion Rogers and Mary E. Swezea, (MD) 19 Mar. 1862.
James Lutta (?) and Mary R. Pierce, (MD) 26 Oct. 1862.
Henry D Gresham and Mary O. C. Leach, (MD) 19 Apr. 1863.
James Snider and Cressey Neal, (MD) 23 Feb. 1865.
Issac Patterson and Emely Jones, (MD) 7Oct. 1863.
Robert Lambert and Elizabeth Tinker, (MD) 21 Jun. 1866.
F. M. Kelley and Margaret Porter, (MD) 11 Oct. 1860.
James Leach and Fanny A. Smith, (MD) 11 July 1866.
Thomas R. Brame and Antimissa O'Dell, (MD) ?? Oct. 1866.
Isaac M. Raymer and Frances Ann Powel, (MD) 4 Oct. 1866.
William Jones and Elisabeth Turley, (MD) 4 Oct. 1866.
George W. Vainyard and Susan G. Brame, (MD) 25 Jan. 1867.
Isom McKeen and Rebecca T. Pouge, (MD) 22 Aug. 1866.
Thomas A. Pince and Louiza I. Cox, (MD) 5 Mar. 1864.
Manuel L. Lawson and Harritt Rebecca White, (MD) 17 Mar. 1867.
George W. Hendricks and Kinian Jane Hardin, (MD) 30 Mar. 1867.
Marke L. Moon and Rachael Adier, (MD) 14 Apr. 1867.
James Maberry and Manurry(?) Baker, (MD) 23 Jun. 1867.
John Sheets and Julia B. Stout, (MD) 4 Jul. 1867.
Joseph Burns and Nancis Sanders, (MD) 21 July 1867.
Andrew A. Parsons and Liza Jane Wheeler, (MD) 8 Aug. 1867.
John Meadows and Margaret Mury, (MD) 28 July 1867.
William R. Gray and Martha A. Rink, (MD) 1 Aug. 1867.
William T. Hewey and Vira Jones, (MD) 26 Sep. 1867.
Cornelius Lafferty and Louiza Jane Long, (MD) 15 Sep. 1867.

Timothy Reeves and Adaline Brown, (MD) 4 Oct. 1867., (CMTS) premarital agreement
William J. O'Dell and Saral A. Cates, (MD) 24 Oct. 1867.
Martin Boin and Elizabeth Rogers, (MD) 10 Oct. 1867.
Timothy Reeves and Adaline Brown, (MD) 4 Oct. 1867.
Anderson Lawson and Stacy Hickson, (MD) 11 Sep. 1867.
Peter Hartridge and Elizabeth Brewer, (MD) 27 Oct. 1867.
Elisha Robertson and Sariah Sweezea, (MD) 10 Nov. 1867.
John M. Brame and Mary L. Hoskins, (MD) 18 Nov. 1867.
Benjamine C. Taylor and Ellen Cates, (MD) 16 Jan. 1868.
Caloway Boyer and Elizabeth Raymour, (MD) 9 Jan. 1868.
George Columbus Condray and Cordele Robertson, (MD) 19 Jan. 1868.
Jackson Maberry and Mary Perteat, (MD) 2 Mar. 1868.
William J. Robertson and Louiza E. Condry, (MD) 15 Mar. 1868.
Fidillo Condry and Tennessee A. Maze, (MD) 22 Mar. 1868.
William Sanders and Mandy Tins, (MD) 9 Feb. 1868.
Charles Malloy and Telitha Spillman, (MD) 15 Mar. 1868.
Charles Joplin and Mary McKinney, (MD), (MD) 20 Feb. 1868.
Anderson Colman and Elizabeth Kelley, (MD) 19 Apr. 1868.
Jonathan Box and Nancy Wiscarver, (MD) 26 Apr. 1868.
(no name) and Melinda Colman, (MD) 31 May, 1868.
James L. Kelley and Sely Hopper, (MD) 23 Jul. 1868.
William Griffin and Mary Ann Snider, (MD) 22 Oct. 1868.
Henry Cloninger and Amanda Fagga, (MD) 1 Oct. 1868.
John P. Norton and Mary E. Kinnard, (MD) 19 Nov. 1868.
Francis M. Spears and Mary Lane, (MD) 22 Nov. 1868.
Henry Davice and Musy M. Joyles, (MD) 9 Sep. 1868.
Peter D. Brame and Lucy Jane O'Dell, (MD) 11Dec. 1868.
Ephraim S. Vinson and Mary Ann Snider, (MD) 7Jan. 1869.
Jefferson Fullington and Elizabeth Carey (?), (MD) 10 Jan. 1869.
William M. Gunn and Matilda E. Crites, (MD) 25 Jan. 1869.
Thomas Fredrick and Martha A. Cronister, (MD) 28 Jan. 1869.
John H. McKinney and Mary Chanbers, (MD) 9 Feb. 1869.
A. Wigen and Manda Lowery, (MD) 28 Feb. 1869.
Thomas D. Thompson and Mary Jane McKinney, (MD) 16 Mar. 1869.
Calvin Carter and Mahaly Giles, (MD) 25 Mar. 1869.
Jackson M. Markham and Clevay Elizabeth Lawson, (MD) 4Apr. 1869.
William O. Turley and Margaret E. Snider, (MD) 7Mar. 1869.
Anthony G. Gresham and Elizabeth Ann Sweazea, (MD) 22 Apr. 1869.
William Smith and Nancy Ann Robertson, (MD) 6 Jun. 1869.
Thomas Gray and Mary Irvin, (MD) 27 Jun. 1869.
William Gilbrith and Rebecca F. Baker, (MD) 9 Sep. 1869.
John Rubinger(?) and Mary Bradshaw, (MD) 10 Oct. 1869.

Ezekiel Furgerson and Nancy A. Box, (MD) 11Aug. 1869.
William A. Gresham and Mary J.S. Ammons, (MD) 4 Dec. 1869.
Hardin Davise and Polley C. Gardner, (MD) 24 Dec. 1869.
Shadric Chilton and Cyntha Coleman, (MD) 7 Nov. 1869.
Silas Alley and Margaret Snider, (MD) 2 Jan. 1870.
Groom (?) and Sophia White, (MD) 21 Jun. 1864.
Jarret S. McCluen and Feeby Hooper, (MD) 6 Mar. 1870.
William C. Colins and Mary M. Robson, (MD) 6 Mar. 1870.
Bates and Nancy Patterson, (MD) 21 Mar. 1870.
Shadrick Chilton and Cyntha Coleman, (MD) 7 Nov. 1869.
James R. Brown and Emily F. Cowen, (MD) 5 Jun. 1870.
Henry F. Long and Mary Ann Long, (MD) 20 Jun. 1870.
Thomas Mabrey and Sarah J. Carter, (MD) 28 Aug. 1870.
John Sanders and Nancy Morris, (MD) 11 Sep. 1870.
John Kinnard and Cele A. Coleman, (MD) 8 Sep. 1870.
James M. Wigers and Rebecca E. Anderson, (MD) 13 Oct. 1870.
Caloway Boyer and Elvira P. Gibbs, (MD) 24 Aug. 1870.
Hezekiah Brotherton and Mary Jane Clay, (MD) 27 Sep. 1870.
Thomas Cloinger and Agness Bess, (MD) 11 Jan. 1870.
Avis Wilson and Lee Ann Vincent, (MD) 20 Oct. 1870.
William Crook and Elizabeth Patterson, (MD) 20 Aug. 1870.
Anderson None and Elizabeth Long, (MD) 20 Aug. 1870.
Rosen Kearby (?) and Matilda King, (MD) 25 Aug. 1870.
Ephraim Vincent and Margaret A. McSpadin, (MD) 8 Jan. 1871.
Charles Gunn and Amanda Condrey, (MD) 22 Jan. 1871.
George S. Glimp and Mary Ann Boyer, (MD) 12 Jan. 1871.
William Nivins and Harreat Ganes, (MD) 12 Jan. 1871.
Samuel Donigan and Mandy Condrey, (MD) 11 Jan. 1871.
Isaac Lafferty and Perlecy Goff, (MD) 27 Mar. 1871.
Abagey Manard and Pernecy Laffertry, (MD) 27 Mar. 1871.
William Scoggin and Arminta House, (MD) 2 Jul. 1871.
George Cowin and Frances Jane Wheeler, (MD) 27 Jul. 1871.
Umphry Jones and Harriet Dildine, (MD) 9 Jul. 1871.
James McCoin and Nancy J. Maynard, (MD) 21 Jun. 1871.
Lewis Beck and Julia Ellis, (MD) 30 Jul. 1871.
William Moore and Elisabeth F. Hanger, (MD) 20 Sep. 1871.
Noah Clark and Emaline Chilton, (MD) 20 Sep. 1871.
James Sanders and Louisa Hooper, (MD) 19 Oct. 1871.
Thomas Gilbraith and Sarah Elisabeth Irvin, (MD) 17 Sep. 1871.
Fines W. Sharp and Lucinda Casinger 24 Nov. 1871.
J. M. Bezley and Isabella Raymer 13 Nov. 1871.
Arch Crolley and Elizabeth Crites, (MD) 22 Nov. 1871.
Richard Maland and Nancy Jane Box, (MD) 10 Dec. 1871.

Robert W. McCane and P.E. Edwards, (MD) 4 Dec. 1871.
Charles Kinnard and Margaret E . Turley, (MD) 23 Nov. 1871.
Joseph L. Hart and J. Rusha Elizabeth Woodard, (MD) 17 Dec. 1871.
James A Carter and Mary J. Gresham, (MD) 14 Dec. 1871.
James W. Snider and Helen V. McSpadden, (MD) 4 Jan. 1872.
Zimri Alley and Sailey Snider, (MD) 8 Feb. 1872.
Johnathan B.L. Richmond and Emily C. Long, (MD) 11 Feb 1872.
Alexander McCaulep (?) and Nancy D. Guinn, (MD) 25 Feb. 1872.
John Cloninger and Martha J. Barker, (MD) 10 Mar. 1872.
Joseph A. Gilbraith and Sarah J. House, (MD) 27 Jun. 1872.
James G. Giles and Ellen Waller, (MD) 7 May 1872.
Theadore B. Wallis and Cynthia S. Crow, (MD) 15 Aug. 1872.
James Clark and Mary Coleman, (MD) 26 Sep. 1872.
M. C. Leach and Lucinda Cox, (MD) 21 Jul. 1872.
J. M. Leach and Dianah Link, (MD) 6 Oct. 1872.
Marion Gunn and Colley Giles, (MD) 30 Jun. 1872.
Anthony Bumgarner and Catharine Jane Hiatt, (MD) 20 Oct. 1872.
Elvey G. Turley and Catherine Kinnard, (MD) 9 Jan. 1873.
Joseph B. Norton and Susan A. Snider, (MD) 15 Dec. 1872.
Robert Jones and Nancy J. Alley, (MD) 19 Jan. 1873.
Robert R. Beaver and Narcissus Piles, (MD) 25 Nov. 1872.
James F. Davis and Sarah E.J. Williams, (MD) 8 Dec. 1872.
Elvis B. Williams and Cyary A. Woods, (MD) 12 Dec. 1872.
Henry Glas and Ara Weeb, (MD) 5 Jan. 1873.
Joseph Shelton and Mary E. Cowin, (MD) 16 Mar. 1873.
Joseph N. Ellis and Almeda Green, (MD) 27 Mar. 1873.
Nathan Pace and Arbuckle Bucy, (MD) 20 Apr. 1873.
David H. Hedgepeth and Margaret E. Snider, (MD) 27 Mar. 1873.
Robert Johnson and Mary West, (MD) 8 Jun. 1873.
Anderson Nunn and Louisa K. Mayner, (MD) 24 Jul. 1873.
Anderson Coleman and Malinda Hixon, (MD) 17 Aug. 1873.
James B. Kennedy and Elizabeth Tinker, (MD) 12 Sep. 1873.
John H. Dollar and S. L. Travis, (MD) 20 Sep. 1873.
Thomas McKinney and Jane Payne, (MD) 3 Nov. 1873.
William Owen and Lurene Sanders 24 Oct. 1873.
William R. Dawson and Sarah Ann Snider, (MD) 6 Nov. 1873.
Pinkney W. Andrews and Sarah E. Brame, (MD) 18 Jan. 1874.
James L. Kelley, Jr. and Emily Cowin, (MD) 18 Jan. 1874.
William Kinnard and Martha Ann Sholar, (MD) 11 Dec 1873.
Merriett M. Windes and Mary A. Snider, (MD) 1 Jan 1874.
Richard Sweazea and Clementine Carter, (MD) 8 Nov 1873.
John H. Rector and Minerva J. Wheeler 2 Jul 1874.
William Reeves and Mary Buchanan, (MD) 27 Sep. 1874.

John Boyer and Santilla Cates 24 Sept. 1874.
George Kinnard and Mrs. Melissa Jane Snider, (MD) 31 Dec. 1875.
Stephen Shumate and Mary A. Stevenson, (MD) 10 Jan. 1875.
J. W. R. Richmond and F. E. Guller (CMTS) Written Consent.
Charles H. Joplin and Alvira S.A. Emry, (MD) 17 Jan 1875.
J. W. R. Richmond and F. E. Fuller, (MD) 22 Nov. 1874.
William Owens and Tennessee P. Webb, (MD) 28 Feb. 1875.
R. W. Wenchell and M.J. Stanley, (MD) 14 Mar.. 1875.
James Hooper and Ann Sanders, (MD) 24 Jan. 1875.
John Longbottom and Susan Brame, (MD) 18 Apr. 1875.
Thomas L. Collins and Mary E. Davis, (MD) 20 May 1875.
F. P. Jackson and Nancy E. Carter, (MD) 30 May 1875.
Marion House and Eliza J. Bridges, (MD) 27 Aug. 1875.
William P. Ake and Emma J. Frazier, (MD) 10 Oct. 1875.
George Wines and Sarah Ann Snider, (MD) 30 Sep. 1875.
Henry Small and Matilda Ann Dawson, (MD) 19 Sep. 1875.
F. M. Kelley and Mary J. Blanchard, (MD) 3 Jul. 1875.
Martin V. Bowen and Melvina C. Tinker, (MD) 21 Apr. 1875.
John W. Kennedy and Rachel J. Milican, (MD) 17 Oct. 1875.
Thomas J. Boyer and Minerva Lankford, (MD) 24 Jan 1876.
William H. H. Stevenson and Nancy E. Jones, (MD) 30 Jan 1876.
Jno. J. McKing and Mary A. McCluskey 2 Jan. 1876.
Nelson Smith and Ellen Case, (MD) 26 Mar. 1876.
Zoell W. Daugherty and Malinda Robesson, (MD) 10 Oct. 1875.
George Johnson and Mary E. Bucy, (MD) 9 Dec. 1875.
Thomas Ramzy and Amandy Smith, (MD) 3 Feb 1876.
Alfred N. Massie and Mahaler Z. Holland, (MD) 9 Apr. 1876.
Vincent Massie and Catharine Neal, (MD) 10 ??, 1876., (CMTS)
    filed 11 Sep. 1876..
Edward Moss and Cuvinia J. Sweazy, (MD) 17 Sep. 1876.
John A. Gresham and Aletha Ballard, (MD) 10 Sep. 1876.
Jacob Angle and Martha Ann Brame, (MD) 24 Oct 1876.
William P. Rector and Sarah Ann Cowin, (MD) 31 Aug. 1876.
James F. Bucy and Sarah Lucinda Green, (MD) 26 Oct. 1876.
William D. Baker and Martha Ellen Collins, (MD) 3 Sep. 1876.
Charles A. Hoskins and Missouri E. Hill, (MD) 8 Oct. 1876.
William T. Coutsell and Elizabeth Smith, (MD) 3 Mar. 1877.
John R. Meadows and S. E. Andrews, (MD) 5 Apr 1877.
John C. Waymeyer and Sarah Boyer, (MD) 4 Feb 1877.
Joseph M. Leach and Sarah Elizabeth Hope, (MD) 22 Feb 1877.
Marion Green and Polly A. Snider, (MD) 12 Apr. 1877.
Joseph M. Tubbs and Malinda Freeman, (MD) 24 Jun. 1877.
Jessie W. Bradshaw and Caroline Hunter, (MD) 1 Jul. 1877.

William R. Snider and Mary C. Turley, (MD) 20 Sep. 1877.
James W. Adare and Mary McDonald, (MD) 28 Sep. 1877.
Mr. Sartin and Anna Pritchett, (MD) 9 Oct 1877.
John J. Frazier, Jr. and Artemisa Kelley, (MD) 11Oct. 1877.
John W. Kelley and Harriet R. Marler 13 Oct. 1877.
Joseph Bumgardner and Mary C. Kever, (MD) 15 Nov. 1877.
Shadrack Jones and Martha Coil, (MD) 25 Nov. 1877.
John Chanson and Sarah Turnbelt, (MD) 30 Sep. 1877.
Arisan Bratcher and Mary Cusinger, (MD) 30 Nov. 1877.
William Kinnard and Martha E. Snider, (MD) 20 Dec. 1877.
George W. Coffee and Carrie Fisher, (MD) 6 Feb. 1878.
James Kinnard and Sarah L. McSpaden, (MD) 7 Feb. 1878.
John Lamert and Melviney Crabtree, (MD) 22 Sep. 1877.
James B. Snider and Sarah B. Kinnard, (MD) 14 Feb. 1878.
Nathaniel L. Mallory and Sophrona C. Wood, (MD) 7 Feb. 1878.
John Marney and Mary A. Goodwin, (MD) 17 Feb. 1878.
Andrew L. Lord and Sarah J. Snider, (MD) 23 Apr. 1878.
Spencer Burris and Cuzic Snider, (MD) 3 Mar 1878.
Isaac C. Clark and Zillie Kinnard, (MD) 5 May 1878.
A. K. Oliver and Malinda Ellis, (MD) 5 May 1878.
Moses L. Copeland and Margret Ann Rose, (MD) 19 May 1878.
Jacob Brakefield and Almeda Boyer, (MD) 14 Apr. 1878.
Anthony Murphy and Sarah A. Mauk, (MD) 5 May 1878.
James M. Meadows and Juda C. Angle, (MD) 27 Apr. 1878.
William H. Parrett and Leety J. Snider, (MD) 11Aug. 1878.
Daniel T. Frazier and Manerva J. Burnham, (MD) 18 Jul. 1878.
James Nickles and Elizbeth Neel, (MD) 18 Aug. 1878.
David C. Norton and Sarah E. Kinnard, (MD) 17 Oct. 1878.
Graves Storm(?) and Lyda Causs(?), (MD) 4 Aug. 1878.
Samuel C. Westen and Anna E. Gross, (MD) 8 Sep. 1878.
Lewis Neel and Lusinda A. Leach, (MD) 12 Sep. 1878.
Harrison A. Holland and Lucindia McCaskill 24 Nov. 1878.
Preston A. Baker and Malinda J. Dawson, (MD) 25 Dec. 1878.
David L. Massie and Mary E. Holland, (MD) 11 Dec. 1878.
Isaac Raymer and Sarah A. Boyer, (MD) 17 Nov. 1878.
Daniel B. Edington and Mary J. Raymer, (MD) 15 Dec. 1878.
Austin Strouptto Lillie Chilton, (MD) 22 Jan. 1879.
William House and Mary J. Hawkins, (MD) 4Feb 1879.
Christian Rumburg and Elizabeth Jane Massie, (MD) 27 Feb. 1879.
Charles Paris and Lucinda Richmond, (MD) 30 Oct. 1878.
Daniel Ashcraft and Martha Sutten, (MD) 27 Oct. 1878.
William W. Lawson and Betty Young, (MD) 30 Dec. 1878.
Nicholas Smith and Narcissus Condrey, (MD) 23 Feb. 1879.

James W. Joplin and Louisa Alice Cole, (MD) 7 Mar. 1879.
John B. Hobs and Mary Elen Housden, (MD) 28 Feb. 1879.
Thomas A. Smith and Sarah Hamerrick, (MD) 1 Jan. 1879.
J. A. Bramhall and Mary A. Mills, (MD) 16 Jun. 1879.
James Lee and Martha A. Snider 24 Aug. 1879.
C. A. Hoskins and Theodosha Stephens, (MD) 25 Sep. 1879.
Charley T. Burden and Julin C. House, (MD) 26 Oct. 1879.
John E. McDonald and Nancy E. Snider, (MD) 28 Aug. 1879.
Alfred P. Payne and Mary C. Snider, (MD) 28 Aug. 1879.
Richard C. Piles and Dollie Cook, (MD) 9 Nov. 1877.
John W. Jucco and Eliza McSpaden, (MD) 23 Nov. 1879.
Joseph C. Carpenter and Nancy A. Ressinger, (MD) 14 Sep. 1879.
Perry Dennon and Mary C. Norris, (MD) 21 Dec. 1879.
William M. Dawson and Sarah Snider, (MD) 28 Dec. 1879.
Elijah Jett and Mary J. Eaton, (MD) 8 Jan. 1880.
Louis H. Hollis and Melinda Jones, (MD) 22 Jan. 1880.
James Lambert and Sary J. West, (MD) 14 April 1864.
William Henson and Mary Cliburn 13 Nov. 1879.
William T. Cimp and Mary H.L. Lewis, (MD) 30 Nov. 1879.
Henry C. Dial and Sarah E. Webber, (MD) 26 Nov. 1879.
Joseph L. Ramer and Scintha A. Boyer, (MD) 4 Dec. 1879.
Thomas B. Sweazea and Sarah C. Edmonds, (MD) 7Mar 1880.
Francis M. Woodruff and Amanda Jane England, (MD) 16 Jan. 1880.
William M. Bay and Oily Fleming, (MD) 25 Nov. 1879.
David Hewit and Sary Jones, (MD) 18 Feb. 1880.
James H. P. Green and Mrs. Nelley B. Lowry 2 May, 1880.
James B. Carson and Hesterann Smith, (MD) 13 May, 1880.
David A. DeSpain and Mary E. Brame, (MD) 28 Mar. 1880.
Winifield S. Stevenson and Canzad S. Mitchell, (MD) 11Jul. 1880.
Moses E. Ellington and Phebe A. Cliburn, (MD) 6 Jul. 1880.
James C. McCready and Mary Plaster, (MD) 3 Jul. 1880.
John Entemann and Milly E. McCamey, (MD) 8 Aug. 1880.
Daniel Snodgrass and Sarah E. Marchbanks, (MD) 1 Aug. 1880.
Alonzo Lingo and Hannah J. Smith, (MD) 22 Aug. 1880.
Thomas Trimon(?) and Mrs. Allis Denison, (MD) 22 Aug. 1880.
Auther II.McCamey and Isadora S. Blackman, (MD) 26 Sep. 1880.
George Kinnard and Nancy Jane Snider, (MD) 16 Sep. 1880.
James Ring and Mrs. Nancy Huff, (MD) 26 Sep. 1880.
Joseph Langley and Nancy McKeen, (MD) 26 Sep. 1880.
Dr. James E. Mosely and Lizzie L. Chilton 24 Nov. 1880.
Jefferson Carson and Mary J. King, (MD) 21 Nov. 1880.
Joseph Mills and Minna Day, (MD) 19 Sep. 1880.
W. W. Carson and Hattie Valentine, (MD) 24 Oct. 1880.

Wm. Rufus Crandell and Minerva C. Hoskins, (MD) 25 Jan. 1880.
James L. Coleman and Malinda Chilton, (MD) 19 Dec. 1880.
Lathan Emery and Sarah J. Renaley (?), (MD) 5 Dec. 1880.
Wm. Lowe and Alsia Wood, (MD) 21 Nov. 1880.
James Edington and Alice J. Call, (MD) 12 Dec. 1880.
Willis A. Allmon and Margaret A. Butts, (MD) 12 Dec. 1880.
Joshua Brown and Mary E. Condry, (MD) 5 Jan 1881.
W.M. Hazlelip and Nancy C. Mills, (MD) 28 Dec. 1880.
John A. Angie and Anna B. Sutterfield, (MD) 12 Dec. 1880.
Isaac Rasnic and Mary F. Sutterfield, (MD), (MD) 23 Dec. 1880.
Allen Dewitt Swezie and Sarah Elizabeth Frazier, (MD) 6 Feb. 1881.
George P. Bush and Mrs. Sarah Mitchell, (MD) 8Feb. 1881.
Lace Counts and Lutitia B. Norris, (MD) 17 Mar. 1881.
Charles B. Rodgers and Luenda A. Buchannan, (MD) 6 Mar. 1881.
Alexander Carter and Sarah E.R. Rose, (MD) 27 Mar. 1881.
William Day and Seliann Crites 24 Apr. 1881.
Samuel M. Long and Theadoria Reeves, (MD) 28 Apr. 1881.
Joshua Tolliver and Mary Patterson, (MD) 6 Mar. 1875.
Lonnon Dinwidey and Polley Lee Collerd, (MD) 31 Mar. 1867.
Alexander Canton and Winney Dinwoody, (MD) 20 Aug. 1867.
Elias Dinwoody and Jannatta Brown, (MD) 5 Sep. 1867.
F. N. Kelley and Margaret Patterson, (MD) 11 Oct. 1860.

Macon County, Missouri, Ballinger Cemetery, Liberty Township, Near of Calleo, MO, Road 612.

Name	Birth	Death
Delbert S. Skinner	Nov. 13, 1904	Feb. 8, 1960
Avel Dirl Skinner, Jr.	1913	1912
Archie Lee Skinner	1935	1935
Virgil Skinner	1924	1924
Sarah J. Skinner	Aug. 25, 1856	May 1, 1931
Caroline Skinner	Jan. 30, 1867	Jul. 10, 1912
W. A. Skinner	Nov. 21, 1862	---
John T. Skinner	Jan. 30, 1847	Jan. 14, 1927
Freddie Skinner, son of C. D. and K. Skinner	Feb. 12, 1891	Aug. ??, 1891
Elvie Skinner, daughter of C. D. and Katie Skinner	Feb. 3, 1882	Apr. 16, 1886
Olie Skinner, daughter of C. D. and K. Skinner	Jan. 15, 1890	Sep. ??, 1890
Katie Skinner	Aug. 23, 1872	Apr. 27, 1903
Therman L. Schwenk	1924	1924
Sidney Skinner	Jul. 27, 1880	May 31, 1899

Name	Birth	Death
Susan F. Skinner	May 29, 1859	Jul. 22, 1880
Maud Skinner, daughter of F. T. and I. F. Skinner	Jul. 19, 1902	Jul. 20, 1904
Sylvie Meyer	May 1, 1902	Sep. 12, 1950
August M. Schwenk	Dec. 21, 1885	Dec. 12, 1956
William Robert Sagaser	Feb. 20, 1874	Nov. 23, 1936
Martha A. Sagaser, *(Age: 49Y 1M 1D)	May 19, 1858	Jun. 20, 1907
Andrew Nelson Sagaser, *(Age: 57Y 7M)	Jan. 1, 1861	Aug. 1, 1918
Mary C. Ballinger	1853	1939
Levi Ballinger	1848	1913
B. H. Ballinger	1852	1930
Other G. Ballinger	Sep. 29, 1891	Jan. 10, 1893
Mattie W. Ballinger	Apr. 22, 1867	Dec. 11, 1908
Oscar T. Ballinger	May 1, 1860	Jan. 2, 1942
Lena Dohring, daughter of L. M. and G. W. Dohring (Age: 16Y 2D)	---	Jul. 26, 1907
Charles F. Dohring, son G. W. and L. M. Dohring, (Age: 19Y 1M 1D)	---	Oct. 6, 1903
Lulu M. Dohring	May 28, 1865	Aug. 4, 1911
Geo. W. Dohring	May 15, 1865	Apr. 9, 1932
Betsy Jane Smith	Apr. 17, 1853	Jun. 19, 1912
Mary B. Wilkins, daughter of H. F. and R. F. Wilkins	Sep. 3, 1900	May 1, 1902
Betty Sagaser Skinner	1872	1953
S. B. Pete Skinner	1870	1934
Chas. Skiner (Age: 2D)	---	1865
Sarah Skinner (Age: 4Y)	---	1859
Katie Skinner (Age: 4Y)	---	1857
Bettie Skinner (Age: 6M)	---	1853
Frank C. Dohring	May 15, 1865	Nov. 30, 1908
Charles Skinner, son of J. T. and Sarah J. Skinner	Jan. 5, 1876	---
Goldie M. Skinner	Apr. 7, 1894	Mar. 13, 1935
Avel D. Skinner	Jan. 25, 1895	Oct. 31, 1937

Audrain County, Missouri, Appleman's Cemetery

Name	Birth	Death
Virgil F. Stites, son of J. R. and Rena Stites	1900	1920

Name	Birth	Death
Rena Frances Stites	1869	1951
John Randolph Stites	1858	1936
Andrew R. Bowne	1852	1921
Annie E. Bowne	1859	1944
Lloyd Bowne	Feb. 10, 1890	Dec. 7, 1959
Jake Bowne	Feb. 14, 1883	Jul. 12, 1968
Rosa Lee Bowne Roberts	Sep. 5, 1879	Jul. 15, 1952
Wm. Silas B. Roberts	Feb. 26, 1880	Jun. 11, 1968
William T. Eckley	Oct. 16, 1935	Oct. 22, 1935
Grant Eckley	1872	1947
Sarah F. Eckley	1875	1945
Kenneth Butler Vanderpool	Jun. 16, 1927	Jul. 25, 1927
Raymond H. Dysart	1897	1919
Okie E. Dysart	1906	1915
Susan K. Dysart	1904	1917
B. F. Vanderpool	Dec. 27, 1979	Mar. 26, 1964
Audella Vanderpool	Dec. 6, 1886	May 19, 1978
Margaret Groves	1874	1959
Marion Groves	1876	1949
Charley L. Vigneron. son of G. N. Vigneron	Feb. 8, 1889	Sep. 20, 1896
George E. Vigneron, son of G. N. Vigneron	Jul. 6, 1887	Oct. 15, 1896
Newton L. Dysart	Nov. 25, 1863	Dec. 12, 1935
Lilla Rich Dysart	Jun. 7, 1869	Mar. 31, 1950
Nancy Bowne, wife of S. J. Bowne	Apr. 18, 1843	May 17, 1910
S. J. Bowne	1845	1930
Adolph Hielscher	1871	1912
Lena Hielscher	1875	1918
Eddie Hielscher	1904	1921
Infant Daughter Hielscher	1908	---
Elgin R. Groves	Aug. 14, 1904	May 29, 1943
Emma Groves	1907	---
Elmer Groves	1895	---
Joseph Eckley	Sep. 28, 1840	Feb. 20, 1918
Cordelia Exckley	Feb. 23, 1843	Apr. 1, 1917
Nellie Barnes	Sep. 15, 1886	Mar. 4, 1888
Elizabeth Barnes, wife of W. S. Barnes (Age: 40Y 2M 15D)	Jan. 16, 1850	Apr. 1, 1890
Minnie Lee Winscott,	Jun. 11, 1883	Jun. 2, 1906

Name	Birth	Death
wife of S. E. Winscott		
Infant Hartley, daughter of T. R. and M. E. Hartley	Jun. 4, 1884	Jun. 4, 1884
Harold W. Swartz	Aug. 27, 1915	Mar. 11, 1936
Charles A. Swartz	Apr. 16, 1893	Apr. 21, 1952
Mary E. Swartz	Jun. 18, 1893	Jun. 2, 1964
Morris Askisson	Jul. 4, 1934	
Inah Lavone Askisson	1935	
Virgil Raymond Adkisson	Aug. 14, 1906	Feb. 23, 1927
J. T. Adkisson	Feb. 19, 1852	May 25, 1924
Elizabeth M. Adkisson	Aug. 12, 1853	---
Elizabeth M. Adkisson	1857	---
Infant Bowne, child of W. A. and Minnie Bowne	---	Jan. 27, 1909
Margaret Ankrom, wife of A. Ankrom	Jul. 18, 1841	Apr. 25, 1901
J. E. Appleman, son of T. and S. A. Appleman	Aug. 9, 1877	Oct. 20, 1886
Arthur Appleman	Feb. 29, 1880	---
Thomas Appleman	1849	1893
Elizabeth Appleman	1853	1919
Edward Appleman	Jun, 23, 1871	Jul. 1, 1943
John Appleman	Feb. 11, 1895	Feb. 13, 1895
Bessie Applemman	Sep. 6, 1872	Nov. 7, 1923
Joseph Appleman	Feb, 11, 1895	Mar. 18, 1895
Pauline Appleman	May 3, 1908	Sep. 18, 1935
Thomas Appleman	Jun. 16, 1896	Feb. 23, 1897
Lurinda J. Adkisson	1862	1944
John H. Adkisson	1860	1923
Infant Hawk, daughter of A. L. and Bette Hawk	Nov. 13, 1901	Nov. 13, 1901
Infant Hawk, son of A. L. and Bette Hawk	Jun. 7, 1904	Jun. 7, 1904
Samuel Defigh	---	---
Cora Defigh, daughter of S. and M. M. Defigh (Age: 9M 1D)	---	Aug. 29, 1872
Infant Hartley, daughter of T. R. and M. E. Hartley	Dec. 28, 1882	Dec. 28, 1992
Martha A. Anderson	1849	1918
William Anderson	1844	1914
George Anderson	Aug. 16, 1873	Mar. 15, 1899
Victoria Anderson	---	Nov. 13, 1880

Name	Birth	Death
(Age: 20D) Malinda Anderson	---	Oct. 10, 1872
(Age: 1Y 10M 6D) Savilla Appleman	---	Jan. 13, 18??
(Age: 69Y) Ollie Teeters	1872	1930
William A. Teeters	1853	1930
Addie Teeters	1860	1894
Minnie E. Appleman	---	May 28, 1881
(Age: 6Y 3M 3D) John Foreaker	1866	1888
Woodrow W. Sheridan	1912	1938
Hattie V. Sheridan	1885	1968
James G. Sheridan	1882	1959

Buchanan County, Missouri, The Bartlett Trust Co., Officers and Directors, 1920, Established. 1906

Name	Office
B. P. Wentner	Chairman of the Board
B. P. Wentner	President
H. A. Westhoff	Vice-President
J. C. Willbrand	Vice-President
J. C. Willbrand	Secretary
J. H. Werner, Jr.	Asst. Secretary
J. C. Willbrand	Cashier
J. H. Werner, Jr.	Asst. Cashier
Wm. Woye, Jr.	Trust Officer
H. A. Westhoff	Director
B. P. Wentner	Director
Chas. H. Oelting	Director
Otto H. Willbrand	Director
J. C. Willbrand	Director

St. Louis County, Missouri, Mississippi Valley Trust Co., 1920, Established 1890.

Name	Office
Julius S. Walsh	Chairman of the Board
Breckinridge Jones	President
William G. Lackey	Vice-President
Frederick Vierling	Vice-President
J. Sheppard Smith	Vice-President
William M. Fitch	Vice-President

Name	Office
Hord Hardin	Vice-President
John R. Longmire	Vice President
Guy C. Phillips	Vice Presidnet
Thos. J. Kavanaugh	Vice-President
James E. Brock	Secretary
Henry C. Ibbotson	Asst. Treasurer
C. Hunt Turner, Jr.	Asst. Secretary
Edwin J. Kropp	Asst. Secretary
Robert W. Fisher	Asst. Secretary
James A. Weaver	Asst. Secretary
Frank C. Ball	Asst. Secretary
Joseph A. Rouveyrol	Asst. Secretary
Frederick Vierling	Trust Officer
A. H. Roudebush	Asst. Trust Officer
Jesse H. Keebaugh	Asst. Trust Officer
Fred A. Gissler	Asst. Trust Officer
Cecil A. Tolin	Asst. Trust Officer

Ship Werra, From Bremen and Southampton to New York, Arrival Date May 31, 1887.

Name	Age	Sex	Occupation	Destination
Anton Koszicki	41	M	Laborer	Missouri
Marianne Koszicki	33	F	Wife	Missouri
Peter Koszicki	17	M		Missouri
Yohaness Koszicki	7	M	Child	Missouri
Anna Koszicki	11	F	Infant	Missouri

Ship City of Richmond from Liverpool to New York, Arrival Date Aug. 19, 1887

Name	Age	Sex	Occupation	Destination
Josel Phillips	55	M	Laborer	St. Louis
Isaac Daviniski	26	M	Laborer	St. Louis

Ship Marsala from Hamburg to New York, Arrival Date Sep. 22, 1887.

Name	Age	Sex	Occupation	Destination
Rickel Weizmann	24	F	Woman	St. Louis
Pese Weizmann	11	F	Infant	St. Louis
Simon Weizmann	4	M	Child	St. Louis

Ship Sorrento from Hamburg to New York, Arrival date Oct. 27, 1887.

Name	Age	Sex	Occupation	Destination
Israel Seidewerk	31	M	Laborer	Missouri

Name	Age	Sex	Occupation	Destination
Mendel Seiewrk	28	M	Laborer	Missouri
Moses Kuzmann	42	M	Laborer	Missouri
Chane Buerger	45	F	Woman	Missouri
Ruche Buerger	3	F	Child	Missouri
Zippe Buerger	11/12	F	Infant	Missouri
Michel Buerger	1	M	Child	Missouri

Ship Waesland from Anterwerp to New York, Arrived Feb. 11, 1888.

Name	Age	Sex	Occupation	Destination
Gottlieb Paule	59	M	Gardner	St. Louis

Ship England from Liverpool to New York, Arrived Feb. 23, 1888.

Name	Age	Sex	Occupation	Destination
Aaron Margolis	40	M	Laborer	St. Louis

Ship The Queen from Liverpool to New York, Arrived Mar. 15, 1888.

Name	Age	Sex	Occupation	Destination
Josef Zakewitz	22	M	Laborer	St. Louis
F. Popensky	22	M	Laborer	St. Louis
Jos. Maschlewitz	26	M	Laborer	St. Louis
K. Jordgewitz	28	M	Laborer	St. Louis
Mathias Moses	21	M	Laborer	St. Louis

Ship Rhein from Bremen to Baltimore, Arrived May 9, 1888

Name	Age	Sex	Occupation	Destination
Joh. Goszczycki	22	M	Laborer	Missouri
Wladisl Tawcznski	32	M	Laborer	Missouri

Ship America from Bremen to Baltimore, Arrived May 20, 1888.

Name	Age	Sex	Occupation	Destination
Michael Latawschinski	22	M	Laborer	Missouri
Valentina Brzeukwicz	18	F	Unknown	Missouri
Ottilie Schmidt	23	F	Unknown	Missouri
Martha Schmidt	2	F	Child	Missouri
George Schimdt	3/12	M	Infant	Missouri
Auguste Schmidt	44	F	Unknown	Missouri
Ottilie Schmidt	21	F	Servant	Missouri
Reinhardt Schmidt	7	M	Child	Missouri
Hermann Schmidt	6	M	Child	Missouri
Martha Schimdt	2	M	Child	Missouri
Jan Belzinsky	42	M	Farmer	Missouri

Name	Age	Sex	Occupation	Destination
Felix Maslowsky	26	M	Tailor	Missouri
Jacob Modersky	13	M	Child	Missouri

Ship Weser from Bremen to Baltimore, Arrived May 24, 1888.

Name	Age	Sex	Occupation	Destination
Rachel Buernk	30	F	Unknown	Missouri
Lea Buernk	7	F	Child	Missouri
Chajem Buernk	5	F	Child	Missouri
Hinde Buernk	4	F	Child	Missouri

Ship The Queen from Liverpool and Queenstown to New York, Arrived Jun. 6, 1888.

Name	Age	Sex	Occupation	Destination
Bas. Sapperstein	32	F	Woman	St. Louis
Schage Sapperstein	5	F	Child	St. Louis
Kissel Sapperstein	3	F	Child	St. Louis
Ber. Sapperstein	1	M	Child	St. Louis
Mig. Dobrzyniski	25	M	Laborer	St. Louis
Chaim Lewin	26	M	Laborer	St. Louis
A. Schwarman	29	M	Laboer	St. Louis
B. Helstein	55	F	Woman	St. Louis
Henry Helstein	11	M	Child	St. Louis
Kackiz Helstein	10	M	Child	St. Louis
Rocklan Helstein	7	M	Child	St. Louis
Duvere Helstein	4	M	Child	St. Louis
Sagoel Helstein	2	M	Child	St. Louis
Solemn Helstein	1	M	Child	St. Louis
J. Malonowski	26	M	Laborer	St. Louis
W. Rubenstein	28	M	Laborer	St. Louis
Johan Robat	16	M	Laborer	St. Louis
Itzig Lewin	23	M	Laborer	St. Louis
M. Jalowicz	29	F	Woman	St. Louis
W. Jalowicz	7	F	Child	St. Louis
J. Jalowicz	4	F	Child	St. Louis
W. Jalowicz	2	F	Child	St. Louis
Chaim Robinson	15	M	Laborer	St. Louis
Fred Harnig	19	M	Laborer	St. Louis
Slate Prieschkowsky	24	M	Laborer	St. Louis

Ship Donau from Bremen to Baltimore, Arived Jun. 13, 1888.

Name	Age	Sex	Occupation	Destination
Konstanty Zukowski	33	M	Laborer	Missouri

Boone County, Missouri, Stephens Female College, 1879-1880, Faculty and Students, Eddlemon Collection.

Name	Comments
Rev. G. L. Black	Board of Curators, Liberty
Rev. H. W. Dodge	Board of Curators, Columbia
J. N. Garnett, M. D.	Board of Curators, Kansas City
Jas. Harris	Board of Curators, Boone Co.
T. H. Hickman	Board of Curators, Boone Co.
W. T. Hickman	Board of Curators, Columbia
R. T. Prewitt	Board of Curators, Columbia
Rev. J. M. Robinson	Board of Curators, Columbia
J. L. Stephens	Board of Curators, Columbia
E. W. Stephens	Board of Curators, Columbia
G. W. Trimble	Board of Curators, Columbia
F. Wilcox	Board of Curators, Boone Co.
Rev. T. W. Barrett	Board of Curators, Jeff. City
James Boggs	Board of Curators, Boone Co.
W. H. Ellis, M. D.	Board of Curators, Cooper Co.
Jas. M. Ellis	Board of Curators, Boone Co.
John G. Herndon	Board of Curators, Howard Co.
J. T. Chandler	Board of Curators, Liberty
Rev. G. W. Hyde	Board of Curators, Boonville
W. T. Maupin, M. D.	Board of Curators, Columbia
N. T. Mitchell, Jr.	Board of Curators, Boone Co.
W. R. Wilhitte	Board of Curators, Boone Co.
R. H. Willis	Board of Curators, Marshall
James Harris	President
E. W. Stephens	Secretary
G. W. Trimble	Treasurer
Rev. J. M. Robinson	Business Agent
J. N. Garnett	Exceutive Committee
J. L. Stephens	Executive Committee
G. W. Trimble	Executive Committee
R. P. Rider	Board of Management, President
Mrs. S. H. Wallace	Board of Management, Matron
Mrs. R. P. Rider	Board of Management, Directress
J. M. Robinson	Board of Management, Business Manager
R. P. Rider	President and Professor of Philosophy and Biblical History
H. W. Dodge	Lecturer on Evidences of

Name	Comments
	Christianity, Chaplain
Mrs. Hattie E. Stone	Professor of History and Literature
R. P. Rider	Professor of Mathematics
Mrs. Hattie E. Stone	Professor of English
Wm. L. Lemmon	Professor of Natural Science
Mamie W. Sampson	Professor of Intermediate School
Mrs. Mary H. Gardner	Teacher of Primary School
Emma F. Rider	Professor of Instrumental Music
Eleanor S. Smith	Professor of Vocal Music
Kate C. Rider	Teacher on Piano
Elanor S. Smith	Professor of Elocution
Wm. L. Lemmon	Teacher of Drawing, Painting and Gymnastics
E. F. Rider	Secretary of the Faculty
Wm. L. Lemmon	Librarian
Susan H. Allen	Student, Liberty
Anna C. Ash	Student, Versailles, IL
Maggie P. Anderson	Student, Columbia
Mattie Anderson	Student, Columbia
Minnie E. Babb	Student, Columbia
Anna Banks	Student, Columbia
Nita Banks	Student, Columbia
Carrie M. Bass	Student, Columbia
Lillian L. Bass	Student, Columbia
Lucie M. Bass	Student, Columbia
Maggie Bass	Student, Columbia
Ella M. Bates	Student, Columbia
Bettie Beasley	Student, Boone Co.
Isa May Berry	Student, Columbia
Evie Blankenbaker	Student, Howard Co.
Emma K. Botts	Student, Howard Co.
Russie C. Boyd	Student, Marshall
Mamie Bradley	Student, Cooper Co.
Nellie Briggs	Student, Columbia
Maggie A. Broughton	Student, Columbia
Lula Brown	Student, Saline Co.
Caddie P. Buckner	Student, Columbia
Laura M. Buckner	Student, Columbia
Maggie P. Buckner	Student, Columbia
Ellie S. Casey	Student, Howard Co.
Georgia A. Casey	Student, Howard Co.
Katie Chandler	Student, Columbia

Name	Comments
Mattie Lee Chandler	Student, Rocheport
Hallie H. Clarkson	Student, Boone Co.
Belle M. Clough	Student, Columbia
Roberta L. Crumbaugh	Student, Columbia
Lida Cunningham	Student, Columbia
Nannie T. DeVier	Student, Boone Co.
Agnes Dinwiddie	Student, Columbia
Laura Dinwiddie	Student, Columbia
Lulu Doran	Student, Cooper Co.
M. Gertie Matthews	Student, Columbia
Jessie O. Matthews	Student, Columbia
Laura A. Matthews	Student, Columbia
Lucie Matthews	Student, Columbia
Allie L. Mason	Student, Carrollton
Helen Martin	Student, Dallas, TX
Ellen McAfee	Student, Columbia
Mary McAfee	Student, Columbia
Carrie McKinney	Student, Boone Co.
Anna McQuitty	Student, Columbia
Lula McQuitty	Student, Columbia
Stella A. Meador	Student, Howard Co.
F. Pearl Mitchell	Student, Boone Co.
Mary Mosier	Student, Saline Co.
Mamie Moss	Student, Columbia
Sallie A. Morehead	Student, Howard Co.
Edna Newman	Student, Columbia
Lula Phipps	Student, Glasgow
Ella S. Potter	Student, Marshall
Amanda Prather	Student, Columbia
Emily Prather	Student, Columbia
Ella Prather	Student, Columbia
Mary Lee Prather	Student, Columbia
R. Y. Prigmore	Student, Dover
Anna Rice	Student, Randolph Co.
Nannie E. Rickey	Student, Centralia
Kate C. Rider	Student, Jacksonville, IL
Harper Riggins	Student, Columbia
Blanche Robinson	Student, Boone Co.
Sallie Robinson	Student, Boone Co.
Anna M. Rowland	Student, Bevier
Vena Russell	Student, Saline Co.
Vallie M. Sands	Student, Keytesville

Name	Comments
Kate M. Sawyer	Student, Jacksonville, IL
Lizzie Schweitzer	Student, Columbia
Nellie W. Dorsett	Student, Columbia
Julia Dorsett	Student, Columbia
Allie Duncan	Student, Columbia
Mattie R. Ellis	Student, Boone Co.
Lizzie Leg. Fisher	Student, Columbia
Estelle C. Fleming	Student, Jefferson City
Nina L. Gardner	Student, Edwardsville, IL
Mattie M. Garner	Student, Richmond
Jennie Halley	Student, Saline Co.
Anna M. Garnett	Student, Saline Co.
Mary A, Greogry	Student, Pettis Co.
Bessie Guitar	Student, Boone Co.
Mattie Guitar	Student, Boone Co.
Mollie Halley	Student, Saline Co.
Lizzie Hancock	Student, Saline Co.
Anna M. Harris	Student, Boone Co.
Maggie B. Harris	Student, Boone Co.
Emma Hayes	Student, Columbia
Cornelia Hickman	Student, Bates. Co.
Mary Hickman	Student, Bates Co.
Mary D. Hickman	Student, Columbia
Sallie Hickman	Student, Boone Co.
Orrie Hickman	Student, Boone Co.
Annie Hodge	Student, Columbia
Lizzie Hodge	Student, Columbia
Mattie F. Hodge	Student, Columbia
Minnie E. Hoffman	Student, Trenton
Bessie S. Hopper	Student, Saline Co.
Tennie Hopper	Student, Saline Co.
Kitty Jacobs	Student, Boone Co.
Coonie (sic) Jacobs	Student, Boone Co.
H. P. Jameson	Student, Montgomery City
Elvira Johnston	Student, Columbia
Eva Johnston	Student, Columbia
Nellie V. Keyser	Student, Howard Co.
M. Gertie Lemmon	Student, Warrensburg
Fannie Lowrey	Student, Boone Co.
Anna Shobe	Student, Boone Co.
Mollie Shobe	Student, Boone Co.
Mary A. Simcoe	Student, Callaway Co.

Name	Comments
Ada L. Smith	Student, Boone Co.
Rose Smith	Student, Howard Co.
Lizzie Summers	Student, Columbia
Mary A. Tatum	Student, Glasgow
Leona Thomson	Student, Saline Co.
Susie Trimble	Student, Columbia
Carrie Todd	Student, Columbia
Nora Todd	Student, Columbia
Lettie Todd	Student, Columbia
Sallie Tuttle	Student, Boone Co.
Hettie Walker	Student, Marshal (sic)
Anna Walker	Student, Cooper Co.
Florence Walker	Student, Cooper Co.
Mary Belle Walker	Student, Cooper Co.
Sallie Lee Wallace	Student, Cooper Co.
Emma Waters	Student, Columbia
Bessie Waters	Student, Columbia
Laura Waters	Student, Columbia
Cora Watson	Student, Columbia
Maggie Watson	Student, Columbia
Stella Watson	Student, Columbia
Lizzie Whalley	Student, Bourbon Co., KY
Effie A. Williams	Student, Pettis Co.
Jennie B. Williams	Student, Pettis Co
Anna Lee Willis	Student, Marshsall
Josie Wilson	Student, Salisbury
Louise Woolfolk	Student, Boone Co.
Anna Woody	Student, Columbia
Annie E. Woods	Student, Howard Co.
Lizzie Yancey	Student, Howard Co.
Nina Young	Student, Columbia
Sallie Young	Student, Columbia

Class of Small Boys

Name	Comments
Jimmy Anderson	Student, Columbia
Walter Anderson	Student, Columbia
Robert P. Bates	Student, Columbia
Eddie Chandler	Student, Columbia
Clarence P. Dodge	Student, Columbia
Willie Dodge	Student, Columbia
Chessie McQuitty	Student, Columbia
Theodore Murphy	Student, Columbia

Name	Comments
James Moss	Student, Columbia
George S. Pratt	Student, Columbia
Willie Pratt	Student, Columbia
Willis Schweitzer	Student, Columbia
Ben W. Dorsett	Student, Columbia
Kenneth Gardner	Student, Edwardsville, IL
Willie Guitar	Student, Boone Co.
Johnnie Lientz	Student, Boone Co.
Willie B. Gentry	Student, Columbia
Eddie Tillery	Student, Columbia
Ben E. Todd	Student, Columbia
Henry Wallace	Student, Pettis Co.
Robbie Wallace	Student, Pettis Co.
Eddie Watson	Student, Columbia
Eddie Woody	Student, Columbia

St. Louis County, Missouri, St. Louis Woman's Exchange, Organized May 15, 1883, Second Annual Report, May, 1885, Eddlemon Collection.

Name	Comments
Mrs. J. D. Lawnin	President, 1884-1885
	President, 1885-1886
Mrs. John B. Henderson	Vice-President, 1884-1885
Mrs. A. S. Barnes	Vice-President, 1884-1885
Mrs. B. K. Maude	Recording Secretary, 1884-1885
	Recording Secretary, 1885-1886
Mrs. Samuel Slawson	Corresponding Secretary, 1884-1885
Mrs. A. A. Gilliam	Treasurer, 1884-1885
	Treasurer, 1885-1886
Mrs. Wm. Patrick	Managing Committee, 1884-1885
	Managing Committee, 1885-1886
Mrs. M. A. Perrine	Managing Committee, 1884-1885
Mrs. C. T. Biser	Managing Committee, 1884-1885
	Managing Committee, 1885-1886
Mrs. Geo. D. Barnard	Managing Committee, 1884-1885
Mrs. E. H. Long	Managing Committee, 1884-1885
	Managing Committee, 1885-1886
	Vice-President, 1885-1886
Mrs. W. L. G. B. Allen	Vice-President, 1885-1886
Mr. James E. Yeatman	Auditor, 1885-1886
Mrs. Wm. Patrick	Managing Committee, 1885-1886
Mrs. Geo. Lynch	Managing Committee, 1885-1886
Mrs. E. Phillips	Managing Committee, 1884-1885

Name	Comments
Mrs. Olive Plant	Managing Committee, 1884-1885
Mrs. T. G. Comstock	Managing Committee, 1884-1885
	Managing Committee, 1885-1886
	Vice-President, 1885-1886
Mrs. J. L. D. Morridon	Vice-President, 1885-1886
Mrs. J. T. Watson	Managing Committee, 1884-1885
	Managing Committee, 1885-1886
Mrs. S. Hermann	Managing Committee, 1885-1886
Mrs. J. D. Malis	Managing Committee, 1885-1886
Mrs. W. H. Niedringhaus	Managing Committee, 1885-1886
Mrs. L. L. Culver	Managing Committee, 1885-1886
Mrs. D. Arnold	Managing Committee, 1885-1886
Mrs. Wm. Forsythe	Managing Committee, 1885-1886
Mr. S. Hermann	Legal Advisor, 1885-1886
Judge J. H. McKeighan	Legal Advisor, 1885-1886
Mr. J. B. Henderson	Legal Advisor, 1885-1886
Mr. D. P. Dyer	Legal Advisor, 1885-1886
Mr. Hugh Crawford	Advisory Committee, 1885-1886
Mr. I. G. Baker	Advisory Committee, 1885-1886
Mr. Wm. M. Senter	Advisory Committee, 1885-1886
Mr. I. N. Mason	Advisory Committee, 1885-1886
Mr. J. R. Lionberger	Advisory Committee, 1885-1886
Mr. Geo. S. Edgell	Advisory Committee, 1885-1886
Mr. James E. Yeatman	Advisory Committee, 1885-1886
Miss C. Gantt	Library Committee, 1885-1886
Miss Addie Hermann	Library Committee, 1885-1886
Miss V. E. Stevenson	Library Committee, 1885-1886
Miss Reinhard	Library Committee, 1885-1886
Miss Jennie L. Edwards	Library Committee, 1885-1886
Miss Mary Sloan	Library Committee, 1885-1886
Miss M. Mayfield	Library Committee, 1885-1886
Miss Mildred Clendennin	Library Committee, 1885-1886
Miss Carrie Plant	Library Committee, 1885-1886
Miss Nellie Plant	Library Committee, 1885-1886
Miss Susie M. Brooks	Library Committee, 1885-1886
Miss Minnie Gamble	Library Committee, 1885-1886
Miss F. Pocock	Library Committee, 1885-1886
Miss Fannie Nesbit	Library Committee, 1885-1886
Mrs. Wallace Hardy	Library Committee, 1885-1886
Mrs. Rebecca Webb	Cash Donor
Mrs. Geo. R. Taylor	Cash Donor
Mrs. J. B. Henderson	Cash Donor

Name	Comments
Mrs. Gerard B. Allen	Cash Donor
Col. Thomas Richerson	Cash Donor
Mrs. Wm. Waters	Cash Donor
Mrs. Ariadne Lawnin	Cash Donor
Mr. Charles Parsons	Cash Donor
Mrs. S. S. Blackwell	Cash Donor
Mrs. M. B. Norman	Cash Donor
Mrs. O. H. Peckham	Cash Donor
Mrs. John O'Fallon	Cash Donor
Mr. Henry T. Mudd	Cash Donor
Mr. Francis Bast	Cash Donor
Mr. H. A. Harstick	Cash Donor
Mr. T. G. Bowman	Cash Donor
Mr. G. C. Peckham	Cash Donor
Mr. Henry Dodge	Cash Donor
Mr. Jno. Crangle	Cash Donor
Mr. Wm. Thompson	Cash Donor
Mr. J. D. Thompson	Cash Donor
Mr. Jno. Homes	Cash Donor
Mr. Charles Gauss	Cash Donor
Mr. Jno. Bast	Cash Donor
Mrs. W. C. Butler	Cash Donor
Mrs. J. S. Dunham	Cash Donor
Mrs. A. B. Thompson	Cash Donor
Mr. Hugh Green	Cash Donor
Mr. Geo. H. Morgan	Cash Donor
Mr. L. B. Ripley	Cash Donor
Mr. A. R. Strain	Cash Donor
Mrs. C. F. Gauss	Cash Donor
Mrs. Wm. C. Orr	Cash Donor
Mrs. Wm. A. Pope	Cash Donor
Mr. John Randall	Cash Donor
Mrs. Wm. Patrick	Cash Donor
Miss Addie Herman	Cash Donor
Mr. Martin Collins	Cash Donor
Mrs. McKeighan	Cash Donor
Mr. Samuel Cupples	Cash Donor
Mrs. Edward Bredell	Cash Donor
Mrs. Alex Cameron	Cash Donor
Dr. J. D. Brooks	Cash Donor
Mrs. Geo. H. Rhea	Cash Donor
Miss Addie Mitchell	Cash Donor

Name	Comments
Mrs. J. D. Lawnin	Cash Donor
Miss Kennedy	Cash Donor
Miss Perry	Cash Donor
Mrs. James Garland	Cash Donor
Miss V. E. Stevenson	Cash Donor
Mr. Geo. Partridge	Cash Donor
Mrs. Edward Manny	Cash Donor
Mrs. Sylvester Laflin	Cash Donor
Mr. E. O. Stanard	Cash Donor
Mrs. Simmons	Cash Donor
Mrs. Nichols	Cash Donor
Mrs. Allen	Cash Donor
Mr. Heoff	Cash Donor
Mr. Lagrove	Cash Donor

Annual Members

Mrs. L. L. Asbrook, Mrs. Denham Arnold, Mrs. S. S. Blackwell, Mrs. C. T. Biser, Mrs. E. H. Bradbury, Mrs. A. Brentano, Mrs. G. D. Barnard, Mrs. L. L. Culver, Miss Susie M. Brookes, Miss T. G. Comstock, Miss J. N. Coruch, Mrs. J. T. Cottrell, Mrs. H. Crawford, Miss M. Clendennin, Mrs. DeStaablier, Mrs. W. R. Edwards, Mrs. J. D. Malin, Miss J. L. Edwards, Mrs. J. E. McKeighan, Mrs. E. S. Foster, Mrs. A. A. Gilliam, Mrs. R. W. Golson, Miss McCluney, Miss M. Mayfield, Mrs. J. W. Gunn, Mrs. H. L. Niedringhaus, Miss Clara Gannt, Miss N. Niedringhaus, Miss Minnie Gamble, Miss Fannie Nisbet, Mrs. Wm. Forsythe, Mrs. S. Hermann, Mrs. S. J. Pettit, Miss Addie Hermann, Mrs. O. H. Peckham, Mrs. Wm. Patrick, Mrs. E. S. Hardy, Mrs. Olive Plant, Mrs. W. S. Humphreys, Mrs. M. A. Perrine, Mrs. J. D. Lawnin, Miss Fannie Pock, Mrs. Geo. Lynch, Mrs. H. C. West, Mrs. E. H. Long, Mrs. J. T, Watson, Mrs. M. Watts, Miss Mamie Woods, Mrs. P. G. Robert, Miss E. White, Miss Reinhart, Miss Carrie Wilkerson, Mrs. S. Slawson, Mrs, Wishart, Mrs. Sessions, Mrs. Settle, Mrs. Jos. Specht, Mrs. Server, Miss V, E, Stevenson, Miss Mary Sloan, Mrs. Geo. Taylor, Mrs. Nannie Wright, Mrs. H. Tyler Wilcox, M.D., Miss Julia Von Schrader, Mrs. C. R. Robertson, Mrs. J. L. D. Morrison, Mrs. Rebecca Webb, Mrs. Sonneschein, Mrs. John Whittaker, Mrs. D. Wilson, Mrs. Marie T. Allen, Mrs. J. B. Henderson, Mrs. Alice B. McKibbin, Mrs. Dr. Brank (sic), Mrs. J. H. Brookes, Mrs. C. L. Goddell, Miss Sue Beeson, Mrs. A. A. Parsons, Mrs. M. B. Pearman, M. D., Mrs. Geo. C. Betts, Mrs. L. L. Culver, Mrs. Olive Plant.

Missourians on the Vietnam War Memorial, Surnames A through C.
Abbenhaus, Jr., Gerald Robert: (ID) 500527765, (Svc) Marines, (Rank) Pfc, (A) 37, (Home) St Louis, MO, (D) Aug. 23, 1986, (B) Oct. 12,

1948, (Race) C, (St) S, (Sex) Male.
Abbott, Jr., Robert Esten: (ID) 56588962 (Svc) Army, (Rank) Pfc, (A) 23, (Home) Pine Lawn, MO, (D) May 8, 1968, (B) Dec. 16, 1944, (Race) C, (St) S, (Sex) Male.
Abernathy, Robert Lloyd: (ID) 44035, (Svc) Air Force, (Rank) Maj., (A) 37, (Home) St Louis, MO, (D) Dec. 17, 1965, (B) Sep. 3, 1928, (Race) C, (St) M, (Sex) Male.
Adams, Harlan Floyd: (ID) 55203556 (Svc) Army, (Rank) SSgt, (A) 37, (Home) Salem, MO, (D) Jun. 21, 1967, (B) May 16, 1930, (Race) C, (St) M, (Sex) Male.
Adams, Oley Neal: (ID) 17440848, (Svc) Air Force, (Rank) SSgt., (A) 28, (Home) Green City, MO, (D) Jun. 17, 1966, (B) Jun. 27, 1937, (Race) C, (St) M (Sex) Male.
Adams, Richard Lyle: (ID) 499485198, (Svc) Army, (Rank) SSgt., (A) 24, (Home) Florissant, MO, (D) Nov. 8, 1969, (B) 19450228, (Race) C, (St) S, (Sex) Male.
Agnew, James William: (ID) 56428619, (Svc) Army, (Rank) Sgt., (A) 21, (Home) New Franklin MO, (D) Apr. 3, 1969, (B) Jun. 8, 1947, (Race)C, (St) S, (Sex) Male.
Allen, Charles Richard: (ID) 2035166, (Svc) Marines, (Rank) LCpl, (A) 21, (Home) St. Louis, MO, (D) Jan. 1, 1966, (B) Dec. 6, 1944, (Race) N, (St) S, (Sex) Male
Allen, Elvin L: (ID) 67162092, (Svc) Army, (Rank) Pfc, (A) 26, (Home) Kansas City, MO, (D) Mar. 8, 1968, (B) Apr. 4, 1941, (Race) N, (St) M, (Sex) Male.
Allen, John Lee: (ID) 493488941, (Svc) Army, (Rank) Pfc, (A) 23, (Home) Smithville, MO, (D) Aug. 6, 1969, (B) Sep. 24, 1945, (Race) C, (St) M, (Sex) Male.
Allen, Otis Lee: (ID) 2404949, (Svc) Marines, (Rank) Pfc, (A) 20, (Home) Steele, MO, (D) May 26, 1968, (B) Mar. 2, 1948, (Race) N, (St) S, (Sex) Male.
Allen, Raymond Eugene: (ID) 55883021 (Svc) Army, (Rank) Sp4, E4, (A) 20, (Home) Independence, MO, (D) Aug. 21, 1967, (B) May 23, 1947, (Race) C, (St) S, (Sex) Male.
Allen, Terry Lee Odis: (ID) 16955933 (Svc) Army, (Rank) Pfc, (A) 19, (Home) Kansas City, MO, (D) Jun. 22, 1967, (B) Dec. 22, 1947, (Race) C, (St) S, (Sex) Male.
Alley, Michael Morris: (ID) 56580882, (Svc) Army, (Rank) Sp4, E4, (A) 21, (Home) Bridgeton, MO, (D) Feb. 12, 1968, (B) Nov. 28, 1946, (Race) C, (St) S, (Sex) Male.
Aly, Leslie Morgan: (ID) 489546464, (Svc) Navy, (Rank) Hn, (A) 22, (Home) De Soto, MO, (D) Sep. 17, 1969, (B) Aug. 12, 1947, (Race) C, (St) M, (Sex) Male.

Mark Thomas: (ID) 486507863, (Svc) Marines, (Rank) Pfc, (A) 21, (Home)Hawk Point, MO, (D) Aug. 12, 1969, (B) Jul. 17, 1948, (Race) C, (St) S, (Sex) Male

Ames, James David: (ID) 67169813, (Svc) Army, (Rank) Sp4, E4, (A) 20, (Home) Florissant, MO, (D) May 14, 1968, (B) Sep. 2, 1947, (Race) C, (St) S, (Sex) Male.

Amos, Thomas Hugh: (ID) 495380196, (Svc) Air Force, (Rank) Maj, (A) 35, (Home) Republic, MO, (D) Jun. 23, 1976, (B) Sep. 25, 1940, (Race) C, (St) M (Sex) Male.

Amrhein, Herbert Franklin: (ID) 497481186, (Svc) Army, (Rank) Sgt Pp, E4, (A) 21, (Home) St Louis, MO, (D) Jul. 18, 1969, (B) Mar. 21, 1948, (Race) C, (St) S, (Sex) Male.

Amstutz, Jr., William Joseph: (ID) 55767237, (Svc) Army, (Rank) Sp4, E4, (A) 20, (Home) St. Louis, MO, (D) Feb. 9, 1966,(B) Dec. 2, 1945, (Race) C, (St) S, (Sex) Male.

Anders, John William: (ID) 495525587, (Svc) Army, (Rank) Cpl Pp, (A) 24, (Home) Waldron, MO, (D) Apr. 1, 1971, (B) Dec. 23, 1946, (Race) C, (St) S, (Sex) Male.

Anderson, George Rogers: (ID) 16996218, (Svc) Army, (Rank) Cpl Pp, (A) 23, (Home) St. Louis, MO, (D) Aug. 16, 1968, (B) Mar. 13, 1945, (Race) N, (St) S, (Sex) Male.

Andreotta, Glenn Urban: (ID) 17701280, (Svc) Army, (Rank) Sp4, E4, (A) 20, (Home) St. Louis, MO, (D) Apr. 8, 1968, (B) Oct. 30, 1947, (Race) C, (St) S, (Sex) Male.

Andresen, Terry Lee: (ID) 496588079, (Svc) Army, (Rank) Pfc, (A) 20, (Home) Morrisville, MO, (D) Nov. 14, 1969, (B) Apr. 5, 1949, (Race) C, (St) M (Sex) Male

Anspach, Robert Allen: (ID) 17289137, (Svc) Army, (Rank) Msg Pp, E7, (A) 33, (Home) Macon, MO, (D) Sep. 11, 1967, (B) Oct. 1, 1933, (Race) C, (St) M (Sex) Male.

Armor, Loyde Dean: (ID) 56584529, (Svc) Army, (Rank) Sp4, E4 (A) 23, (Home) Broseley, MO, (D) Jan. 10, 1968, (B) Apr. 14, 1944, (Race) C, (St) M (Sex) Male.

Arnold, Steven Ernest: (ID) 489563736, (Svc) Army, (Rank) Sp5, (A) 21, (Home) Holden, MO, (D) Oct. 5, 1969, (B) Oct. 2, 1948, (Race) C, (St) M (Sex) Male.

Asbury, David Charles: (ID) 17662383, (Svc) Army, (Rank) Sgt., (A) 22, (Home) Foley, MO, (D) Jun. 25, 1969, (B) Jan. 23, 1947, (Race) C, (St) S, (Sex) Male.

Ashford, Jr., Bill: (ID) 56592739, (Svc) Army, (Rank) Sp4, E4 (A) 20, (Home) St Louis, MO, (D) Mar. 21, 1969 (B) Oct. 6, 1948, (Race) N, (St) S, (Sex) Male

Aspey, Darrell Wayne: (ID) 495481943, (Svc) Army, (Rank) Cpl Pp, (A)

23, (Home) Belton, MO, (D) Feb. 27, 1970, (B) Nov. 26, 1946, (Race) C, (St) M (Sex) Male

Asquith, William Robert: (ID) 492542533, (Svc) Army, (Rank) Pvt., (A) 20, (Home) Louisiana, MO, (D) Nov. 19, 1970, (B) Mar. 25, 1950, (Race) C, (St) S, (Sex) Male.

Atkison, Charles Leon: (ID) 496567632, (Svc) Marines, (Rank) LCpl, (A) 19, (Home) St Joseph, MO, (D) Sep. 21, 1969, (B) Oct. 12, 1949, (Race) C, (St) S, (Sex) Male

Austermann, Jr. Raymond A.: (ID) 2286518, (Svc) Marines, (Rank) Pfc, (A) 19, (Home) St Louis, MO, (D) Apr. 2, 1967, (B) Apr. 29, 1947, (Race) C, (St) S, (Sex) Male

Austin, Tyrone Wagner: (ID) 2200259, (Svc) Marines, (Rank) Cpl, E4, (A) 22, (Home) St Louis, MO, (D) May 2, 1968, (B) Sep. 6, 1945, (Race) N (St) M, (Sex) Male

Ayer, Jr., Herley: (ID) 55252532 (Svc) Army, (Rank) Sfc, E7, (A) 36, (Home) Kahoka, MO, (D) Jan. 17, 1968, (B) Feb. 6, 1931, (Race) C, (St) M, (Sex) Male

Ayers, Jarel Wayne: (ID) 17748266, (Svc) Army, (Rank) Pfc, (A) 21, (Home) Lamar, MO, (D) Dec. 31, 1966, (B) Sep. 1, 1945, (Race) C, (St) S, (Sex) Male

Backy, Thomas Alan: (ID) 16994663, (Svc) Army, (Rank) Pfc, (A) 19, (Home) Festus, MO, (D) Feb. 9, 1968, (B) Mar. 12, 1948, (Race) C, (St) S, (Sex) Male.

Badger, Thomas Albert: (ID) 56581011 (Svc) Army, (Rank) Sp4, E4, (A) 22, (Home) Arnold, MO, (D) Jan. 30, 1968, (B) Jul. 21, 1945, (Race) C, (St) M, (Sex) Male.

Bagley, Jack Lawrence: (ID) 495461054 (Svc) Army, (Rank) 1Lt, (A) 24, (Home) Marshfield, MO, (D) Oct. 27, 1970, (B) Npov. 7, 1945, (Race) C, (St) M, (Sex) Male.

Baker, Gary Paul: (ID) 490568984 (Svc) Army, (Rank) Sgt Pp, E4, (A) 21, (Home) Monroe City, MO, (D) May 11, 1970, (B) Feb. 12, 1949, (Race) C, (St) S, (Sex) Male.

Baker, Michael Ray: (ID) 16994222 (Svc) Army, (Rank) Pfc, (A) 21, (Home) St. Louis, MO, (D) Jan. 5, 1968, (B) May 27, 1946, (Race) C, (St) S, (Sex) Male.

Baker, Jr., Rennie Joe: (ID) 491460982 (Svc) Army, (Rank) Cpl Pp, (A) 25, (Home) Dixon, MO, (D) Jul. 11, 1969, (B) May 26, 1944, (Race) C, (St) M, (Sex) Male.

Baker, Thomas Michael: (ID) 56588123 (Svc) Army, (Rank) Cpl Pp, (A) 20, (Home) Fulton, MO, (D) May 19, 1968, (B) Jun. 5, 1947, (Race) C, (St) S, (Sex) Male.

Baker, Willie Cecil: (ID) 55815333, (Svc) Army, (Rank) Pvt Pp, E1, (A)

22, (Home) St Louis, MO, (D) Aug. 28, 1967, (B) Mar. 19, 1945, (Race) N, (St) S, (Sex) Male.

Balcom, Joel Arnold: (ID) 498469935, (Svc) Navy, (Rank) Hm3, E4 (A) 22, (Home) Independence, MO, (D) Nov. 3, 1969, (B) Jul. 26, 1947, (Race) C, (St) M (Sex) Male.

Ballay, James Vincent: (ID) 488544645, (Svc) Army, (Rank) Sgt, (A) 21, (Home) Monett, MO, (D) May 12, 1970, (B) Jan. 4, 1949, (Race) C, (St) M, (Sex) Male.

Bamvakais, Jr., John Robert: (ID) 17728982, (Svc) Army, (Rank) Sgt Pp, E4, (A) 20, (Home) Jefferson City, MO, (D) Sep. 28, 1967, (B) Aug. 29, 1947, (Race) C, (St) S, (Sex) Male.

Bancroft, Stephen Wayne: (ID) 492528021, (Svc) Army, (Rank) Cpl Pp, (A) 22, (Home) Brentwood, MO, (D) Jul. 29, 1970, (B) Mar. 15, 1948, (Race) C, (Mar) M (Sex) Male.

Barber, Johnie Ray: (ID) 55986934, (Svc) Army, (Rank) Sp4, E4 (A) 20, (Home) Kansas City, MO, (D) Jan. 28, 1968, (B) Jan. 2, 1948, (Race) C, (St) S, (Sex) Male.

Barham, Larry Gene: (ID) 53811973, (Svc) Army, (Rank) Pfc, (A) 22, (Home) Portageville, MO, (D) Feb. 6, 1968, (B) Sep. 11, 1945, (Race) C, (St) S, (Sex) Male.

Barker, Larry Lee: (ID) 55986208, (Svc) Army, (Rank) Cpl Pp, (A) 20, (Home) Independence, MO, (D) Sep. 9, 1967, (B) Dec. 16, 1946, (Race) C, (St) M (Sex) Male.

Barnes, John Henry: (ID) 56584001, (Svc) Army, (Rank) Pfc, (A) 20, (Home) St. Louis, MO, (D) Nov. 12, 1967, (B) Ap. 18, 1947, (Race) C, (St) S, (Sex) Male.

Barnett, Jr., Billie Joe: (ID) 56584918, (Svc) Army, (Rank) Sp4, (A) 20, (Home) Overland, MO, (D) Nov. 7, 1967, (B) Jun. 25, 1947, (Race) C, (St) S, (Sex) Male.

Bartell, Larry Michael: (ID) 56591350, (Svc) Army, (Rank) Pfc, (A) 21, (Home) Hazelwood, MO, (D) Dec. 27, 1968, (B) Jul. 14, 1947, (Race) C, (St) S, (Sex) Male.

Bartle, Richard Paul: (ID) 55811597, (Svc) Army, (Rank) Sp4, (A) 22, (Home) Villa Ridge, MO, (D) Sep. 22, 1966, (B) Oct. 19, 1943, (Race) C, (St) S, (Sex) Male.

Barton, James Paul: (ID) W3154304, (Svc) Army, (Rank) Wo, W1, (Home) Bates City, MO, (D) Mar. 19, 1967, (B) Mar. 1, 1943, (Race) C, (St) M, (Sex) Male.

Basnett, Jerry Dale: (ID) 2273572, (Svc) Marines, (Rank) Cpl, E4 (A) 21, (Home) Columbia, MO, (D) May 12, 1967 (B) Mar. 12, 1946, (Race) C, (St) M, (Sex) Male.

Bateman, Raymond: (ID) 2404878, (Svc) Marines, (Rank) Pfc, (A) 18,

(Home) St Louis, MO, (D) Jul. 7, 1968, (B) Aug. 11, 1949, (Race) N, (St) S, (Sex) Male.

Bates, Robert W: (ID) 55983621 (Svc) Army, (Rank) Sp4, E4 (A) 20, (Home) Independence, MO, (D) Aug. 17, 1967, (B) Aug. 4, 1947, (Race) C, (St) S, (Sex) Male.

Batesel, Dennis Gordon: (ID) 491540571 (Svc) Army, (Rank) Sp4, E4, (A) 21, (Home) Hocomo, MO, (D) Aug. 26, 1970, (B) Jul. 31, 1949, (Race) C, (St) S, (Sex) Male.

Batts, Percill: (ID) 493545660, (Svc) Marines, (Rank) Lcpl, (A) 22, (Home) St. Louis, MO, (D) Feb. 12, 1970, (B) Aug., 14, 1947, (Race) N, (St) M (Sex) Male.

Bauer, James Phillip: (ID) 2273570, (Svc) Marines, (Rank) Pfc, (A) 21, (Home) St. Louis, MO, (D) Jan. 26, 1967, (B) Jul. 6, 1945, (Race) C, (St) S, (Sex) Male.

Baum, Rory Michael: (ID) 490549866, (Svc) Army, (Rank) Cpl Pp, (A) 21, (Home) Creve Coeur, MO, (D) Jul. 28, 1969, (B) May 27, 1948, (Race) C, (St) S, (Sex) Male.

Bax, Bernard Herman: (ID) 488603913, (Svc) Army, (Rank) Pfc, (A) 19, (Home) Dixon, MO, (D) May 8, 1970, (B) Mar. 15, 1951, (Race) C, (St) S, (Sex) Male.

Baxter, Bobbie Ray: (ID) 548348476, (Svc) Army, (Rank) Sfc, E7, (A) 40, (Home) St Louis, MO, (D) Feb. 25, 1970, (B) Jan. 4, 1930, (Race) C, (St) M, (Sex) Male.

Baxter, Larry Lee: (ID) 67162600, (Svc) Army, (Rank) Pfc, (A) 21, (Home) Pierce City, MO, (D) May 12, 1969, (B) Nov. 7, 1947, (Race) C, (St) S, (Sex) Male.

Bean, Donald Wayne: (ID) 963774, (Svc) Marines, (Rank) Smaj., E8, (A) 42, (Home) Holt, MO, (D) Mar. 11, 1968, (B) Jan. 16, 1926, (Race) C, (St) M, (Sex) Male.

Beckmann, Louis Martin: (ID) 56596866, (Svc) Army, (Rank) Pfc, (A) 25, (Home) St Louis, MO, (D) Mar. 17, 1969, (B) Jun. 24, 1943, (Race) C, (St) S, (Sex) Male.

Beeler, George Fredrick: (ID) 527726357, (Svc) Army, (Rank) Sp4, E4 (A) 20, (Home) Lancaster, MO, (D) Jul. 28, 1970, (B) Oct. 11, 1949, (Race) C, (St) S, (Sex) Male.

Beers, Jr., Carl William: (ID) 2434670, (Svc) Marines, (Rank) Pfc, (A) 19, (Home) St Louis, MO, (D) Jan. 3, 1969, (B) Jul. 12, 1949, (Race) C, (St) M (Sex) Male.

Beesley, Gary Evans: (ID) 17726035, (Svc) Army, (Rank) Pfc, (A) 21, (Home) St Louis, MO, (D) Jun. 22, 1967, (B) Jan. 31, 1946, (Race) C, (St) S, (Sex) Male.

Behrens, Peter Claus: (ID) 499485375, (Svc) Army, (Rank) Wo, (A) 26, Home) Newburg, MO, (D) Dec. 4, 1970, (B) Nov. 28, 1944, (Race)

C, (St) S, (Sex) Male.

Beile, Fred: (ID) 17514426, (Svc) Army, (Rank) Cpl, E4, (A) 26, (Home) St. Louis, MO, (D) Mar. 14, 1967, (B) Aug. 14, 1940, (Race) C, (St) M, (Sex) Male.

Belinge, Richard Lewis: (ID) 55987673 (Svc) Army, (Rank) Pfc, (A) 22, (Home) Springfield, MO, (D) Mar. 26, 1968, (B) Aug. 31, 1945, (Race) C (St) S, (Sex) Male.

Bell, Dean Allan: (ID) 55985550 (Svc) Army, (Rank) Sp5, (A) 21, (Home) Kansas City, MO, (D) Sep. 6, 1968, (B) Jun. 24, 1947, (Race) C, (St) S, (Sex) Male.

Bell, Ronald Eugene: (ID) 2377629, (Svc) Marines, (Rank) Pfc, (A) 19, (Home) St. Joseph, MO, (D) Jun. 9, 1968, (B) Sep. 26, 1948, (Race) C, (St) S, (Sex) Male.

Beltz, John David: (ID) 17698346 (Svc) Army, (Rank) Sgt., (A) 20, (Home) St. Louis, MO, (D) Nov. 14, 1966, (B) May 26, 1946, (Race) C, (St) S, (Sex) Male.

Bemboom, Herbert Donald: (ID) 489544276, (Svc) Army, (Rank) Sgt., (A) 21, (Home) Independence, MO, (D) Jul. 9, 1970, (B) Aug. 21, 1948, (Race) C, (St) S, (Sex) Male.

Bennett, Jr., James Harrell: (ID) 68370, (Svc) Air Force, (Rank) Cpt., (A) 31, (Home) St Louis, MO, (D) Oct. 30, 1967, (B) Jun. 1, 1936, (Race) C, (St) M (Sex) Male.

Benton, Carroll Joe: (ID) 490569630, (Svc) Army, (Rank) Sgt., (A) 19, (Home) Cape Girardeau, MO, (D) Jun. 12, 1971, (B) Sep. 23, 1951, (Race) C, (St) S, (Sex) Male.

Berhowe, Marvin Richard: (ID) 497504345, (Svc) Army, (Rank) Pfc, (A) 21, (Home) Independence, MO, (D) Nov. 16, 1969, (B) Jun. 14, 1948, (Race) C, (St) M, (Sex) Male.

Berry, Elmer Eugene: (ID) 17520808, (Svc) Army, (Rank) SSgt., (A) 32, (Home) St. Joseph, MO, (D) Feb. 26, 1966, (B) Jun. 3, 1933, (Race) C, (St) M (Sex) Male.

Betebenner, David Lee: (ID) 55988237, (Svc) Army, (Rank) Sgt Pp, E4, (A) 22, (Home) Alba, MO, (D) May 6, 1968, (B) Mar. 9, 1946, (Race) C, (St) M, (Sex) Male.

Bezold, Steven Neil: (ID) 499487561, (Svc) Army, (Rank) Cpt., (A) 24, (Home) Mc Kittrick, MO, (D) Oct. 29, 1968, (B) Jun. 12, 1944, (Race) C, (St) S, (Sex) Male.

Biggs, Jimmy Dean: (ID) 2451993, (Svc) Marines, (Rank) Pfc, (A) 19, (Home) Kansas City, MO, (D) Dec. 7, 1968, (B) Aug. 31, 1949, (Race) C, (St) S, (Sex) Male.

Biglieni, Charles Robert: (ID) 493540413, (Svc) Army, (Rank) Sgt. Pp, E4, (A) 21, (Home) Republic, MO, (D) Mar. 5, 1971, (B) Apr. 26, 1949, (Race) C, (St) M, (Sex) Male.

Biondo, Martin: (ID) 56585994, (Svc) Army, (Rank) Sp4, E4, (A) 22, (Home) Kirkwood, MO, (D) Mar. 19, 1968, (B) Nov. 7, 1945, (Race) C, (St) S, (Sex) Male.

Bishop, Ronald Burk: (ID) 523640592, (Svc) Army, (Rank) SSgt., (A) 21, (Home) Hazelwood, MO, (D) Sep. 17, 1969, (B) Aug. 17, 1948, (Race) C, (St) M (Sex) Male.

Blacksten, Billy Joe: (ID) O5241991, (Svc) Army, (Rank) 1Lt, (A) 23, (Home) Versailles, MO, (D) Feb. 4, 1968, (B) Feb. 1, 1945, (Race) C, (St) M, (Sex) Male.

Blair, Terry Lee: (ID) 493563694, (Svc) Army, (Rank) Sp4, E4, (A) 20, (Home) Kansas City, MO, (D) Mar. 7, 1971, (B) Apr. 12, 1950, (Race) C, (St) S, (Sex) Male.

Blake, Richard Thomas: (ID) 496529861, (Svc) Army, (Rank) Sgt., (A) 21, (Home) Malden, MO, (D) Jul. 29, 1969, (B) Feb. 23, 1948, (Race) C, (St) M, (Sex) Male.

Blankenship, James Oris: (ID) O5331259, (Svc) Army, (Rank) 1Lt, (A) 24, (Home) Independence, MO, (D) Jan. 9, 1968, (B) Oct. 23, 1943, (Race) C, (St) M, (Sex) Male.

Blanton, Kenneth Gene: (ID) 55816307, (Svc) Army, (Rank) Sp4, E4 (A) 21, (Home) Florissant, MO, (D) Mar. 21, 19670, (B) Aug. 16, 1945, (Race) C, (St) M, (Sex) Male.

Blassie, Michael Joseph: (ID) 490526882, (Svc) Air Force, (Rank) 1Lt, (A) 24, (Home) St Louis, MO, (D) May 11, 1972, (B) Apr. 4, 1948, (Race) C, (St) S, (Sex) Male.

Blattel, David Lee: (ID) W3155811, (Svc) Army, (Rank) Cwo, W2, (A) 22, (Home) Scott City, MO, (D) May 5, 1968, (B) Oct. 27, 1945, (Race) C, (St) S, (Sex) Male.

Blevins, Frank Lee: (ID) 17693831, (Svc) Army, (Rank) Pfc, (A) 23, (Home) Kansas City, MO, (D) Aug. 8, 1966, (B) Nov. 28, 1942, (Race) C, (St) S, (Sex) Male.

Bliss, Benjamin Charles: (ID) 56432372, (Svc) Army, (Rank) Sp4, E4 (A) 20, (Home) Crane, MO, (D) May 10, 1969, (B) Feb. 21, 1949, (Race) C, (St) S, (Sex) Male.

Boardman, Michael Kenneth: (ID) 2305853, (Svc) Marines, (Rank) LCpl, (A) 19, (Home) Sikeston, MO, (D) Jul. 19, 1967, (B) Jun. 23, 1948, (Race) C, (St) S, (Sex) Male.

Boatman, Elmer Lee: (ID) 2200242, (Svc) Marines, (Rank) Pfc, (A) 21, (Home) Wayland, MO, (D) Sep. 18, 1966, (B) Jan. 25, 1945, (Race) C, (St) S, (Sex) Male.

Bobo, Leon Nelson: (ID) 500569241, (Svc) Army, (Rank) Sp4, E4, (A) 19, (Home) St. Louis, MO, (D) May 21, 1970, (B) Jan. 25, 1951, (Race) N, (St) S, (Sex) Male.

Bockewitz, Carl Edward: (ID) 088778, (Svc) Marines, (Rank) Cpt, (A) 28,

(Home) Bourbon, MO, (D) Feb. 28, 1967, (B) Feb. 16, 1939, (Race) C, (St) S, (Sex) Male.

Boever, David Richard: (ID) 56590679, (Svc) Army, (Rank) Pfc, (A) 19, (Home) St Louis, MO, (D) Aug. 16, 1968, (B) Sep. 30, 1948, (Race) C, (St) S, (Sex) Male.

Boggs, Donnie Rex: (ID) 499582448, (Svc) Army, (Rank) Sp4, E4, (A) 19, (Home) Walnut Grove, MO, (D) Apr. 26, 1970, (B) Nov. 14, 1950, (Race) C, (St) S, (Sex) Male.

Bohon, Ronald Eugene: (ID) 2240076, (Svc) Marines, (Rank) Pfc, (A) 20, (Home) St Joseph, MO, (D) Mar. 23, 1967, (B) Sep. 6, 1946, (Race) C, (St) M (Sex) Male.)

Bonderer, Thomas Edward: (ID) 55986677, (Svc) Army, (Rank) Sgt., (A) 24, (Home) Chillicothe, MO, (D) May 1, 1968, (B) Mar. 5, 1944, (Race) C, (St) S, (Sex) Male.

Bonds, Michael David: (ID) 493582400, (Svc) Army, (Rank) Pfc, (A) 18, (Home) St Louis, MO, (D) May 6, 1971, (B) May 24, 1952, (Race) C, (St) S, (Sex) Male.

Bonnarens, Frank Owen: (ID) O73613, (Svc) Army, (Rank) Maj., (A) 36, (Home) Browning, MO, (D) Sep. 19, 1968, (B) Feb. 11, 1932, (Race) C, (Mar) M, (Sex) Male.

Bono, Ben Dominic: (ID) 2273633, (Svc) Marines, (Rank) LCpl., (A) 20, (Home) O'Fallon, MO, (D) May 14, 1967, (B) Dec. 1946, (Race) C, (St) S, (Sex) Male.

Borawski, James David: (ID) 2239656, (Svc) Marines, (Rank) Pfc, (A) 20, (Home) North Kansas City, MO, (D) May 3, 1967, (B) Aug. 25, 1946, (Race) C, (St) S, (Sex) Male.

Boston, Kenneth Dean: (ID) 498508017, (Svc) Army, (Rank) Pfc, (A) 21, (Home) Lathrop, MO, (D) Feb. 12, 1970, (B) Dec. 8, 1948, (Race) C, (St) S, (Sex) Male.

Boswell, Joe Roscoe: (ID) 1909754, (Svc) Marines, (Rank) SSgt., (A) 28, (Home) Steele, MO, (D) Jan. 25, 1969, (B) May 23, 1940, (Race) N, (St) S, (Sex) Male.

Bourne, Lawrence Gilbert: (ID) 16995132, (Svc) Army, (Rank) Sp4, E4, (A) 19, (Home) St Louis, MO, (D) Oct. 31, 1968, (B) Feb. 4, 1949, (Race) N, (St) S, (Sex) Male.

Bowdern, Jr., Robert James: (ID) 56586432, (Svc) Army, (Rank) Sp4, E4, (A) 20, (Home) Pagedale, MO, (D) Apr. 27, 1968, (B) Jul. 2, 1947, (Race) C, (St) S, (Sex) Male.

Bowman, Ronald Leon: (ID) 2177701, (Svc) Marines, (Rank) Pfc, (A) 21, (Home) Warrensburg, MO, (D) Aug. 23, 1966, (B) Oct. 7, 1944, (Race) C, (St) S, (Sex) Male.

Boyd, Roy Bradley: (ID) 56428759, (Svc) Army, (Rank) Sp4, E4 (A) 21, (Home) Windsor, MO, (D) Mar. 29, 1969, (B) Jan. 27, 1948,

(Race) C, (St) S, (Sex) Male.
Boyer, Dennis Michael: (ID) 491423978, (Svc) Army, (Rank) Sp5, (A) 26, (Home) St Joseph, MO, (D) Apr. 21, 1970, (B) Sep. 17, 1943, (Race) C, (St) M, (Sex) Male.
Boyer, James Roger: (ID) 17662193, (Svc) Army, (Rank) Sp4, E4 (A) 20, (Home) St Louis, MO, (D) Sep. 22, 1967, (B) Oct. 3, 19146, (Race) C, (St) S, (Sex) Male.
Boyles, Jerry Lee: (ID) 55986790, (Svc) Army, (Rank) Sp4, E4 (A) 19, (Home) Foster, MO, (D) Apr. 18, 1968, (B) Nov. 8, 1948, (Race) C, (St) S, (Sex) Male.
Bozikis, Ronald Henry: (ID) 499522062, (Svc) Army, (Rank) SSgt., (A) 22, (Home) St Louis, MO, (D) Oct. 25, 1969, (B) Sep.10, 1947, (Race) C, (St) S, (Sex) Male.
Braden, Terry Lee: (ID) 7717247, (Svc) Navy, (Rank) Sn, (A) 20, (Home) Liberty, MO, (D) Jan. 23, 1967, (B) Oct. 20, 1946, (Race) C, (St) M, (Sex) Male.
Bradley, Sylvan Keith: (ID) O5513621, (Svc) Army, (Rank) Cpt., (A) 28, (Home) Irondale, MO, (D) Nov. 10, 1966, (B) Apr. 26, 1938, (Race) C, (St) M (Sex) Male.
Brandom, Jr., Thomas M.: (ID) 00024482, (Svc) Air Force, (Rank) Maj., (A) 43, (Home) Liberty, MO, (D) Apr. 25, 1969, (B) Dec. 3, 1925, (Race) ?, (St) ?, (Sex) Male.
Branson, Jerry Leon: (ID) 2225150, (Svc) Marines, (Rank) Pfc (A) 20, (Home) Owensville, MO, (D) Sep. 19, 1966, (B) Sep. 2, 1946, (Race) C, (St) S, (Sex) Male.
Branson, Jr., Ralph Alton: (ID) 56588094, (Svc) Army, (Rank) Pfc, (A) 20, (Home) Vienna, MO, (D) Mar. 17, 1968, (B) Nov. 1, 1947, (Race) C, (St) S, (Sex) Male.
Brashears, Ronald Lee: (ID) 56433104, (Svc) Army, (Rank) Pfc (A) 20, (Home) Stanberry, MO, (D) Jun. 5, 1969, (B) Nov. 6, 1948, (Race) C, (St) S, (Sex) Male.
Breeding, Wayne Peter Earl: (ID) 17661716, (Svc) Army, (Rank) Pfc, (A) 19, (Home) Eureka, MO, (D) Oct. 9, 1965, (B) Apr. 13, 1946, (Race) C, (St) S, (Sex) Male.
Brennan, James Aloyisus: (ID) 2130937, (Svc) Marines, (Rank) Cpl, E4, (A) 23, (Home) Creve Coeur, MO, (D) Jan, 31, 1968, (B) Jan. 26, 1945, (Race) C, (St) S, (Sex) Male.
Bright, Jr., Thomas: (ID) 56431753, (Svc) Army, (Rank) Sp4, E4 (A) 21, (Home) Warrensburg, MO, (D) Mar. 12, 1969, (B) Apr. 20, 1947, (Race) N, (St) S, (Sex) Male.
Brock, Terrance Lee: (ID) 56586684, (Svc) Army, (Rank) Sp4, E4 (A) 22, (Home) Cape Girardeau, MO, (D) Jan. 4, 1969, (B) Aug. 21, 1946, (Race) C, (St) S, (Sex) Male.

Brockman, Verndean Arthur: (ID) 17297834, (Svc) Army, (Rank) Sfc, E7 (A) 31, (Home) Sedalia, MO, (D) 19631116 (B) 19320609, (Race) C, (St) S, (Sex) Male.

Brooks, Edward Allen: (ID) 56431974 (Svc) Army, (Rank) Pfc (A) 20, (Home) Springfield, MO, (D) May 20, 1969, (B) Dec. 3, 1948, (Race) C, (St) S, (Sex) Male.

Brooks, Franklin Eugene: (ID) 55825264 (Svc) Army, (Rank) Pfc (A) 21, (Home) Napton, MO, (D) Dec. 10, 1966, (B) Apr. 28, 1945, (Race) C, (St) S, (Sex) Male.

Brooks, Larry Lee: (ID) 56590062 (Svc) Army, (Rank) Sp4, E4 (A) 21, (Home) Salem, MO, (D) Feb. 24, 1969, (B) Feb. 22, 1948, (Race) C, (St) M, (Sex) Male.

Brown, Clarence: (ID) 487566648 (Svc) Army, (Rank) Sp4, E4 (A) 21, (Home) St Louis, MO, (D) Aug. 23, 1970, (B) Apr. 4, 1949, (Race) N, (St) S, (Sex) Male.

Brown, Daniel L: (ID) 55870348, (Svc) Army, (Rank) Pfc (A) 21, (Home) St. Louis, MO, (D) Dec. 26, 1966, (B) Apr. 22, 1945, (Race) N, (St) S, (Sex) Male.

Brown, Dierother: (ID) 17641587, (Svc) Army, (Rank) SSgt., (A) 23, (Home) St. Louis, MO, (D) Feb. 1, 1968, (B) Feb. 29, 1944, (Race) N, (St) M (Sex) Male.

Brown, Galen Charles: (ID) 56432375, (Svc) Army, (Rank) Sp4, E4, (A) 20, (Home) Cassville, MO, (D) May 13, 1969, (B) Feb. 8, 1949, (Race) C, (St) S, (Sex) Male.

Brown, Harry Lee: (ID) 17539269, (Svc) Army, (Rank) Sp4, E4, (A) 27, (Home) St. Louis, MO, (D) Nov. 21, 1968, (B) May 13, 1941, (Race) N, (St) M, (Sex) Male.

Brown, Harve Edward: (ID) 2146018, (Svc) Marines, (Rank) Pfc, (A) 19, (Home) Kansas City, MO, (D) Dec. 2, 1966, (B) Nov. 27, 1947, (Race) C, (St) S, (Sex) Male.

Brown, III, Harvey Lee: (ID) 16870385, (Svc) Army, (Rank) Sp4, E4, (A) 21, (Home) St Louis, MO, (D) Nov. 1967, (B) Mar. 18, 1946, (Race) N, (St) M, (Sex) Male.

Brown, Jr., Howard Eugene: (ID) 494567099, (Svc) Navy, (Rank) Sn, (A) 19 (Home) Lebanon, MO, (D) Oct. 9, 1970, (B) Oct. 16, 1950, (Race) C, (St) S, (Sex) Male.

Brown, James Richard: (ID) 17723679, (Svc) Army, (Rank) Pfc, (A) 18, (Home) Sedalia, MO, (D) Jul. 23, 1966, (B) Aug. 9, 1947, (Race) C, (St) S, (Sex) Male.

Bruton, Carl Leon: (ID) 558683609, (Svc) Army, (Rank) Pfc (A) 20, Home) Seligman, MO, (D) Apr. 14, 1970, (B) Feb. 7, 1950, (Race) C, (St) M (Sex) Male.

Buckner, Anthony Eugene: (ID) 55986833, (Svc) Army, (Rank) Pfc (A)

19, (Home) Sedalia, MO, (D) Nov. 19, 1967, (B) Dec. 7, 1947, (Race) N, (St) S, (Sex) Male.

Budzinski, Lawrence Joseph: (ID) 56591262, (Svc) Army, (Rank) Sgt. Pp., E4, (A) 23, (Home) St. Ann, MO, (D) Apr. 24, 1969, (B) Sep. 20, 1945, (Race) C, (St) S, (Sex) Male.

Buell, Craig Harold: (ID) 17747953, (Svc) Army, (Rank) Sp5, (A) 23, (Home) Kansas City, MO, (D) Feb. 12, 1968, (B) May 9, 1944, (Race) C, (St) S, (Sex) Male.

Buffington, Larry Daniel: (ID) 497424001, (Svc) Army, (Rank) Sgt Pp., E4, 29, (Home) St. Louis, MO, (D) May 5, 1970, (B) Jul. 4,1940, (Race) C, (St) S, (Sex) Male.

Bullerdick, Gary Allen: (ID) 496480092, (Svc) Army, (Rank) Cwo, (A) 22, (Home) Arnold, MO, (D) Feb. 4, 1970, (B) Dec. 19, 1947, (Race) C, (St) M (Sex) Male.

Bumiller, Robert Oscar: (ID) 56588723, (Svc) Army, (Rank) Sp4, E4, (A) 20, (Home) La Due, MO, (D) Aug. 9, 1968, (B) Sep. 22, 1947, (Race) C, (St) S, (Sex) Male.

Bunch, Larry Dale: (ID) 487441204, (Svc) Marines, (Rank) SSgt., (A) 27, (Home) Glenair, MO, (D) Oct. 20, 1969, (B) Aug. 26, 1942, (Race) C, (St) M, (Sex) Male.

Buntion, Charles Wayne: (ID) 491604957, (Svc) Army, (Rank) Sp4, E4, (A) 19, (Home) Ironton, MO, (D) Mar. 31, 1972, (B) Mar. 16, 1953, (Race) C, (St) M, (Sex) Male.

Burford, John Shelby: (ID) O84920, (Svc) Army, (Rank) Maj., (A) 33, (Home) Cape Girardeau, MO, (D) Aug. 30, 1967, (B) Jun. 13, 1934, (Race) C, (St) M, (Sex) Male.

Burks, Jr., Virgil: (ID) 56590100 (Svc) Army, (Rank) Pfc, (A) 22, (Home) Sikeston, MO, (D) Apr. 25, 1969, (B) Nov. 8, 1946, (Race) C, (St) S, (Sex) Male.

Burnett, Jr., Charles C.: (ID) 1563028, (Svc) Marines, (Rank) SSgt., (A) 27, (Home) St. Joseph, MO, (D) May 14, 1967, (B) Dec. 21, 1939, (Race) C, (St) S, (Sex) Male.

Burnett, Curters Joseph: (ID) 497589602, (Svc) Army, (Rank) Pvt., (A) 19, (Home) Sikeston, MO, (D) Nov. 21, 1970, (B) Feb. 20,1951, (Race) N, (St) S, (Sex) Male.

Burnett, Gary Ray: (ID) 17702791, (Svc) Army, (Rank) Sgt., (A) 22, (Home) Union, MO, (D) Mar. 5, 1968, (B) Dec. 21, 1945, (Race) C, (S) S, (Sex) Male.

Burns, Jr., John Robert: (ID) 0101776, (Svc) Marines, (Rank) 2Lt, (A) 24, (Home) St. Louis, MO, (D) Jan. 27, 1968, (B) Jan. 23, 1944, (Race) C, (St) S, (Sex) Male.

Burrow, Leonard: (ID) 27535147, (Svc) Army, (Rank) SSgt., (A) 33, (Home) Ferguson, MO, (D) Sep. 17, 1966, (B) Jun. 7, 1933,

(Race) C, (St) M, (Sex) Male.

Burruano, Samuel Vincent: (ID) 497547895, (Svc) Army, (Rank) Sp4, E4, (A) 19, (Home) St. Louis, MO, (D) Jul. 23, 1969, (B) Nov. 21, 1949, (Race) C, (St) S, (Sex) Male.

Busch, Elwin Harry: (ID) 3057045, (Svc) Air Force, (Rank) Cpt, (A) 35, (Home) Cape Girardeau, MO, (D) Jun. 9, 1967, (B) Jan. 11, 1932, (Race) C, (St) M (Sex) Male.

Bush, Steven Clarence: (ID) 56589003, (Svc) Army, (Rank) Cpl Pp, (A) 19, (Home) Grubville, MO, (D) Jun. 3, 1968, (B) Jul. 13, 1948, (Race) C, (St) S, (Sex) Male.

Butler, Jimmie Joe: (ID) 497500883, (Svc) Marines, (Rank) Sgt., (A) 22, (Home) Bernie, MO, (D) Nov. 1, 1969, (B) Nov. 4, 1946, (Race) C, (St) M, (Sex) Male.

Byrd, Gary Dean: (ID) 55840544, (Svc) Army, (Rank) SSgt., (A) 21, (Home) Houstonia, MO, (D) Oct. 13, 1967, (B) Dec. 21, 1945, (Race) C, (St) M, (Sex) Male.

Cabrini, John Richard: (ID) 2213044, (Svc) Marines, (Rank) LCpl., (A) 20, (Home) Kansas City, MO, (D) May 30, 1967, (B) Jan. 27, 1947, (Race) C, (St) S, (Sex) Male.

Cady, Stephen Michael: (ID) 490544043, (Svc) Army, (Rank) Pfc, (A) 21, (Home) St. Louis, MO, (D) Oct. 13, 1970, (B) Jul. 14, 1949, (Race) C, (St) S, (Sex) Male.

Caffery, Howard Eugene: (ID) 498523099 (Svc) Army, (Rank) Sgt Pp., E4 (A) 20, (Home) St. Louis, MO, (D) Jun. 30, 1970, (B) Dec. 10, 1949, (Race) C, (St) S, (Sex) Male.

Cagley, James Nelson: (ID) 55823927, (Svc) Army, (Rank) Sp4, E4, (A) 21, (Home) Independence, MO, (D) Nov. 23, 1966, (B) Jan. 8, 1945, (Race) C, (St) M, (Sex) Male.

Cahall, James Warren: (ID) 55871642, (Svc) Army, (Rank) Sp4, E4, (A) 20, (Home) Mexico, MO, (D) Jan. 15, 1967, (B) May 8, 1946, (Race) C, (St) S, (Sex) Male.

Cain, Glennie Wayne: (ID) 53813421, (Svc) Army, (Rank) Sgt Pp,, E4 (A) 20, (Home) Caruthersville, MO, (D) Apr. 8, 1969, (B) May 15, 1948, (Race) C, (St) M (Sex) Male.

Cain, Jerry Maurice: (ID) 17701157, (Svc) Army, (Rank) Pfc, (A) 18, (Home) St. Louis, MO, (D) Feb. 8, 1966, (B) Jul. 17, 1947, (Race) N, (St) S, (Sex) Male.

Caldwell, Floyd Dean: (ID) 430566004 (Svc) Army, (Rank) SSgt., (A) 37, (Home) St Louis, MO, (D) Dec. 14, 1971, (B) Apr. 15, 1934, (Race) C, (St) M, (Sex) Male.

Callahan, Thomas Francis: (ID) 2356842, (Svc) Marines, (Rank) LCpl., (A) 19, (Home) St. Louis, MO, (D) Nov. 17, 1968, (B) Oct. 25, 1949, (Race) C, (St) S, (Sex) Male.

Callihan, Lyndal Ray: (ID) 2361303, (Svc) Marines, (Rank) Cpl, E4 (A) 19, (Home) Kansas City, MO, (D) Aug. 29, 1968, (B) May 16, 1949, (Race) C, (St) S, (Sex) Male.)

Calmese, Albert: (ID) 500568669, (Svc) Army, (Rank) Cpl Pp, (A) 20, (Home) St.Louis, MO, (D) Jul. 27, 1977, (B) Feb. 14, 1950, (Race) N, (St) S, (Sex) Male.

Campbell, John Allen: (ID) 2273609, (Svc) Marines, (Rank) Cpl, E4 (A) 20, (Home) Russellville, MO, (D) Aug. 13, 1967, (B) Dec. 24, 1946, (Race) C, (St) S, (Sex) Male.

Campbell, Larry Gene: (ID) 2212926, (Svc) Marines, (Rank) Cpl, E4, (A) 20, (Home) St. Joseph, MO, (D) Aug. 19, 1967. (B) Dec. 21, 1946, (Race) C, (St) S, (Sex) Male.

Campbell, Robert Crawford: (ID) 55986886 (Svc) Army, (Rank) Pfc, (A) 20, (Home) Independence, MO, (D) Dec. 10, 1967, (B) Apr. 5, 1947, (Race) C, (St) S, (Sex) Male.

Campbell, Jr., William L.: (ID) 496468488, (Svc) Marines, (Rank) LCpl., (A) 26, (Home) Kansas City, MO, (D) Jan. 8, 1970, (B) May 11, 1943, (Race) C, (St) M, (Sex) Male.

Candrl, Bruce Charles: (ID) 488501629, (Svc) Army, (Rank) Sgt., (A) 23, (Home) St. Louis, MO, (D) Jul. 14, 1970, (B) Oct. 2, 1946, (Race) C, (St) S, (Sex) Male.

Caplan, Laurence Curtis: (ID) 55986854, (Svc) Army, (Rank) Sgt., (A) 21, (Home) Kansas City, MO, (D) May 29, 1968, (B) May 6, 1947, (Race) C, (St) S, (Sex) Male.

Carlyle, Donald Richard: (ID) 56595291, (Svc) Army, (Rank) Pfc, (A) 20, (Home) East Prairie, MO, (D) Jan. 24, 1969, (B) Aug. 4, 1948, (Race) C, (St) S, (Sex) Male.

Carnett, Dennie Lynn: (ID) 255684827, (Svc) Army, (Rank) Sgt., (A) 26, (Home) Kennett, MO, (D) May 24, 1970, (B) Jul. 18, 1943, (Race) C, (St) M, (Sex) Male.

Carnoske, Robert Thomas: (ID) 55870320, (Svc) Army, (Rank) Pfc, (A) 22, (Home) St. Louis, MO, (D) Feb. 26, 1967, (B) Apr. 17, 1944, (Race) C, (St) S, (Sex) Male.

Carrico, Jr., Chester Calvin: (ID) 491528759, (Svc) Marines, (Rank) Pfc, (A) 20, (Home) Joplin, MO, (D) Feb. 1, 1970, (B) Oct. 16, 1949, (Race) C, (St) S, (Sex) Male.

Carroll, Jr., Roger William: (ID) 490423122, (Svc) Air Force, (Rank) Maj. (A) 33, (Home) Kansas City, MO, (D) Sep. 21, 1972, (B) Jul. 20, 1939, (Race) C, (St) M, (Sex) Male.

Carson, Lawrence Howard: (ID) 2020400, (Svc) Marines, (Rank) Cpl, E4, (A) 24, (Home) Springfield, MO, (D) May 31, 1968, (B) Dec. 22, 1943, (Race) C, (St) S, (Sex) Male.

Carson, Tyrone Bruce: (ID) 17618042, (Svc) Army, (Rank) Sgt., (A) 24,

(Home) North Kansas City, MO, (D) May 30, 1965, (B) May 25, 1941, (Race) C, (St) S, (Sex) Male.

Carter, Jerry Ray: (ID) 2266077, (Svc) Marines, (Rank) LCpl., (A) 22, (Home) Imperial, MO, (D) Jun. 29, 1967, (B) Sep. 8, 1944, (Race) C, (St) M, (Sex) Male.

Cartier, Victor John: (ID) 2502640, (Svc) Marines, (Rank) Pfc, (A) 19, (Home) Webster Groves, MO, (D) Apr. 8, 1969, (B) Sep. 7, 1949, (Race) C, (St) S, (Sex) Male.

Carver, Harold Leroy: (ID) 2240371, (Svc) Marines, (Rank) Pfc, (A) 19, (Home) Joplin, MO, (D) Apr. 5, 1967, (B) Aug. 6, 1947, (Race) C, (St) S, (Sex) Male.

Casebolt, Henry Clayton: (ID) 1933907, (Svc) Marines, (Rank) Cpl, E4 (A) 24, (Home) St. Joseph, MO, (D) Feb. 28, 1966, (B) Jan. 31, 1942, (Race) C, (St) S, (Sex) Male.

Cash, James Ronald: (ID) 56598032 (Svc) Army, (Rank) Pfc (A) 21, (Home) St Louis, MO, (D) Jun. 28, 1969, (B) Jun. 28, 1948, (Race) C, (St) S, (Sex) Male.

Cason, Jr., George Gilbert: (ID) 2146081, (Svc) Marines, (Rank) Cpl, E4, (A) 21, (Home) St. Joseph, MO, (D) May 31, 1968 (B) Nov. 27, 1946, (Race) C, (St) S, (Sex) Male.

Cassmeyer, Jr., Victor Paul: (ID) 489485916, (Svc) Army, (Rank) Cpl Pp, (A) 21, (Home) Jefferson City, MO, (D) Sep. 9, 1969, (B) Sep. 2, 1948, (Race) C, (St) S, (Sex) Male.

Cawley, Richard Ernest: (ID) B614617, (Svc) Navy, (Rank) Hn, (A) 20, (Home) St. Joseph, MO, (D) Apr. 13, 1968, (B) May 18, 1947, (Race) C, (St) S, (Sex) Male.

Chambers, Udell: (ID) 67170023, (Svc) Army, (Rank) Pfc, (A) 20, (Home) Kirkwood, MO, (D) Jun. 21, 1968, (B) Feb. 22, 1948, (Race) N, (St) S, (Sex) Male.

Champion, Gerald Alan: (ID) 2273584, (Svc) Marines, (Rank) Pfc, (A) 21, (Home) St. Louis, MO, (D) May 31, 1967, (B) Mar. 28, 1946, (Race) N, (St) S, (Sex) Male.

Chandler, Charles William: (ID) O5339338 (Svc) Army, (Rank) Cpt, (A) 25, (Home) Jefferson City, MO, (D) Apr. 26, 1969, (B) Aug. 8, 1943, (Race) C, (St) M, (Sex) Male.

Chandler, Joe Wayne: (ID) 55872299, (Svc) Army, (Rank) Sp4, E4 (A) 20, (Home) St Louis, MO, (D) Mar. 27, 1967, (B) Dec. 6, 1946, (Race) C, (St) S, (Sex) Male.

Channel, Billy Gene: (ID) 498606865 (Svc) Army, (Rank) Sgt., (A) 19, (Home) Kansas City, MO, (D) Apr. 10, 1971, (B) Sep. 22, 1951, (Race) C, (St) S, (Sex) Male.

Chappell, John Monroe: (ID) 17225733, (Svc) Air Force, (Rank) TSgt (A)

36, (Home) St. Louis, MO, (D) Dec. 17, 1965, (B) Nov. 2, 1929, (Race) C, (St) M, (Sex) Male.

Chasteen, Roger Wilson: (ID) 2265875, (Svc) Marines, (Rank) Pfc, (A) 20, (Home) Crestwood, MO, (D) May 10, 1967, (B) Apr. 11, 1947, (Race) C, (St) S, (Sex) Male.

Cherry, Allen Sheldon: (ID) 3082436, (Svc) Air Force, (Rank) Cpt, (A) 30, (Home) University City, MO, (D) Aug. 9, 1967, (B) Sep. 14, 1936, (Race) C, (St) M, (Sex) Male.

Cheshire, Gary Allen: (ID) 492546525, (Svc) Army, (Rank) Pfc, (A) 19, (Home) St. Louis, MO, (D) Jan. 30, 1970, (B) Jun. 8, 1950, (Race) C, (St) M, (Sex) Male.

Child, Ronald William: (ID) 2286612, (Svc) Marines, (Rank) Cpl, E4, (A) 21, (Home) St. Louis, MO, (D) May 5, 1968, (B) Mar. 25, 1947, (Race) C, (St) S, (Sex) Male.

Childers, Estill Lee: (ID) 2195935, (Svc) Marines, (Rank) LCpl., (A) 21, (Home) Slater, MO, (D) Sep. 24, 1966, (B) Jul. 13, 1945, (Race) C, (St) S, (Sex) Male.

Childress, George W: (ID) 55872500, (Svc) Army, (Rank) Cpl Pp, (A) 20, (Home) Holcomb, MO, (D) Jul. 23, 1967, (B) Feb. 21, 1947, (Race) C, (St) M, (Sex) Male.

Chittwood, James Phillip: (ID) 492446376, (Svc) Army, (Rank) 1Lt, (A) 23, (Home) Raytown, MO, (D) Jul. 29, 1969, (B) Feb. 18, 1946, (Race) C, (St) S, (Sex) Male.

Chitwood, Fred Allen Jr: (ID) 16991017, (Svc) Army, (Rank) Sp4, E4 (A) 19, (Home) Bridgeton, MO, (D) Aug. 21, 1968, (B) Apr. 13, 1949, (Race) C, (St) S, (Sex) Male.

Chorlins, Richard David: (ID) 495466751, (Svc) Air Force, (Rank) Cpt., (A) 24, (Home) University City, MO, (D) Jan. 11, 1970, (B) Jul. 16, 1945, (Race) C, (St) M, (Sex) Male.

Christensen, Roger Lee: (ID) 493543568 (Svc) Army, (Rank) Sp4, E4, (A) 20, (Home) Macon, MO, (D) Dec. 5, 1971, (B) Jan. 23, 1951, (Race) C, (St) M (Sex) Male.

Christofferson, Scott Andrew: (ID) 17729663 (Svc) Army, (Rank) Sp4, E4, (A) 19, (Home) St. Louis, MO, (D) Oct. 8, 1967, (B) Nov. 5, 1947, (Race) C, (St) S, (Sex) Male.

Claggett, John Allen: (ID) 490546821 (Svc) Army, (Rank) Cpl Pp, (A) 21, (Home) Union, MO, (D) May 20, 1970, (B) Aug. 31, 1948, (Race) C, (St) S, (Sex) Male.

Clark, Dale Lee: (ID) 2131124, (Svc) Marines, (Rank) LCpl (A) 19, (Home) Jefferson City, MO, (D) Aug. 19, 1966, (B) Sep. 18, 1946, (Race) C, (St) S, (Sex) Male.

Clark, Larry Gene: (ID) 2427400, (Svc) Marines, (Rank) Pfc, (A) 19, (Home) Kansas City, MO, (D) Jun. 15, 1968, (B) Dec. 30, 1948,

(Race) C, (St) S, (Sex) Male.
Clarkson, Jay Owen: (ID) 529669384, (Svc) Army, (Rank) Cpl Pp, (A) 21, (Home) Creve Coeur, MO, (D) Apr. 15, 1970, (B) Feb. 27, 1949, (Race) C, (St) S, (Sex) Male.
Claspill, Larry Vernal: (ID) 55986233, (Svc) Army, (Rank) Sp4, E4 (A) 19, (Home) Kansas City, MO, (D) Feb. 5, 1968, (B) Jul. 7, 1948, (Race) C, (St) S, (Sex) Male.
Claverie, Richard Lee: (ID) 56580217, (Svc) Army, (Rank) Sp4, E4 (A) 23, (Home) Maplewood, MO, (D) Mar. 4, 1968, (B) Dec. 30, 1944, (Race) C, (St) S, (Sex) Male.
Claxton, Richard Rex: (ID) 2502308, (Svc) Marines, (Rank) Pfc, (A) 22, (Home) Eldon, MO, (D) Jun. 13, 1969, (B) Dec. 19, 1946, (Race) C, (St) S, (Sex) Male.
Clay, Charles Edward: (ID) 55657964, (Svc) Army, (Rank) Sgt Pp., E4, (A) 31, (Home) East Prairie, MO, (D) Feb. 26, 1969, (B) May 12, 1937, (Race) C, (St) M, (Sex) Male.
Clayton, Bennie Clifford: (ID) 488566269, (Svc) Army, (Rank) Sgt., (A) 21, (Home) Agency, MO, (D) Oct. 21, 1969, (B) Mar. 19, 1948, (Race) C, (St) S, (Sex) Male.
Cleaver, Donald Gene: (ID) 19346602, (Svc) Air Force, (Rank) SSgt., (A) 37, (Home) Joplin, MO, (D) 19681003 (B) 19310730, (Race) C, (St) M, (Sex) Male.
Clemmon, Edward L: (ID) 19880434, (Svc) Army, (Rank) Sp4, E4 (A) 19, (Home) St. Louis, MO, (D) Dec. 18, 1967, (B) Dec. 30, 1947, (Race) N, (St) S, (Sex) Male.
Cleve, Reginald David: (ID) 499505657, (Svc) Army, (Rank) Wo, (A) 23, (Home) Farmington, MO, (D) Mar. 22, 1971, (B) Aug. 2, 1947, (Race) C, (St) M, (Sex) Male.
Clifton, Robert Harrison: (ID) 499484931, (Svc) Army, (Rank) Sp4, E4, (A) 23, (Home) Arnold, MO, (D) Oct. 23, 1971, (B) Jan. 12, 1948, (Race) C, (St) M, (Sex) Male.
Clubbs, Charles Earl: (ID) 56598011, (Svc) Army, (Rank) Pfc., (A) 21, (Home) St. Louis, MO, (D) Jun. 22, 1969, (B) Mar. 1, 1948, (Race) C, (St) M (Sex) Male.
Cobb, Ronald David: (ID) 2131086, (Svc) Marines, (Rank) LCpl., (A) 20, (Home) Poplar Bluff, MO, (D) Apr. 29, 1968, (B) Nov. 25, 1947, (Race) C, (St) S, (Sex) Male.
Coffman, Clyde Lee: (ID) 492543416, (Svc) Army, (Rank) Sp5, (A) 20, (Home) Warrensburg, MO, (D) Apr. 4, 1970, (B) Nov. 3, 1949, (Race) C, (St) S, (Sex) Male.
Colbert, John Wayne: (ID) 56592222, (Svc) Army, (Rank) Pfc., (A) 21, (Home) Kinder, MO, (D) Nov. 23, 1968, (B) Dec. 7, 1946, (Race) C, (St) M, (Sex) Male.

Coleman, James Edward: (ID) 55984729, (Svc) Army, (Rank) Pfc., (A) 19, (Home) Kansas City, MO, (D) May 26, 1967, (B) Sep. 25, 1947, (Race) C, (St) S, (Sex) Male.

Coleman, James Francis: (ID) 56582618, (Svc) Army, (Rank) Sgt., (A) 20, (Home) Festus, MO, (D) Feb. 29, 1968, (B) Aug. 4, 1947, (Race) C, (St) S, (Sex) Male.

Coleman, Lonald Ray: (ID) 490506702, (Svc) Army, (Rank) Sgt., (A) 22, (Home) De Soto, MO, (D) Feb. 8, 1971, (B) Aug. 11, 1948, (Race) C, (St) S, (Sex) Male.

Collins, Arlie Ray: (ID) 56592817, (Svc) Army, (Rank) Sp4, E4, (A) 21, (Home) Willow Springs, MO, (D) Apr. 13, 1969, (B) Mar. 5, 1948, (Race) C, (St) S, (Sex) Male

Collins, Arlin Darrell: (ID) 56586507, (Svc) Army, (Rank) Sgt., (A) 20, (Home) Elsberry, MO, (D) Aug. 28, 1968, (B) Oct. 5, 1947, (Race) C, (St) S, (Sex) Male.

Collins, Donald Clifton: (ID) 491540574, (Svc) Army, (Rank) Sp4, E4, (A) 20, (Home) West Plains, MO, (D) Aug. 13, 1970, (B) Aug. 21, 1949, (Race) C, (St) S, (Sex) Male.

Cozmbs, Clifford Dale: (ID) 2502461, (Svc) Marines, (Rank) Pfc, (A) 19, (Home) Marquand, MO, (D) Feb. 25, 1969, (B) Aug. 19, 1949, (Race) C, (St) S, (Sex) Male.

Combs, Phillip Eugene: (ID) 2480789, (Svc) Marines, (Rank) Pfc, (A) 19, (Home) Grandview, MO, (D) May 10, 1969, (B) Feb. 25, 1950, (Race) C, (St) M (Sex) Male.

Conner, Donnie Ray: (ID) 495605831, (Svc) Marines, (Rank) LCpl ., (A) 19, (Home) St. Peters, MO, (D) Feb. 14, 1973, (B) Jul. 20, 1953, (Race) C, (St) S, (Sex) Male.

Cook, Charles Herman: (ID) 2379407, (Svc) Marines, (Rank) Pfc, (A) 25, (Home) New Haven, MO, (D) Feb. 1, 1968, (B) Apr. 3, 1942, (Race) C, (St) S, (Sex) Male.

Cook, Jay Alan: (ID) 56589436 (Svc) Army, (Rank) Pfc., (A) 25, (Home) High Ridge, MO, (D) May 6, 1968, (B) Mar. 29, 1943, (Race) C, (St) S, (Sex) Male.

Cook, Robert Edward: (ID) 16991170 (Svc) Army, (Rank) Sp4, E4, (A) 19, (Home) Overland, MO, (D) Apr. 6, 1968, (B) Aug. 8, 1948, (Race) C, (St) S, (Sex) Male.

Cook, Scott Howard: (ID) 56586402 (Svc) Army, (Rank) Pfc., (A) 19, (Home) Pacific, MO, (D) Dec. 30, 1967, (B) Jan. 29, 1948, (Race) C, (St) S, (Sex) Male.

Cooper, Gary Robert: (ID) 17724060 (Svc) Army, (Rank) Sp4, E4, (A) 21, (Home) Bosworth, MO, (D) Nov. 19, 1967, (B) Jul. 14, 1946, (Race) C, (St) S, (Sex) Male.

Cooper, Richard Lee: (ID) 16994649 (Svc) Army, (Rank) Sp4, E4 (A) 23,

(Home) Richmond Heights, MO, (D) Sep. 15, 1968, (B) Nov. 3, 1944, (Race) C, (St) M, (Sex) Male.

Cope, Charles Alfred: (ID) 56588588 (Svc) Army, (Rank) Pfc., (A) 20, (Home) St. Louis, MO, (D) May 15, 1968, (B) Jan. 27, 1948, (Race) C, (St) S, (Sex) Male.

Copeland, Norman Ottis: (ID) 2149681, (Svc) Marines, (Rank) Cpl, E4, (A) 20, (Home) De Soto, MO, (D) Feb. 5, 1968, (B) Jul. 19, 1947, (Race) C, (St) M, (Sex) Male.

Copeland, Robert: (ID) 1999889, (Svc) Marines, (Rank) Cpl, E4, (A) 21, (Home) Berkeley, MO, (D) Dec. 14, 1966, (B) Jan. 12, 1945, (Race) C, (St) S, (Sex) Male.

Cordia, Michael James: (ID) 56582027, (Svc) Army, (Rank) Sp4, E4, (A) 20, (Home) Richwoods, MO, (D) Mar. 20, 1968, (B) Aug. 3, 1947, (Race) C, (St) S, (Sex) Male.

Corp, Jerry Marsh: (ID) 492562125, (Svc) Army, (Rank) Pfc., (A) 20, (Home) Tecumseh, MO, (D) Apr. 21, 1970, (B) Apr. 14, 1950, (Race) C, (St) S, (Sex) Male.

Cortor, Jr., Francis Edwin: (ID) 499482636 (Svc) Army, (Rank) Sgt (A) 22, (Home) Festus, MO, (D) Oct. 21, 1969, (B) May 23, 1947, (Race) C, (St) S, (Sex) Male.

Couch, Jacky Ray: (ID) B509462, (Svc) Navy, (Rank) Swf3, E4, (A) 24, (Home) St. Louis, MO, (D) Jan. 12, 1968, (B) Nov. 1, 1943, (Race) C, (St) M, (Sex) Male.

Coult, Gerry Don: (ID) 496569757 (Svc) Army, (Rank) Sp4, E4, (A) 20, (Home) Chillicothe, MO, (D) Jul. 22,1971, (B) Jan. 7, 1951, (Race) C, (St) S, (Sex) Male.

Cowen, Harold Edward: (ID) 500440516, (Svc) Navy, (Rank) Ams1, (A) 28, (Home) Eminence, MO, (D) Sep. 20, 1971, (B) Mar. 22, 1943, (Race) C, (Mar) M, (Sex) Male.

Cowsert, Kenneth William: (ID) 496506250 (Svc) Army, (Rank) Pfc, (A) 19, (Home) Pacific, MO, (D) Mar. 10, 1970, (B) Mar. 31, 1950, (Race) C, (St) S, (Sex) Male.

Cox, James Allen: (ID) 2240191, (Svc) Marines, (Rank) Cpl, E4, (A) 21, (Home) Independence, MO, (D) May 18, 1969, (B) Oct. 25, 1947, (Race) C, (St) S, (Sex) Male.

Cox, Martin: (ID) 17241455 (Svc) Army, (Rank) Sfc, E7, (A) 36, (Home) Warrensburg, MO, (D) Apr. 7, 1966, (B) Nov. 18, 1929, (Race) C, (St) M, (Sex) Male.

Crabtree, James Otis: (ID) 2036732, (Svc) Marines, (Rank) Cpl, E4, (A) 20, (Home) Bethany, MO, (D) Jun. 7, 1965, (B) Mar. 12, 1945, (Race) C, (St) S, (Sex) Male.

Craig, James Herbert: (ID) 492506519, (Svc) Army, (Rank) Sp5, (A) 20, (Home) Walnut Shade, MO, (D) May 23, 1970, (B) Jul. 11, 1949,

(Race) C, (St) M, (Sex) Male.
Craighead, Terry Dean: (ID) 55815158 (Svc) Army, (Rank) Pfc., (A) 23, (Home) Fulton, MO, (D) Aug. 2, 1966, (B) Nov. 11, 1942, (Race) C, (St) S, (Sex) Male.
Cramer, Donald Martin: (ID) 569646147 (Svc) Army, (Rank) Cwo, (A) 27, (Home) St Louis, MO, (D) May 31, 1973, (B) Jan. 12, 1946, (Race) C, (St) S, (Sex) Male.
Cramer, Robert Michael: (ID) 076778, (Svc) Marines, (Rank) (A) 32, (Home) Stoutland, MO, (D) Jan. 8, 1968, (B) Sep. 24, 1935, (Race) C, (St) M, (Sex) Male.
Crane, II, William Joseph: (ID) 493583905 (Svc) Army, (Rank) Pfc, (A) 21, (Home) Kansas City, MO, (D) Jan. 27, 1972, (B) Jan. 16, 1951, (Race) C, (St) S, (Sex) Male.
Crawford, James J.: (ID) 487448186, (Svc) Air Force, (Rank) Cpt, (A) 30, (Home) St. Joseph, MO, (D) Feb. 3, 1972, (B) Dec. 6, 1941, (Race) ?, (St) ?, (Sex) Male.
Crawford, Jr., John Nelson: (ID) 487444495, (Svc) Army, (Rank) Sp6, (A) 29, (Home) Kansas City, MO, (D) Aug. 7, 1970, (B) Oct. 22, 1940, (Race) C, (St) S, (Sex) Male.
Crawford, Robert Dean: (ID) 55987113, (Svc) Army, (Rank) Pfc., (A) 19, (Home) Springfield, MO, (D) Oct. 24, 1967, (B) Mar. 10, 1948, (Race) C, (Mar) M, (Sex) Male.
Crawford, William Thomas: (ID) 17368102, (Svc) Air Force, (Rank) A1C, E4 (A) 33, (Home) Windsor, MO, (D) May 16, 1965, (B) May 11, 1932, (Race) C, (St) M, (Sex) Male.
Crockran, James: (ID) 2273686, (Svc) Marines, (Rank) Pvt., E1 (A) 20, (Home) St. Louis, MO, (D) Mar. 4, 1968, (B) Jul. 23, 1947, (Race) N, (St) S, (Sex) Male.
Crook, Oren Lee: (ID) 489566959, (Svc) Army, (Rank) Sp4, E4 (A) 20, (Home) Doniphan, MO, (D) Mar. 6, 1970, (B) Jun. 15, 1949, (Race) C, (St) S, (Sex) Male.
Crook, Thomas Hiram: (ID) 2067712, (Svc) Marines, (Rank) Pvt, E1 (A) 22, (Home) Kansas City, MO, (D) May 17, 1968, (B) Jun. 25, 1945, (Race) C, (St) S, (Sex) Male.
Crosby, Louis John: (ID) 499521379, (Svc) Army, (Rank) Sgt Pp,, E4, (A) 21, (Home) St. Louis, MO, (D) Jul. 3, 1970, (B) May 20, 1949, (Race) C, (St) S, (Sex) Male.
Cross, Gary Lee: (ID) 56431607, (Svc) Army, (Rank) Sp4, E4 (A) 19, (Home) Hopkins, MO, (D) Apr. 9, 1969, (B) Sep. 8, 1949, (Race) C, (St) S, (Sex) Male.
Cross, Thomas John: (ID) 495567477, (Svc) Army, (Rank) Sp4, E4 (A) 20, (Home) Bevier, MO, (D) Jan. 1, 1970, (B) Feb. 7, 1949, (Race) C, (St) S, (Sex) Male.

Crow, Larry Edwin: (ID) 489547697, (Svc) Army, (Rank) Sgt., (A) 20, (Home) Kirksville, MO, (D) Oct. 11, 1969, (B) Feb. 18, 1949, (Race) C, (St) S, (Sex) Male.

Crow, Lindsey Houston: (ID) W2215898, (Svc) Army, (Rank) CWO, (A) 34, (Home) Viola, MO, (D) Nov. 18, 1965, (B) Jan. 1, 1931, (Race) C, (St) S, (Sex) Male.

Crowder, Neal Steven: (ID) 500544363, (Svc) Army, (Rank) Sgt., (A) 22, (Home) Bourbon, MO, (D) Mar. 13, 1971, (B) Mar. 27, 1948, (Race) C, (St) S, (Sex) Male.

Cullers, Ronald Kenneth: (ID) 092158, (Svc) Marines, (Rank) 2Lt, (A) 23, (Home) Shelbina, MO, (D) Jul. 15, 1966, (B) Jul. 25, 1942, (Race) C, (St) M, (Sex) Male.

Cunningham, Donnie Lee: (ID) 490586715, (Svc) Army, (Rank) Sgt., (A) 20, (Home) Gideon, MO, (D) Nov. 18, 1970, (B) Mar. 4, 1950, (Race) C, (St) S, (Sex) Male.

Cunningham, Wells Eldon: (ID) O92421, (Svc) Army, (Rank) Cpt., (A) 26, (Home) St. Joseph, MO, (D) Aug, 17, 1966, (B) Nov. 19, 1939, (Race) C, (St) S, (Sex) Male.

Cureton, Ronnie Charles: (ID) 2240061, (Svc) Marines, (Rank) LCpl., (A) 19, (Home) Kansas City, MO, (D) Mar. 23, 1968, (B) Aug. 11, 1948, (Race) C, (St) S, (Sex) Male.

Currier, Jr., Gordon Leroy: (ID) 55986184 (Svc) Army, (Rank) Pfc., (A) 22, (Home) Independence, MO, (D) Jan. 31, 1968, (B) Jan. 24, 1946, (Race) C, (St) S, (Sex) Male.

Curry, Marvin Ellis: (ID) 55766100, (Svc) Army, (Rank) Sp4, E4, (A) 22, (Home) St Louis, MO, (D) Oct. 31, 1965, (B) Feb. 10, 1943, (Race) C, (St) S, (Sex) Male.

Cutbirth, Richard Eugene: (ID) 2377740, (Svc) Marines, (Rank) LCpl (A) 19, (Home) Marionville, MO, (D) May 28, 1968, (B) Feb. 28, 1949, (Race) C, (St) S, (Sex) Male.

Randolph County, Missouri, Pensioners on the Roll of Jan. 1, 1883 living in Randolph County, U. S. Pension Bureau.

Chinece Routt: (PO) Cairo, (C) 111,941, (CMTS) Widow, (ALWD) Dec., 1868.

Henry Shultz: (PO) Cairo, (C) 125,158, (CMTS) G. A. W. Left Hip, (ALWD) ?.

Dicey Bobbitt: (PO) Cairo, (C) 32,698, (CMTS) Widow, War 1812, (ALWD) Sep., 1882

John Mariels: (PO) Cairo, (C) 159,401, (CMTS) G. S. W. Right Shoulder, (ALWD) ?.

John Hammon: (PO) Cairo, (C) 188,736, (CMTS) Dis. Eyes, (ALWD) ?.

Sarah A. Campbell: (PO) Higbee, (C) 196,751, (CMTS) Widow, (ALWD) Jul., 1882.
Thomas J. Parrick: (PO) Higbee, (C) 31,424, (CMTS) Inj. to Back, (ALWD) ?.
Michael Perkins: (PO) Higbee, (C) 206,975, (CMTS) Inj. to Back, Hip & C., (ALWD) Apr., 1882.
Jacob A. Baker: (PO) Higbee, (C) 180,852, (CMTS) Inj. to Left Shoulder, (ALWD) Jan., 1881.
Tetitah Snoddy: (PO) Higbee, (C) 157,987, (CMTS) Widow, (ALWD) May, 1872.
Mary Patterson: (PO) Higbee, (C) 197,524, Dep. Mother, (ALWD) Oct., 1882.
Amanda M. Perkins: (PO) Higbee, (C) 197,165, (CMTS) Dep. Mother, (ALWD) Sep., 1882.
Noah Blackford: (PO) Higbee, (C) 161,985, (CMTS) G. S. W. Left Foot, (ALWD) Aug., 1879.
Alexr. J. Romesburg: (PO) Huntsville, (C) 38,290, (CMTS) Wd. Left Elbow, (ALWD) ?.
Harriet Davis: (PO) Huntsville, (C) 18,800, (CMTS) Widow, War 1812, (ALWD) Feb., 1879.
Henry H. Bergstresser: (PO) Huntsville, (C) 192,049, (CMTS) G. S. W. Left Thigh, (ALWD) Jun., 1881.
Jacob S. Miller: (PO) Huntsville, (C) 192,751, (CMTS) Necrosis Right Leg, (ALWD) Jul., 1881.
Clara A. Henderson: (PO) Huntsville, (C) 182,969, (CMTS) Widow, (ALWD) Feb., 1879.
Patsy F. S. Foot: (PO) Huntsville, (C) 32,062, (CMTS) Widow, War 1812, (ALWD) Dec., 1881.
Elijah C. Musick: (PO) Huntsville, (C) 146,645, (CMTS) G. S. W. Neck, (ALWD) Jun., 1877.
Rhoda Artman: (PO) Huntsville, (C) 7,010, (CMTS) Widow, War 1812, (ALWD) Jun., 1878.
Milly Fullington: (PO) Huntsville, (C) 15,750, (CMTS) Widow, War 1812, (ALWD) Jan., 1879.
Susan Blankenship: (PO) Huntsville, (C) 19,233, (CMTS) Widow, War 1812, (ALWD) Feb. 1879.
Andrew Knittle: (PO) Huntsville, (C) 201,708, (CMTS) G. S. W. Left Thigh, (ALWD) Jan., 1882,
Elizabeth Roberts: (PO) Huntsville, (C) 113,619, (CMTS) Widow, (ALWD) May, 1868.
Elizabeth Carver: (PO) Huntsville, (C) 181,048, (CMTS) Widow. (ALWD) May, 1878.
Zarilda Walker: (PO) Huntsville, (C) 150,639, (CMTS) Widow, (ALWD) ?.

Martha F. Collins: (PO) Huntsville, (C) 158,364, (CMTS) Widow, (ALWD) Jun., 1872.
Mathew Perkins: (PO) Huntsville, (C) 195,608, (CMTS) Minor of, (ALWD) May, 1882.
Mildred Peyton: (PO) Huntsville, (C) 7,875, (CMTS) Widow, War 1812, (ALWD) Aug., 1878.
Isabella Moreton: (PO) Jacksonville, (C) 163,283, (CMTS) Widow, (ALWD) Dec., 1873.
Henry Reynolds: (PO) Jacksonville, (C) 162,516, (CMTS) Inj. to Right Hand, (ALWD) ?.
Susan J. Durham: (PO) Jacksonville, (C) 190,637, (CMTS) Widow & C., (ALWD) Dec., 1880.
Hannah Green: (PO) Jacksonville, (C) 158,893, (CMTS) Widow, (ALWD) Jul., 1872
Elizabeth Daniel: (PO) Jacksonville, (C) 25,476, (CMTS) Widow, War 1812, (ALWD) Jul., 1879.
Catharine Boone: (PO) Jacksonville, (C) 154,079, (CMTS) Widow, (ALWD) Oct., 1871.
Thomas Stuck: (PO) Jacksonville, (C) 209,603, (CMTS) G. S. W. Right Hand, (ALWD) May, 1872.
Nancy G. Wright: (PO) Jacksonville, (C) 21,844, (CMTS) Widow, War 1812, (ALWD) Apr., 1879.
Adam Shaner: (PO) Jacksonville, (C) 152,982, (CMTS) G. S. W. Right Leg, Varicose Veins, (ALWD) May, 1878.
William McCanne, Sr. : (PO) Huntsville: (C) 16,286, (CMTS) Surv. War 1812, (ALWD) Apr., 1872.
Sarah A. Lee: (PO) Jacksonville, (C) 46,058, (CMTS) Widow, (ALWD) ?.
Wm. Henrickson: (PO) Moberly, (C) 73,571, (CMTS) Wd. Left Breast & Lung, (ALWD) ?.
Aim Long (sic) Peacha: (PO) Moberly, (C) 129,792, (CMTS) Dep. Mother, (ALWD) May, 1869.
Cyrus L. Hughes: (PO) Moberly, (C) 102,466, (CMTS) Wd. of Throat, (ALWD) ?.
Moses J. Buskirk: (PO) Moberly, (C) 56,371, (CMTS) Partial loss of sight, (ALWD) ?.
Jeremiah D. Ribble: (PO) Moberly, (C) 131,152, (CMTS) G. S. W. Left Leg, (ALWD) ?.
Marcellus A. Hayes: (PO) Moberly, (C) 192,160, (CMTS) Chro. Diarrhea, (ALWD) Jun., 1881.
Levi Kitchen: (PO) Moberly, (C) 131,681, (CMTS) Inj. to Abdomen, (ALWD) Feb., 1878.
John Kennedy: (PO) Moberly, (C) 111,471, (CMTS) G. S. W. Right Shoulder, (ALWD) ?.

Jared K. Kimball: (PO) Moberly, (C) 216,522, (CMTS) Chronic Diarrhea, (ALWD) Aug., 1882.
Walter Kennedy: (PO) Moberly, (C) 221,463, (CMTS) G. S. W. Left Lower Jaw, (ALWD) Mar., 1882.
Caroline Naugle: (PO) Moberly, (C) 118,540, (CMTS) Widow, (ALWD) Sep., 1868.
Eliza Norman: (PO) Moberly, (C) 185,845, (CMTS) Widow, (ALWD) Oct., 1879.
Mary Smith: (PO) Moberly, (C) 33,345, (CMTS) Widow, (ALWD) ?.
Emeline Carter: (PO) Moberly, (C) 182,322, (CMTS) Widow, (ALWD) Oct., 1878.
Henrietta Smith: (PO) Moberly, (C) 178,672, (CMTS) Widow, (ALWD) Sep., 1877.
Enoch Derkin: (PO) Moberly, (C) 203,253, (CMTS) Shell wd. rt. side and one knee, (ALWD) Feb., 1882.
John Williams: (PO) Moberly, (C) 14,008, (CMTS) G. S. W. Left Arm, (ALWD) ?.
Selina Woodward: (PO) Moberly, (C) 196,930, (CMTS) Widow, (ALWD) Aug., 1882.
Sophie B. Campbell: (PO) Moberly, (C) 175,948, (CMTS) Widow and Child, (ALWD) Jan. 1877.
Nancy Collins: (PO) Moberly, (C) 188,981, (CMTS) Widow, (ALWD) May, 1880.
Mary E. Westbrook: (PO) Moberly, (C) 196,879, (CMTS) Widow and Child, (ALWD) Jul., 1881.
Addie Williams: (PO) Moberly, (C) 195,055, (CMTS) Widow, (ALWD) Apr., 1882.
William Coney: (PO) Moberly, (C) 202,068, (CMTS) Dis of Heart & Eyes, (ALWD) ?.
Frank Hayden: (PO) Moberly, (C) 198,480, (CMTS) G. S. W. both Thighs, (ALWD) Nov., 1881.
Chester C. Carter: (PO) Moberly, (C) 183,440, (CMTS) Dis. of Heart and lungs, (ALWD) Mar., 1882.
William D. Butler: (PO) Moberly, (C) 63,902, (CMTS) G. S. W. Right Hand, (ALWD) ?.
Robert Bailey: (PO) Moberly, (C) 123,019, (CMTS) G. S. W. Right Arm, (ALWD) ?.
George Conway: (PO) Moberly, (C) 217,514, (CMTS) Scurvy an Gangrene, (ALWD) Aug., 1881.
Erastus D. Lair: (PO) Moberly, (C) 126,867, (CMTS) Inj. to Right Hand, (ALWD) Feb., 1874.
Eli Mix, II: (PO) Moberly, (C) 179,824, (CMTS) Inj. to Abdomen, (ALWD) Dec., 1880.

Albert Emmons: (PO) Moberly, (C) 172,986, (CMTS) Minor of, (ALWD) Apr., 1876

William D. Watts: (PO) Moberly, (C) 162,327, (CMTS) Loss of fourth finger on right hand, (ALWD) Sep., 1879.

Caroline Farmer: (PO) Moberly, (C) 141,426, (CMTS) Widow and Child, (ALWD) Mar., 1870.

Rocksana Armstrong: (PO) Moberly, (C) 197,708, (CMTS) Widow, (ALWD) Nov., 1882.

Joseph L. Satterlee: (PO) Moberly, (C) 220,509, (CMTS) Inj. to Breast and dis. of Lung, (ALWD) Nov., 1882.

George Scott: (PO) Moberly, (C) 196,549, (CMTS) G. S. W. right breast, (ALWD) ?.

John Sullivan: (PO) Moberly, (C) 178,200, (CMTS) G. S. W. Right Shoulder, (ALWD) ?.

Gideon Wright: (PO) Moberly, (C) 192,476, (CMTS) Loss of right index finger, (ALWD) Jul., 1881.

Charles Wageman: (PO) Moberly, (C) 167,766, (CMTS) Inj. to Back and Head, (ALWD) May, 1880.

Willis Thompson: (PO) Moberly, (C) 204,999, (CMTS) Saber Left Wrist, (ALWD) Mar., 1882.

Richard Ashby: (PO) Moberly, (C) 210,157, (CMTS) Diarrhea and dis. of Abd. Vis., (ALWD) Jun., 1882.

Joseph E. Barclay: (PO) Moberly, (C) 217,294, (CMTS) Inj. to Abdomen,(ALWD) Aug., 1882.

Dureet Bruce: (PO) Moberly, (C) 7,584, (CMTS) Surv., War 1812, (ALWD) Nov., 1871.

Elijah Williams: (PO) Moberly, (C) 5,023, (CMTS) Surv., War 1812, (ALWD) Sep., 1871.

Elizabeth Kelly: (PO) Moberly, (C) 72,664, (CMTS) Widow, (ALWD) ?.

Edwin Smart: (PO) Moberly, (C) 197,485, (CMTS) Rheumatism, (ALWD) Nov., 1881.

George P. Shedd: (PO) Moberly, (C) 177,565, (CMTS) G. S. W. Right Thigh, (ALWD) Oct., 1880.

Millie Irwin: (PO) Moberly, (C) 152,180, (CMTS) Widow, (ALWD) Jul., 1871.

Ruth Ann Pierce: (PO) Moberly, (C) 26,309, (CMTS) Widow, War 1812, (ALWD) Apr., 1879.

Byron Pierce: (PO) Moberly, (C) 212,926, (CMTS) G. S. W. Left Thigh, (ALWD) Jun., 1882.

Hattie M. Hulett: (PO) Moberly, (C) 196,907, (CMTS) Widow and Child, (ALWD) Aug., 1882.

Elizabeth H. Graves: (PO) Moberly, (C) 22,193, (CMTS) Widow, War 1812, (ALWD) Apr. 1879.

Emily G. Miller: (PO) Moberly, (C) 187,100, (CMTS) Widow, (ALWD) Feb., 1880.

Polly Dodson: (PO) Mt. Airy, (C) 22,200, (CMTS) Widow, War 1812, (ALWD) Apr., 1879.

Jacob Burger: (PO) Perche, (C) 179,971, (CMTS) Chr. rheum., (ALWD) Dec., 1880.

Elisha W. Howell: (PO) Randolph, (C) 185,351, (CMTS) G. S. W. Left Leg, (ALWD) Mar., 1881.

William H. Johnson: (PO) Randolph, (C) 128,466, (CMTS) G. S. W. Right Hard, (ALWD) ?.

Ellen Deer: (PO) Renick, (C) 133,315, (CMTS) Dep. Mother, (ALWD) Oct., 1869.

Eliza Lewis: (PO) Renick, (C) 162,689, (CMTS) Dep. Mother, (ALWD) Aug., 1873.

Lucy M. Grant: (PO) Renick, (C) 11,699, (CMTS) Widow, War 1812, (ALWD) Nov., 1878.

Howell County, Missouri, Willow Springs High School Graduates, 1895-1913.

Name	Year
Lina Dawes	1895
Agnes Davis	1895
Edna Stiles	1895
Susie Hinds	1895
Phrona Lovan	1895
Elsie Stanley	1895
Pearl Bartley	1895
Susie Bartley	1896
Tressie Stanley	1896
Lelia Hill	1896
Harry Baldridge	1896
Egbert E. Randal	1896
Ethel Scott	1896
Walter Tarleton	1896
Sylvia Higgins	1897
Fay Voohers	1897
Edith Lovewell	1897
Settie Feathergill	1897
Ethel Lovewell	1897
Birdie Hays	1899
Bertha Harris	1899

Name	Year
Nell Rankin	1899
Warren Whitman	1899
Mary W. Campbell	1900
Anna Angerback	1901
Lizzie Ferguson	1901
Fannie Anson	1901
Maude Lovan	1901
Carrie Anson	1902
Eva Loftis	1902
Bertha Waller	1903
Flora Besheer	1904
Homer Fergusson	1904
Ivan Rowe	1904
Ray Comley	1904
Mabelia O'Bannon	1905
Elmer Abernathy	1905
Cecil Vosburg	1905
Maude Switzer	1905
Archie Anderson	1905
Manie Davis	1905
Goldie Dougherty	1906
Nellie Sass	1906
T. Orval Ferguson	1906
Lola Hutchinson	1906
Claude Besheer	1906
Sam Davis	1906
Minnie Payne	1907
Millard Shibley	1907
Guy Koons	1907
Frank Sass	1907
Maybelle Lovan	1908
Harold Rowe	1908
Willa Redding	1908
Harold Yonker	1908
Ellen Crosby	1909
Naomi Martin	1909
Laurel B. Johnson	1909
Edna O'Bannon	1909
Roy Kendig	1910
Wayne Turner	1910
Harry Fleming	1910
Lucille Howard	1910

Name	Year
Edna Benton	1910
Ruth Holland	1910
Viola Zenor	1910
Atrelle LeCompte	1910
Leona Davis	1912
Adolph Sass	1912
Stanley Barnes	1913
Willie Preston	1913
Helen Osmun	1913
Paul Redding	1913

Registered Coal Oil Inspectors for Missouri, 1903.

    C. S. Orcutt: (AREA) Adair Co., (LOC) Adair Co., (AD) Jun. 23, 1903, (EXPD) Jun. 20, 1904.

    Paul F. Limrick: (AREA) Savannah and Andrew Co., (LOC) Andrew Co., (AD) Jun. 23, 1903, (EXPD) Jun. 9, 1905.

    J. M. Wolfe: (ARE) Tarkio, (LOC) Atchison Co., (AD) Dec. 9, 1902, (EXPD) Jul. 2, 1904.

    Joseph P. Dobyns: (AREA) Mexico, (LOC) Audrain Co., (AD) Jan. 17, 1903, (EXPD) Jan. 17, 1905.

    R. A. Garner: (AREA) Monett, (LOC) Barry Co., (AD) Nov. 1, 1901, (EXPD) Nov. 1, 1903.

    Geo. W. B. Garrett: (AREA) Lamar, (LOC) Barton Co., (AD) Dec. 14, 1901, (EXPD) Dec. 13, 1903.

    Mary J. Wade: (AREA) Bates Co., (LOC) Bates Co., (AD) Aug. 11, 1902, (EXPD) Oct. 17, 1903.

    W. W. DeJarmatt: (AREA) Warsaw, (LOC) Benton Co., (AD) Aug. 30, 1902, (EXPD) Aug. 30, 1904.

    Watson Laws: (AREA) Columbia, (LOC) Boone Co., (AD) Jun. 4, 1904, (EXPD) Apr. 29, 1905.

    Robert L. Hope: (AREA) Centralia, (LOC) Boone Co., (AD) Jun. 24, 1902, (EXPD) Jun. 14, 1904.

    E. S. Hays: (AREA) Buchanan Co., (LOC) Buchanan Co., (AD) May 21, 1901, (EXPD) May 17, 1903.

    Chas. P. Cargill: (AREA) St. Joseph, (LOC) Buchanan Co., (AD) Jun. 25, 1903, (EXPD) Jun. 25, 1905.

    Thos. M. Johnson: (AREA) Poplar Bluff, (LOC) Butler Co., (AD) Jun. 25, 1903, (EXPD) Oct. 17, 1903.

    Williams J. Brent: (AREA) Fulton, (LOC) Callaway Co., (AD) Jul. 6, 1903, (EXPD) Jul. 2, 1905.

    Geo. E. Chappell: (AREA) City of Cape Girardeau, (LOC) Cape Girardeau Co., (AD) Dec. 16, 1901, (EXPD) Dec. 18, 1903.

Chas. S. Sinnard: (AREA) Carrollton and Carroll Co., (LOC) Carroll Co., (AD) Jan. 8, 1902, (EXP) Sep. 7, 1903.

James M. McGhee: (AREA) Carter Co., (LOC) Carter Co., (AD) Mar. 12, 1902, (EXPD) Mar. 16, 1904.

Newton Walker: (AREA) Pleasant Hill, (LOC) Cass Co., (AD) Mar. 27, 1903, (EXPD) Mar. 30, 1905.

Chas. J. G. Clasby: (AREA) El Dorado Springs, (LOC) Cedar Co., (AD) Jun. 9, 1902, (EXPD) May 8, 1904.

J. G. Gallemore: (AREA) Salisbury, (LOC) Chariton, (AD) May 21, 1903, (EXPD) May 21, 1905.

G. D. Kennedy: (AREA) Brunswick, (LOC) Chariton, (AD) Jan. 19, 1903, (EXPD) Dec. 21, 1904.

S. J. Montgomery: (AREA) Clark Co., (LOC) Clark Co., (AD) Nov. 22, 1901, (EXPD) Nov. 4, 1903.

W. M. Gardiner: (AREA) Clay Co., (LOC) Clay Co., (AD) Jun. 29, 1903, (EXPD) Feb. 8, 1905.

Lewis H. Bell: (AREA) Liberty, (LOC) Clay Co. (AD) Feb. 14, 1903, (EXP) May 9, 1904.

Jno. H. Mynatt: (AREA) Cameron, (LOC) Clinton Co., (AD) Sep. 2, 1902, (EXPD) Sep. 2, 1904.

James S. Scanlan: (AREA) Plattsburg, (LOC) Clinton Co., (AD) Dec. 15, 1902, (EXPD) Dec, 15, 1904.

V. J. Kaiser: (AREA) Jefferson City, (LOC) Cole Co., (AD) Jan. 15, 1903, (EXPD) Jan. 18, 1905.

Joseph W. Miller: (AREA) Boonville, (LOC) Cooper Co., (AD) May 15, 1902, (EXPD) May 11, 1904.

William Terry: (AREA) Dade Co., (LOC) Dade Co., (AD) Feb. 18, 1903, (EXPD) Feb. 14, 1905.

O. I. Thurmond: (AREA) Kennet, (LOC) Dunklin Co., (AD) Jun. 1, 1903, (EXPD) Feb. 210, 1905.

J. R. Gallemore: (AREA) Washington, (LOC) Franklin Co., (AD) Aug. 28, 1902, (EXPD) Jul. 18, 1904.

Paul Gregory: (AREA) Gentry Co., (LOC) Gentry Co., (AD) Jul. 14, 1902, (EXPD) Jul. 15, 1904.

S. W. Hatheway: (AREA) Stanberry, (LOC) Gentry Co., (AD) Aug. 2, 1902, (EXPD) Jul. 8, 1904.

J. B. Jewell: (AREA) Springfield, (LOC) Greene Co., (AD) Nov. 28, 1902, (EXPD) Dec. 1, 1904.

M. G. Kennedy: (AREA) Trenton, (LOC) Grundy, (AD) Mar. 22, 1902, (EXPD) Mar. 26, 1904.

George Peak: (AREA) Bethany, (LOC) Harrison Co., (AD) Jun. 23, 1903, (EXPD) Jun. 29, 1905.

Chas. H. Whitaker, Jr.: (AREAA) Clinton, (LOC) Henry Co., (AD) Apr. 23, 1902, (EXPD) Feb. 20, 1904.

Jonas H. Dearmont: (AREA) Mound City, (LOC) Holt Co., (AD) Mar. 16, 1903, (EXPD) Mar. 10, 1905.

W. F. Potts: (AREA) Fayette, (LOC) Howard, (AD) Jun. 21, 1902, (EXPD) Jun. 23, 1904.

Earle Evans: (AREA) West Plains, (LOC) Howell, (AD) Nov. 25, 1902, (EXPD) Nov. 21, 1904.

Raymond Austin: (AREA) Willow Springs, (LOC) Howell Co., (AD) Dec. 10, 1902, (EXPD) May 27, 1904.

Henry Adolph: (AREA) Ironton, (LOC) Iron Co., (AD) Mar. 11, 1903, (EXPD) Feb. 21, 1905.

J. S. Wallace: (AREA) Independence, (LOC) Jackson Co., (AD) Dec. 10, 1901, (EXPD) Dec. 6, 1903.

Thomas Philllips: (AREA) Kansas City, (LOC) Jackson, (AD) Jun. 18, 1903, (EXPD) Jun. 18, 1905.

W. N. Johnson: (AREA) Webb City, (LOC) Jasper, (AD) Mar. 29, 1902, (EXPD) Jan. 10, 1904.

Mathew George: (AREA) Joplin, (LOC) Jasper Co., (AD) Aug. 5, 1902, (EXPD) Aug. 9, 1904.

S. F. Sankey: (AREA) Holden, (LOC) Johnson Co., (AD) May 6, 1902, (EXPD) May 5, 1904.

S. H. Coleman: (AREA) Warrenburg, (LOC) Johnson Co., (AD) Dec. 13, 1902, (EXPD) Dec. 16, 1904.

Phil Donnelly: (AREA) Lebanon, (LOC) Laclede Co., (AD) Jun. 16, 1902, (EXPD) May 30, 1904.

Chas. H. Barron: (AREA) Lexington, (LOC) Lafayette Co., (AD) Dec. 30, 1902, (EXPD) Sep. 28, 1904.

T. H. Gilmer: (AREA) Pierce City, (LOC) Lawrence Co., (AD) Mar. 31, 1902, (EXPD) Mar. 29, 1904.

John M. McNatt: (AREA) Aurora, (LOC) Lawrence Co., (AD) May 15, 1902, (EXPD) May 13, 1904.

Thos. A. Nelson: (AREA) Canton, (LOC) Lewis Co., (AD) Aug. 29, 1901, (EXPD) Sep. 2, 1903.

W. F. Haldeman: (AREA) La Belle, (LOC) Lewis Co., (AD) Apr. 3, 1903, (EXPD) Apr. 2, 1904.

John E. Worsham: (AREA) Lincoln Co., (LOC) Lincoln Co., (AD) Nov. 29, 1902, (EXPD) Nov. 10, 1904.

W. P. Conger: (AREA) Linn Co., (LOC) Linn Co., (AD) Apr. 26, 1903, (EXPD) Apr. 26, 1905.

J. R. Middleton: (AREA) Livingston Co., (LOC) Livingston, (AD) Mar. 16, 1903, (EXPD) Dec. 28, 1904.

Thos. Gibson: (AREA) McDonald Co., (LOC) McDonald Co., (AD) Nov. 11, 1902, (EXPD) Oct. 26, 1904.

J. L. Baity: (AREA) Macon Co., (LOC) Macon Co., (AD) Jan. 17, 1903, (EXPD) Jan. 23, 1904.

James J. O'Conner: (AREA) Madison Co., (LOC) Madison Co., (AD) Aug. 21, 1901, (EXPD) Sep. 9, 1903.

B. F. Brown: (AREA) Hannibal, (LOC) Marion Co., (AD) Nov. 7, 1902, Nov. 8, 1904.

William Hirons: (AREA) Princeton, (LOC) Mercer Co., (AD) Jul. 8, 1903, (EXPD) Jul.. 22, 1905.

Robert L. Shelby: (AREA) Charleston, (LOC) Mississippi Co., (AD) Sep. 29, 1902, (EXPD) Sep. 28, 1904.

J. A. Bertram: (AREA) California, (LOC) Moniteau Co., (AD) Jun. 6, 1903, (EXP) Aug. 29, 1904.

Robert C. Petrsol: (AREA) Monroe Co., (LOC) Monroe Co., (AD) Feb. 9, 1903, (EXPD) 17, 1905.

James R. Appling: (AREA) Montgomery Co., (LOC) Montgomery Co., (AD) Jun. 1901, (EXPD) Jun. 10, 1903.

H. Clark Armstrong: (AREA) Neosho, (LOC) Newton Co., (AD) Jun. 25, 1903, (EXPD) Sep. 7, 1903.

Sam T. Kennedy: (AREA) Maryville, (LOC) Nodaway Co., (AD) Nov. 1, 1901, (EXPD) Oct. 31, 1903.

H. E. Wright: (AREA) Parnell, (LOC) Nodaway Co., (AD) Jun. 6, 1903, (EXPD) May 31, 1905.

Joseph A. Bowers: (AREA) Sedalia, (LOC) Pettis, (AD) Jan. 22, 1902, (EXPD) Jan. 21, 1904.

J. W. Poole: (AREA) Rolla, (LOC) Phelps Co., (AD) Jun. 1, 1902, (EXPD) Jun. 1, 1904.

Perry A. Ballard: (AREA) Platte Co., (LOC) Platte Co., (AD) Jul. 9, 1902, (EXPD) Jun. 28, 1904.

C. W. Whitmore: (AREA) Unionville, (LOC) Putnam Co., (AD) Feb. 3, 1903, (EXPD) Feb. 4, 1905.

Geo. W. Young: (AREA) Ralls Co., (LOC) Ralls Co., (AD) Jul. 10, 1903, (EXPD) Jul. 9, 1905.

J. T. Coates: (AREA) Moberly, (LOC) Randolph Co., (AD) Apr. 17, 1903, (EXPD) Apr. 1905.

John R. Gant: (AREA) Ray Co., (LOC) Ray Co., (AD) Feb. 6, 1903, (EXPD) Feb. 18, 1905.

William V. Ellis: (AREA) Ripley Co., (LOC) Ripley Co., (AD) Nov. 13, 1901, (EXPD) Nov. 11, 1903.

J. B. Weseman: (AREA) St. Charles City, (LOC) St. Charles Co., (AD) Sep. 17, 1902, (EXPD) Aug. 31, 1904.

J. Y. Wilson: (AREA) Oseola, (LOC) St. Clair Co., (AD) Mar. 24, 1902, (EXPD) Mar. 24, 1904.
W. B. Laurie: (AREA) Saline Co., (LOC) Saline Co., (AD) Jan. 23, 1902, (EXPD) Jan. 18, 1904.
Elijah Gwinn: (AREA) Slater, (LOC) Saline Co., (AD) Saline Co., (AD) Mar. 27, 1903, (EXPD) Mar. 13, 1905.
J. R. Rippey, Jr.: (AREA) Schulyer Co., (LOC) Schulyer Co., (AD) Jun. 1, 1903, (EXPD) Aug. 13, 1904.
Henry Beckman, Jr.: (AREA) Scotland Co., (LOC) Scotland Co., (AD) Aug. 29, 1902, (EXPD) Aug. 23, 1904.
E. M. Davis: (AREA) Shannon Co., (LOC) Shannon Co., (AD) Mar. 5, 1902, (EXPD) Mar. 10, 1902.
Robert T. Sparks: (AREA) Shelbina, (LOC) Shelby Co., (AD) Jan. 28, 1903, (EXPD) Dec. 17, 1904.
A. J. Thrower: (AREA) Dexter, (LOC) Stoddard, (AD) Jan. 16, 1902, (EXPD) Jan. 17, 1904.
J. F. Woody: (AREA) Bloomfield, (LOC) Stoddard, (AD) Dec. 13, 1902, (EXPD) Oct. 23, 1904.
C. A. Schoene: (AREA) Sullivan Co., (LOC) Sullivan Co., (AD) Aug. 15, 1901, (EXPD) Aug. 30. 1904.
D. A. Martin: (AREA) Nevada, (LOC) Vernon Co., (AD) Nov. 7, 1902, (EXPD) Aug. 2, 1904.
J. N. Holmes: (AREA) Piedmont, (LOC) Wayne Co., (AD) Oct. 30, 1901, (EXPD) Oct. 19, 1903.
William Sanders: (AREA) Williamsville, (LOC) Wayne Co., (AD) Nov. 3, 1902, (EXPD) Nov. 1, 1904.
W. J. Flynn: (AREA) St. Louis City, (LOC) St. Louis Co., (AD) Jun. 12, 1902, (EXPD) Jun. 18, 1904.

Hickory County, Missouri, Antioch Cemetery, West of Pittsburg, Hwy J to County Round 275 South.

Name	Birth	Death
B. Harry Amiss	Aug. 16, 1888	Oct. 20, 1918
Isabell Amiss	1862	1932
Louis E. Amis	1860	1946
Ada Lee Arthurs	Sep. 4, 1904	Sep. 1, 1978
Darrel F. Arthurs	1912	1988
Nellie M. Bailey	Apr. 23, 1899	Aug. 7, 1899
Fannie M. Bailey	Jan. 18, 1876	May 15, 1899
Simmie D. Bake	Mar. 23, 1884	Jan. 4, 1963
Iva Jane Bake	Jun. 13, 1885	May 15, 1959
J. W. Barnes	Dec. 19, 1873	Feb. 24, 1920
May Barnes	Jan. 28, 1878	Jun. 28, 1958

Name	Birth	Death
Annice Barnes	Feb. 26, 1909	Mar. 10, 1909
Otus L. Barnes	Mar. 31, 1903	Feb. 9, 1921
Elvie Barnes	Mar. 18, 1913	Jan. 31, 1955
Betty Sue Barnes	Mar. 6, 1938	Mar. 8, 1938
Wm. Hobart Barnes	Jun. 26, 1911	Dec. 31, 1968
Joyce Kay Bastion	Jul. 4, 1942	Jul. 10, 1942
Rosa C. Bastion	Jul. 13, 1884	Mar. 14, 1966
Sadie Bastion	---	---
Chas. E. Bastion	May 18, 1859	Feb. 1, 1920
Emmett Bastion	Jun. 17, 1933	Nov. 18, 1979
Mabel Bastion	Jul. 27, 1915	---
Nicholas Bastion	Oct. 16, 1913	---
J. Baxter	Mar. 9, 1844	---
Salina L. Baxter	Feb. 12, 1852	Dec. 2, 1916
Amy C. Beishline	Feb. 14, 1887	Mar. 19, 1970
Elizabeth E. Bertram	Nov. 18, 1847	Nov. 23, 1847
Abe Bertram	Oct. 12, 1843	Nov. 28, 1922
Fena Bigler	Nov. 7, 1875	Aug. 21, 1932
Monroe Bigler	Apr. 4, 1869	Jan. 10, 1951
Gettie Bigler	Feb. 19, 1890	May 2, 1965
N. C. Bigler	Jan. 12, 1880	Aug. 2, 1952
J. W. Bigler	Mar. 18, 1863	Apr. 11, 1885
Helen M. Boney	Jul. 23, 1913	Jul. 1, 1985
Peter T. Bowen	Jul. 8, 1881	Oct. 1, 1959
Callie Bowen	Aug. 23, 1888	Apr. 28, 1955
Henry R. Bowen	May 5, 1883	Jul. 22, 1948
Bonnie B. Bowen	Oct. 14, 1882	---
Rebecca J. Bowen	Oct. 21, 1853	Mar. 2, 1907
Chas. W. Bowen	Jan. 28, 1849	Jan. 29, 1885
William H. Branham	May 1, 1875	Dec. 24, 1956
Martha E. Branham	Dec, 31, 1876	Oct. 14, 1954
Samuel J. Branham	Mar. 18, 1905	Apr. 7, 1907
Wilma Branham	Jun. 12, 1909	Jul. 29, 1987
James Branham	May 18, 1902	Aug. 18, 1981
Johnny Brannon	Mar. 3, 1865	Mar. 31, 1944
Martha Brannon	May 13, 1865	Jul. 1, 1948
Harry Brannon	Dec. 14, 1892	Apr. 29, 1917
Mary E. Brannon	Nov. 16, 1841	Jun. 17, 1924
Martha J. Brannon	Feb. 19, 1859	Nov. 11, 1879
George N. Brannon	Jan. 7, 1872	Aug. 15, 1874
Wm. F. Brannon	Dec. 20, 1877	Feb. 22, 1878
Harriet A. Breshears	Feb. 29, 1843	Dec. 27, 1891

Name	Birth	Death
Rosa Bridges	Jan. 19, 1914	Oct. 22, 1984
Fronia Bridges	Oct. 9, 1895	Oct. 26, 1923
Clarence Briggs	Oct. 9, 1897	Jun. 4, 1986
Sarah E. Brown	Sep. 29, 1854	Sep. 26, 1856
William A. Brown	Dec. 26, 1852	Jul. 25, 1853
Artie Bush	Nov. 11, 1888	Jun. 6, 1965
Brant Bush	Dec. 18, 1887	Dec. 7, 1963
Ellen Campbell	Apr. 19, 1869	Sep. 5, 1946
Smith Campbell	Aug. 6, 1862	Jul. 18, 1930
M. Mildred Campbel	Feb. 7, 1902	---
Clyde Campbell	Aug. 2, 1898	Jan. 9, 1964
Bertie Lee Chaney	Jul. 5, 1935	---
Edna Mae Chaney	Mar. 20, 1905	---
B. H. Chaney	Oct. 21, 1900	---
Derhl Max Chaney, Jr.	Aug. 4, 1942	Feb. 19, 1946
Palmer Clark	Feb, 25, 1886	Ayg. 27, 1969
Dora Clark	May 26, 1903	Dec. 26, 1979
Joseph H. Clark	1853	1900
Malinda J. Clark	1855	1925
Hiram Henry Clark	Feb. 7, 1888	Mar. 23, 1966
Heather Lynn Cline	1981	---
Letha Lee Cloyed	Sep. 21, 1888	Mar. 7, 1920
Alpha Colston	Mar. 21, 1875	Mar. 21, 1875
Elbert Colston	Feb. 22, 1874	Sep. 23, 1874
Julia Colston	Aug. 30, 1878	Aug. 30, 1878
R. H. Conley	Jun. 7, 1861	Jul. 20, 1954
Martha E. Conley	Dec. 25, 1857	Jan. 8, 1936
Della May Conley	Nov. 22, 1889	Jul. 22, 1901
Purley Conley	May 1, 1887	Sep. 14, 1887
William T. Coon	Sep. 1, 1869	Sep. 5, 1954
Margaret A. Coon	Jun. 20, 1880	Oct. 23, 1957
E. W. Coon	Dec. 20, 1846	Jan. 24, 1931
Martha Coon	Dec. 20, 1846	May 26, 1936
Rhoda E. Costelow	May 25, 1852	Dec. 8, 1888
Ralph W. Courier	Mar. 13, 1895	Aug. 4, 1872
Cora Craddick	Jun. 3, 1910	---
Walter W. Craddick	Jul. 23, 1902	Feb. 1, 1989
Loran J. Creed	Dec. 17, 1905	Aug. 1, 1909
Jasper Creed	Nov. 27, 1901	Oct. 18, 1971
Nannie Creed	Jul. 26, 1902	Apr. 4, 1957
Isabell Darby	Oct. 13, 1876	Feb. 4, 1922

Name	Birth	Death
James A. Darby	Nov. 2, 1873	Oct. 28, 1926
Isaac D. Darby	Feb. 21, 1875	Oct. 31, 1955
Ruth M. Darby	Feb. 27, 1885	Oct. 26, 1966
Arthur Davis	Jun. 24, 1880	May 24, 1963
Lou M. Davis	Sep. 15, 1880	Jul. 9, 1924
Wm. Joseph Davis	Jan. 25, 1919	Jan. 28, 1919
Maudie Dehart	Mar. 14, 1893	Jan. 16, 1872
Homer Dehart	May 26, 1890	Jun. 3, 1964
Norma J. Dehart	May 1, 1934	---
Raymond Dehart	Oct. 7, 1930	Aug. 10, 1984
Harold Eugene DeWeese	Aug. 16, 1931	Jan. 28, 1971
Keith Eaton	Jan. 23, 1923	Sep. 3, 1984
Aleene Eaton	Dec. 27, 1930	---
Charles Randolph Ellis, Jr.	Dec. 23, 1919	---
Julien Bell Fisher	1849	1879
Joseph Monrow Fisher	Feb. 8, 1863	Mar. 4, 1863
Alfred C. Floyd	Jun. 21, 1911	Feb. 14, 1966
Romey Floyd	Nov. 19, 1913	Aug. 20, 1963
Dorothy Floyd	Mar. 21, 1916	Oct. 18, 1945
Callie L. Floyd	May 29, 1908	Dec. 13, 1928
James A. Floyd	May 11, 1873	Mar. 22, 1939
Bertha E. Floyd	Apr. 2, 1884	Jun. 8, 1958
Wilford Allen Floyd	Jan. 5, 1925	Aug. 11, 1949
Mabel K. Floyd	Jan. 5, 1912	---
Nycus J. Floyd	Dec. 9, 1909	---
Andro Floyd	Jun. 10, 1888	Feb. 6, 1933
Gale Floyd	Feb. 24, 1933	Feb. 15, 1934
Hubert Lee Floyd	Nov. 14, 1927	Aug. 13, 1953
Julia Floyd	Jul. 11, 1906	Jun. 1, 1985
Wm. T. Floyd	Jan. 9, 1905	Dec. 3, 1987
Thomas Floyd	Dec. 25, 1846	May ??, 1921
Ava Clifford Floyd	1926	1926
A. R. Floyd	Feb. 15, 1897	Jul. 27, 1899
M. E. Floyd	Oct. 23, 1900	Feb. 15, 1902
Elivra Floyd (Age: 70Y 10M 18D)		Mar. 9, 1953
Edward A. Floyd (Age: 82Y 3M 10D)		Jul. 14, 1959
W. H. Floyd	Nov. 8, 1880	Feb. 9, 1959
Lydia M. Floyd	Jan. 24, 1886	Dec. 26, 1966
John W. Floyd	1890	1960
Virgie L. Floyd	1895	Jan. 15, 1975
Loren Gerald Floyd	Sep. 17, 1924	Mar. 21, 1986
Ethel Floyd	Mar. 29, 1904	---

Name	Birth	Death
Leonard Floyd	Apr. 10, 1902	Dec. 12, 1963
George L. Floyd	Nov. 5, 1921	Aug. 29, 1967
Elizabeth P. Floyd	1847	Feb. 28, 1879
George F. Fowler	Oct. 27, 1898	Nov. 25, 1927
Aubra C. Fowler	Apr. 17, 1898	Sep. 4, 1988
Andro N. Fowler	Dec. 28, 1903	Dec. 16, 1973
Shelley Denise Fowler	Dec. 25, 1963	---
Kenton Fraser Fowler	Apr. 10, 1928	Feb. 11, 1962
Andro F. Fowler	Jul. 31, 1862	May 22, 1945
Ida M. Fowler	Nov. 1, 1863	Sep. 14, 1945
Lydia Fowler	Jan. 26, 1894	Nov. 11, 1919
Harry J. Fowler	Sep. 21, 1900	Jun. 1, 1960
Flora M. Fowler	Aug. 2, 1898	Aug. 17, 1981
Gene Fowler	Sep,.20, 1892	Feb. 6, 1897
Susan J. Fowler	Jul. 24, 1869	May 1, 1959
Purdy Fowler	Mar. 3, 1860	Jan. 18, 1955
Jamison George Fowler	Jul. 20, 1975	Dec. 2, 1975
Rose I. Fowler	Feb. 2, 1902	Nov. 11, 1988
Doris Lee Fowler	Oct. 16, 1918	Jul. 21, 1988
Wm. Frank Fowler	Oct. 4, 4, 1918	Nov. 3, 1983
Joeann Frazier	Feb. 16, 1860	Feb. 25, 1948
Isaac W. Frazier	Feb. 14, 1850	Jul. 12, 1907
Mary L. Frazier	Apr. 2, 1890	Jul. 5, 1949
Clara A. Fugate	Jul. 21, 1867	May 5, 1949
Leta May Gargus (Age: 70Y)		Mar. 27, 1990
Arvilla R. Glenn	Sep. 4, 1880	Apr. 12, 1961
Ida F. Gleen	May 18, 1884	Mar. 16, 1971
Zelma N. Glenn	Jan. 23, 1914	---
W. Earl Glenn	Mar. 30, 1907	Jul. 25, 1983
Alice Mae Godfrey	1893	1943
Wm. M. Grisham	1858	1950
Virda E. Grisham	1871	1909
Elmer Halbert	Dec. 30, 1884	Feb. 2, 1903
Matilda C. Halbert	Apr. 30, 1850	Jan. 28, 1903
Wm. H. Halbert	Dec. 25, 1844	Feb. 25, 1922
Joe G. Hardy	Jan. 30, 1921	---
Fran R. Hardy	Mar. 25, 1919	Jul. 29, 1982
Willie D. Hastain	May 4, 1842	Feb. 17, 1863
Helen Lavern Hellums	Sep. 2, 1921	---
Effie Hellums	Oct. 8, 1895	Apr. 1, 1985
Lawrence Hellums	Jan. 28, 1898	Oct. 17, 1967
Steven Bruce Higginbotham	May 4, 1949	Apr. 9, 1971

Name	Birth	Death
Ruth Evelyn Higginbotham	Aug. 14, 1918	Apr. 23, 1983
Nancy Ellen Hobson	Mar. 7, 1852	Jan. 14, 1919
John Hobson	Jun. 15, 1851	May 11, 1911
Loyd Hobson	Sep. 15, 1905	Apr. 23, 1906
Clifford Lee Hobson (Age: 32Y 6M)		Jul. 17, 1945
Creth Hollingswoth	1890	1935
Roy D. Hollingsworth	Sep. 5, 1909	Sep. 1, 1965
Mildred Darby	Feb. 6, 1912	---
Rena Holt	Apr. 18, 1886	Sep. 11, 1923
Barbara Hooper	Jul. 27, 1855	Nov. 16, 1915
William Hooper	Sep. 5, 1842	Jul. 18, 1914
H. P. Houser	Jan. 4, 1884	Dec. 8, 1969
Nell Belle Houser	Dec. 7, 1886	Feb. 9, 1964
Frank W. Houser	Sep. 8, 1913	Apr. 2, 1981
Marilou Houser	Sep. 15, 1917	---
Cleo Hunt	Jan. 20, 1899	Apr. 19, 1899
Effie P. Hunt	Jul. 4, 1874	Jun. 29, 1905
Bessie P. Jenkins	Dec. 19, 1883	Aug. 31, 1979
James A. Jenkins	Sep. 27, 1879	Jan. 5, 1952
Nula B. Johnson	Mar. 19, 1903	Jan. 8, 1968
Robert Lee Johnson	1911	1924
Elpha Jones	Nov. 29, 1888	Nov. 26, 1976
Perry Jones	Feb. 22, 1885	Oct. 18, 1965
Sigel Jones	Jan. 21, 1862	Dec. 16, 1940
Elizabeth Jones	Aug. 16, 1867	Mar. 21, 1909
A. O. Kearney	1884	1962
Bonnie B. Kearney	Oct. 14, 1882	Jul. 22, 1968
Orval Kearney	Oct. 27, 1882	Jan. 6, 1972
Henry Elmer Kelley	Nov. 24, 1894	Aug. 10, 1985
Elsie Ann Kelley	Nov. 13, 1897	Jan. 28, 1989
Fern Kicenski	Jan. 4, 1928	Sep. 27, 1950
Charley Guy Kincaid	Oct. 26, 1889	May 26, 1975
Ora Blanche Kincaid	Mar. 22, 1895	Aug. 29, 1976
Ora F. Kincaid	1877	1913
Retha J. Kincaid	1881	1953
B. A. Kincaid	Sep. 22, 1902	Sep. 14, 1903
Harriet F. Kincaid	Jul. 17, 1858	Aug. 8, 1939
George F. Kincaid	Feb. 17, 1844	Sep. 13, 1928
Artie A. Kincaid	Dec. 11, 1879	Aug. 1, 1951
Pearl Kincaid	Jul. 30, 1880	Dec. 14, 1952
Hooly Frank Kincaid	Jan. 11, 1906	Sep. 19, 1967
Will Knight	Nov. ??, 1867	Jan. 26, 1945

Name	Birth	Death
Jessie Knight	Apr. 15, 1879	Jul. 24, 1944
Barbara Knight	Jul. 22, 1914	---
Martin Leach	Sep. 16, 1890	Dec. 11, 1976
Benton Lightfoot	Aug. 17, 1897	---
Atha Lightfoot	Oct. 25, 1898	Jun. 5, 1980
Theodore Lightle	1928	1990
Tempa Locke	Jul. 10, 1888	Sep. 21, 1971
Mary B. Luttrell	May 10, 1848	Oct. 26, 1921
Catherine Luttrell	1843	1897
Ida Mallonee	Mar. 24, 1893	Nov. 4, 1983
Ben L. Mallonee	My 20, 1889	Mar. 5, 1981
Len G. Mallonee	Sep. 2, 1870	Nov. 15, 1942
Atha C. Mallonee	Oct. 5, 1883	Jun. 16, 1970
Benjamin L. Mallonee	Jan. 20, 1848	Jul. 1, 1914
Lucy K. Mallonee	Aug. 7, 1850	May 4, 1918
Edward Mallonee	1921	1989
Edward Kendall Mallonee	May 20, 1889	May 24, 1963
Arthur Wilbur Manuel	1912	1978
Irene Adele Manuel	1911	1981
M. America Martin	Mar. 25, 1851	Nov. 25, 1918
Samuel James Martin	Dec. 20, 1853	Sep. 2, 1930
James Mimsey	Oct. 14, 1881	Jun. 2, 1948
Mary Martin	1879	1956
Emma Mccaslin	1889	1963
John P. McCaslin	1879	1964
Walter McCoy	Apr. 8, 1862	Mar. 19, 1916
Ella F. McCoy	Oct. 31, 1871	Mar. 25, 1961
Eva McCoy	Nov. 8, 1902	May 29, 1981
Ralph L. McCoy	Mar. 13, 1902	Jan. 26, 1944
Ivan Glenn McCoy	Feb. 12, 1911	Oct. 21, 1944
Joe Anne McCoy	Mar. 20, 1939	---
Fern McCoy	Apr. 22, 1914	---
Joseph E. McCoy	Aug. 31, 1904	Jun. 22, 1972
Mary McCoy	Jun. 7, 1947	Aug. 14, 1982
Harold Lee McCoy	Jul. 24, 1944	---
Wm. E. McCoy	Sep. 12, 1892	Feb. 20, 1893
Fratie Miller	Nov. 10, 1878	Apr. 19, 1961
Wm. Riley Miller	Mar. 7, 1863	Jul. 13, 1939
Sarah F. Miller	May 20, 1875	Jul. 24, 1944
Wm. Earless Miller (Age: 68Y 10M 9D)		Mar. 23, 1958
Eddie H. Miller	Oct. 17, 1877	Feb. 10, 1946
May B. Miller	May 1, 1884	Aug. 13, 1931

Name	Birth	Death
Inez Miller	Jan. 20, 1902	Aug. 24, 1909
Clarence R. Miller	Oc. 17, 1904	Aug. 25, 1905
Elzie I. Miller	Jun. 7, 1903	Jun. 13, 1962
Laura Ethel Miller	Aug. 38, 1906	---
George Hayden Miller	Jun. 11, 1907	Dec. 10, 1987
Georgia Irene Miller	Oct. 2, 1927	---
Hazel Mae Miller	Dec. 12, 1910	Jun. 30, 1975
Audie Miller	Nov. 25, 1909	---
Jesse L. Miller	Jan. 12, 1889	May 24, 1958
Lily B. Miller	Jun. 21, 1893	Sep. 24, 1983
Judith B. Miller	Jul. 26, 1940	Jul. 31, 1940
George P. Miller	Jul. 7, 1854	Aug. 22, 1936
Mary L. Miller	Aug. 8, 1858	May 5, 1943
Lester Miller	Oct. 9, 1900	Nov. 29, 1909
Lottie Miller	Jan. 27, 1899	Feb. 8, 1899
Earl Miller	May 8, 1896	Jul. 12, 1896
Vernie F. Miller	Jan. 27, 1895	Jul. 29, 1895
Amos Miller	May 1, 1887	Jun. 30, 1889
Ida Miller	Sep. 4, 1883	Feb. 18, 1899
Mary M. Miller	Nov. 28, 1859	Jul. 24, 1898
Buley F. Miller	Jun, 20, 1898	Jul. 30, 1898
Mary E. R. Miller	Feb. 7, 1870	Sep. 3, 1885
Ethel Miller	Jul. 16, 1896	Dec. 20, 1896
S. L. Miller	Nov. 13, 1896	Oct. 18, 1901
Della Marie Oldaker	Jul. 14, 1919	Oct. 12, 1919
Isabelle Pitts	Sep. 10, 1866	Oct. 22, 1943
C. C. Pitts	Nov. 25, 1861	Aug. 4, 1937
Charley C. Pitts	1893	1970
Betty Lou Pitts	July. 4, 1925	Jan. 28, 1945
Evert Pitts	Jul. 7, 1887	Jun. 22, 1952
Hattie Pitts	Oct. 13, 1887	Jan. 15, 1980
Zena Pitts	Aug. 23, 1913	---
Loren Pitts	Jul. 8, 1910	Jan. 9, 1988
Ada Pitts	Dec, 19, 1902	Oct. 7, 1918
Curtis H. Pitts	Dec. 26, 1880	Dec. 8, 1960
Lula Pitts	Apr. 22, 1883	Mar. 18, 1904
Vergie E. Pitts	May 12, 1884	Feb. 11, 1970
Helen M. Pitts	Aug. 10, 1907	---
Cecil L. Pitts	Jan. 5, 1903	Aug. 23, 1965
Perry Pitts	Mar. 2, 1883	Dec. 3, 1957
Le Vernia Pitts	May 29, 1884	Jun. 3, 1971
Sarah E. Pitts	Apr. 27, 1854	Jun. 3, 1899

Name	Birth	Death
Blanche C. Pittss	Dec. 2, 1860	Jul. 13, 1889
George Pittss	Nov. 17, 1851	Sep. 18, 1923
Arthur Pitts	Dec. 24, 1884	Mar. 3, 1934
Edith Pitts	Jul. 31, 1886	---
Andrew J. Pitts	Jan. 8, 1907	Dec. 17, 1971
Neta M. Pitts	Feb. 13, 1912	Jan. 9, 1949
Ulysses G. Pitts	Feb. 25, 1868	Jul. 3, 1928
Norma E. Pitts	Dec. 10, 1887	Jan. 4, 1889
Gerald L. Pitts	Jun. 5, 1928	Mar. 30, 1934
Clester T. Pitts	Mar. 23, 1905	Jan. 1, 1966
Fae Pitts	Oct. 17, 1905	---
Thomas Pitts	Apr. 1, 1842	Mar. 3, 1883
Oliver Pitts	Apr. 22, 1878	Apr. 23, 1881
Dena Ward Pitts	Oct. 18, 1881	Oct. 3, 1902
Martha G. Pitts	Mar. 19, 1847	Nov. 24, 1913
Y. J. Pitts	Jun. 10, 1848	Dec. 2, 1924
Carol M. Pitts	Jun. 11, 1853	Oct. 14, 1881
Wm. Newton Pitts	Feb. 10, 1845	Feb. 13, 1940
Anna Pitts	Jul. 23, 1878	Mar. 19, 1902
Henrietta Pitts	Mar. 6, 1870	Jan. 10, 1872
John J. Pitts	Jan. 5, 1847	Dec. 11, 1887
Stella Pitts	Dec. 2, 1891	Feb. 7, 1892
Fayette Pitts	1868	1920
Artency Pitts	1872	1941
Thos. Pitts	1868	1914
Melvina Pitta	1873	1946
Joseph Pitts	Aug. 6, 1899	Aug. 28, 1972
Artie Pitts	1895	1920
Mary E. Pitts	Dec. 24, 1841	Jan. ??, 1875
Charles E. Quick	Dec. 11, 1872	Apr. 21, 1945
Dona A. Quick	Jun. 26, 1888	May 6, 1960
Lyle B. Quick	1935	1938
David F. Quick	1971	1971
Clara Mae Quick	Jul. 31, 1907	Sep. 16, 1978
Elmer Quick	Aug. 7, 1886	Oct. 28, 1968
Henry W. Quick	Mar. 25, 1908	Feb. 27, 1960
Chloe Quick	Nov. 23, 1919	---
Inez R. Quick	Jan. 26, 1917	---
Lindsey A. Quick	Jan. 23, 1913	Jul. 28, 1979
Charles E. Rake	Jul. 21, 1892	Jun. 5, 1981
Oliver Rentfrow	Jan. 23, 1883	Jan. 23, 1883
Elijah L. Reser	Sep. 16, 1871	Apr. 21, 1941

Name	Birth	Death
William F. Reser	Jun. 2, 1869	Feb. 20, 1938
Olie Reser	Jul. 2, 1878	Sep. 24, 1950
Ethel Reser	Nov. 5, 1906	Oct. 8, 1918
Ira Reser	Apr. 12, 1884	Aug. 29, 1957
Lottie Reser	Oct. 15, 1886	Aug. 25, 1968
Alma Reser	Aug. 1, 1901	Aug. 18, 1902
Vergie Reser	Dec. 22, 1899	Aug. 17, 1900
Racy Reser	Jul. 23, 1895	Jul. 6, 1896
Sigel Reser	Sep. 13, 1862	Dec. 16, 1940
Lela Reser	Nov. 11, 1895	Jul. 30, 1896
Elsie Richards	Feb. 25, 1908	---
Archie B. Richards	Nov. 3, 1907	May 7, 1989
Edith G. Richards	Sep. 22, 1905	Aug. 26, 1970
Noah Richards	May 31, 1902	Aug. 20, 1990
Nancy C. Richards	Dec. 27, 1874	May 11, 1968
James C. Richards	Feb. 23, 1870	Jul. 14, 1954
Artie Lee Richards	Dec. 16, 1902	Nov. 4, 1904
George P. Richardson	May 6, 1858	Mar. 11, 1917
Jerusha Richardson	Jun. 4, 1862	Feb. 10, 1924
Icel Pearl Richardson	Oct. 22, 1889	Sep. 19, 1931
Carrie L. Robbins	Apr. 15, 1898	Oct. 18, 1983
Elijah N. Robbins	Sep. 14, 1884	Jul. 5, 1970
Oscar O. Sapp	Feb. 23, 1886	Mar. 8, 1957
Lizzie L. Sapp	Nov. 15, 1891	---
Zella J. Sawyers	Aug. 11, 1906	Mar. 1, 1934
Lorene Shelton	Mar. 6, 1909	---
Oval N. Shelton	Aug. 7, 1905	Jan. 12, 1982
Daniel E. Shelton	Dec. 28, 1870	Mar. 20, 1930
Henrietta Shelton	Oct. 24, 1878	Jun. 13, 1943
Barbara Jane Simmons	Dec. 3, 1955	---
Curtis M. Simmons	Mar. 11, 1896	Dec. 5, 1968
Rhua J. Simmons	Apr. 1, 1904	Jun. 5, 1960
Edward D. Simmons	May 24, 1893	Oct. 10, 1901
Lucy May Smart	Mar. 26, 1905	Dec. 19, 1981
Edwin M. Smith	Mar. 20, 1873	Oct. 19, 1936
E. M. Smith	Jun. 20, 1840	Sep. 3, 1928
Lela Myrl Snow	Mar. 19, 1902	Oct. 1, 1909
Emma Spillman	Jun. 29, 1877	Oct. 21, 1893
E. H. Spillman	1851	1927
William E. Spillman	Sep. 26, 1872	Dec. 15, 1960
Maud M. Spillman	May 17, 1875	Sep. 28, 1966
Mayme Kemper Smillman	Nov. 28, 1901	Jul. 27, 1974

Name	Birth	Death
John T. Spillman	Apr. 26, 1912	---
Marjoir J. Starkey	Jan. 5, 1931	Jan. 6, 1983
Marion F. Starkey	Sep. 4, 1928	---
Amos O. Stout	Jul. 17, 1905	Oct. 27, 1972
Cordelia Stout	Feb. 2, 1866	May 9, 1954
Elijah H. Stout	Jul. 7, 1867	Apr. 30, 1907
John W. Stout	May 22, 1845	May 17, 1913
Isabell Stout	Oct. 2, 1847	Sep. 30, 1888
Margaret E. Stout	Feb. 7, 1874	Jan. 10, 1886
Julia L. Straw	Mar. 8, 1885	Jun. 13, 1905
Marvin Sunderland	Sep. 19, 1857	Mar. 23, 1893
Annis Swanson	Feb. 23, 1904	---
Hilmer J. Swanson	Dec. 15, 18896	Dec. 18, 1972
Wlliam P. Thurman	Mar. 6, 1865	Apr. 1, 1940
Sarah A. Thurman	Jul. 4, 1869	Aug. 15, 1957
John W. Triggs	Nov. 16, 1869	Apr. 12, 1956
Mima May Tucker	Aug. 27, 1911	Jul. 8, 1974
Louis Nelson Tucker	Nov. 8, 1911	---
John W. Tucker	Jan. 30, 1848	Mar. 26, 1869
J. Orlie Vaughn	Aug. 6, 1890	Sep. 11, 1946
Alma Vaughn	Jul. 28, 1891	Apr. 6, 1978
Frank R. Wheeler	1895	1920
Roy Williams	Jul. 24, 1886	Sep. 7, 1935
Bertha B. Williams	Jan. 7, 1888	Jun. 24, 1974
Jordan W. Williams	Jul. 23, 1879	May 3, 1951
Vannia Williams	Apr. 8, 1882	May 16, 1969
Betty Jean Williams	1922	1988
Chester Williams	1909	---
Ernest Williamson	Jan. 14, 1880	Sep. 27, 1958
Lillie Williamson	Sep. 23, 1889	Jul. 17, 1986
Vernia Winfrey	Aug. 22, 1891	Mar. 20, 1958
Richard L. Winfrey	Sep. 11, 1880	Mar. 30, 1968
Alma Winfrey	Nov. 28, 1908	---
Luther B. Winfrey	Mar. 1, 1890	Dec. 18, 1897
Earl Winfrey	Oct. 8, 1895	Mar. 29, 1896
Jasper N. Winfrey	Feb. ??, 1850	Jan. 21, 1931
Rebecca J. Winfrey	Dec. 8, 1857	Apr. 29, 1934

<u>Maries County, Missouri, Will of William S. Thompson, Filed January 27, 1892</u>

In the name of God, Amen. I, William S. Thompson, of Boone Township, in Maries County Missouri, being of sound mind and memory, and considering the uncertainty of life, do hereby make, ordain, publish, and declare this to be my last will and testament; that is to say: First After all my lawful debits are paid and discharged, which are few, and the expenses of my funeral shall have been paid, the residue of my estate I give, devise, bequeath, and dispose of as follows, to-wit: To my son F. J. Thompson and my daughter Mary V. Thompson, to share and share a like, the following described Real Estate, situate, in Maries County Missouri, as follows to-wit: The South half of the South East quarter of section thirty, and the North East quarter of section thirty one and the North West quarter of the South East quarter of section thirty one and the North half of the North West quarter of section thirty one and the South East quarter of the North West quarter of Section Thirty one all in township forty one of Range Eleven west. Also seven acres more or less, as follow, commencing at the North corner of Section thirty six township forty one range twelve, Thence running South forty eight rods and eighteen links, thence West in a right angle twenty rods and seventeen links, thence north in a right angle forty eight rods and eighteen links, thence in an easternly direction twenty rods and seventeen links, and containing seven acres more or less, and situate in Miller County Missouri, said above and forgiving real estate contains in all four hundred and seven acres more or less.

Second to my daughter Peggy Jane, wife of John H. West, and to the heirs of her body now living, or that may here after be born, I give, bequeath and devise the following described real estate, situate in Maries County Missouri, to-wit: the northeast quarter of the southeast quarter of section thirty also the North half of the South West quarter of section Twenty nine,also, the southeast quarter of the northnest quarter of section twenty nine, also the SouthWest Quarter of the North East quarter of section Twenty nine, all in Township Forty one, of Range Eleven west and containing in all Two hundred acres more or less.

Third To my daughter Nancy B., wife of W. A. West, I give and bequeath the sum of Five Dollars and no more.

Fourth To my son, F. J. Thompson, I give and bequeath, one horse mule and two cows, also one third of all the sheep and hogs that are owned by me at the time of my death, also one set of blacksmith tools, now owned by me, also one third part of all farming implements, that may be on hand at the time of my death.

Fifth To my son in law, John H. West. I give and bequeath one yellow on clay bank horse about nine years old.

Sixth To my daughter Mary V. Thompson. I give and bequeath, one deep bay horse, with white spot in forehead, and about three years old past, Also one mare mule going on three years of age and about 13 1/2 hands high, and mouse colored, Also two cows, and one third of all the sheep and hogs owned by me at the time of my death, Also one third of all the farm implements and machinery that may be on hand and owned by me at the time of my death.

Seventh To my daughter Peggy Jane, wife of John H. West I give and bequeath, one two year old heifer and two calves, Also one third of all the sheep and hogs and farm implements and machinery that may be owned by me at the time of my death.

Eighth To my grand-daughter Rosey Lee West. I give and bequeath one heifer calf one year old past. Also one bed and bedding and one bedsted.

Ninth To my son F. J. Thompson, Mary V. Thompson and Peggy Jane, wife of John H. West, I give and bequeath one two horse wagon, Also one log wagon, and it is my request that they keep said wagons and use the same in common.

Tenth To my son, F. J. Thompson, Mary V. Thompson and Peggy Jane, wife of John H. West, I give and bequeath all my personal property not herein before mentioned, of every kind and description, including notes and evidences of debt of every character and kind what so ever, that may be in my possession, or be owning to me at the time of my death, which said personal property shall be equally divided between my son F. J. Thompson, my daughter Mary V. Thompson and Peggy Jane, wife of John H. West.

Eleventh To my daughter Mary V. Thompson I give and bequeath all of my house hold and kitchen furniture including beds and bedding and bed steds, except that heretofore give to my grand-daughter Rosa Lee West.

And I do hereby make, constitute and appoint Gib Crismon, to be Executor of this my last will and testament.

In witness whereof I have hereunto subscribed my name and affixed my seal this twenty second day of December 1891

William S. Thompson.

The above instrument was subscribed by the above named William S. Thompson in our presence, and acknowledged by him to each of us; and at the same time he published and declared the said instrument so subscribed to be his last will and testament, and we at the testator's request and in his presence, have signed our names as witnesses thereto, and written opposite our names our respective paces of residence.

Jackson J. Holmes, St. Thomas; James B. Holmes, St. Thomas; Filed this Jan. 27, 1892, John O. Holmes, Probate Judge

SURNAME INDEX

ABBENHAUS, 153
ABBOT, 79
ABBOTT, 79 154
ABERNATHY, 154 179
ABRAMS, 40
ADAMS, 21 24 28-29 32-33 41-42 54-56 79 154
ADAMSON, 80
ADARE, 135
ADDISON, 56
ADIER, 130
ADKINS, 12 29
ADKISSON, 140
ADOLPH, 182
AGNEW, 154
AGY, 54
AINSWORTH, 54-55
AKE, 134
AKEY, 56
ALBERT, 23 43 50
ALBIN, 56
ALDRIDGE, 80 129
ALEXANDER, 38 54 56 80 124
ALKIRE, 9
ALLAN, 56
ALLCORN, 28
ALLEMAN, 56

ALLEN, 12 21-22 27 29 37 40 47-48 55 80 146 150 152-154
ALLEY, 132-133 154
ALLGOOD, 56
ALLISON, 37 39
ALLMON, 137
ALLYN, 56
ALMOND, 80
ALY, 154
AMBERS, 80
AMES, 155
AMIS, 184
AMISS, 184
AMMONS, 132
AMOS, 155
AMRHEIN, 155
AMSDEN, 32 49
AMSTUTZ, 155
ANDERS, 80 155
ANDERSON, 12 16-17 29 36 53 55-56 65 80 85 132 140-141 146 149 155 179
ANDREOTTA, 155
ANDRESEN, 155
ANDREW, 56
ANDREWS, 80 133-134
ANEMA, 56

ANGEL, 23 27
ANGERBACK, 179
ANGIE, 137
ANGLE, 27 37-38 134-135
ANKROM, 140
ANNO, 80
ANSELL, 124
ANSON, 179
ANSPACH, 155
APPLEMAN, 140-141
APPLING, 183
ARCHER, 80 121
ARMOR, 155
ARMSTRONG, 54 56 177 183
ARNOLD, 56 151 153 155
ARTHUR, 56
ARTHURS, 184
ARTMAN, 80 174
ARYGLE, 10
ASBERRY, 18 20 29 45-46
ASBROOK, 153
ASBURY, 155
ASH, 146
ASHBY, 80 177
ASHCRAFT, 135
ASHENHURST, 56
ASHER, 12-14 17-19 30 42 80
ASHFORD, 155
ASHMORE, 56
ASHWORTH, 80
ASKISSON, 140
ASPEY, 155
ASQUITH, 156
ASSING, 56
ATKINS, 49 80
ATKINSON, 122-123
ATKISON, 156
AULDRIDGE, 55
AUSTERMANN, 156
AUSTIN, 80 156 182
AYER, 156
AYERS, 1 156
BABB, 25 146
BABER, 80
BABOCK, 80

BACAN, 56
BACKY, 156
BACON, 56
BADGER, 156
BAGLEY, 156
BAILEY, 31 52 54 80 176 184
BAIRD, 53 55
BAITY, 183
BAKE, 184
BAKER, 11 14 18 20-21 26 29 35 40
    45-46 52 56 80 125-126 130-131
    134-135 151 156 174
BALCOM, 157
BALDRIDGE, 178
BALDWIN, 57 80
BALES, 57 78 128
BALEY, 80
BALKE, 38
BALL, 42 48 57 142
BALLARD, 80 134 183
BALLAY, 157
BALLINGER, 138
BAMVAKAIS, 157
BANCROFT, 157
BANE, 80
BANKS, 146
BANTA, 80
BARBER, 18 50 54 57 157
BARCLAY, 177
BARDSLEY, 44 57
BARFIELD, 32
BARHAM, 157
BARKER, 22 54 57 80 133 157
BARLOW, 50
BARNARD, 150 153
BARNES, 11 13 20-21 28 32-34 37
    43-46 48-51 53 55 57 80 121 139
    150 157 180 184-185
BARNETT, 157
BARON, 34
BARRETT, 57 145
BARRON, 182
BARTELL, 157
BARTELS, 57
BARTHOLOME, 57`

BARTLE, 157
BARTLETT, 18 57
BARTLEY, 178
BARTON, 12-14 17-19 28 34 37-38 44 48 51-52 57 157
BASNETT, 157
BASS, 146
BAST, 152
BASTION, 185
BATEMAN, 157
BATES, 30 80 132 146 149 158
BATESEL, 158
BATTS, 158
BAUER, 158
BAUGHMAN, 129
BAUM, 158
BAUMAN, 80
BAX, 158
BAXTER, 21 27 80 158 185
BAY, 11 28 30 42 44 136
BAYNE, 121
BEAN, 80 158
BEARD, 23-24
BEARDEN, 27
BEASLEY, 53 146
BEASLY, 80
BEATTY, 9
BEAUMONT, 80
BEAVER, 133
BECK, 16 30 132
BECKHAM, 80
BECKMAN, 184
BECKMANN, 158
BEDWELL, 80
BEELER, 9-10 53 158
BEERS, 158
BEERY, 82
BEESLEY, 158
BEESON, 153
BEGLE, 82
BEHNKE, 57
BEHRENS, 158
BEILE, 159
BEISER, 57
BEISHLINE, 185

BELCHER, 82
BELINGE, 159
BELL, 19 21 47 57 82 159 181
BELLE, 38
BELLER, 125
BELTZ, 159
BELZINSKY, 143
BEMBOOM, 159
BENINGTON, 53
BENNER, 82
BENNETT, 53 82 159
BENSON, 26 57
BENTON, 159 180
BERGSTRESSER, 174
BERGSTROM, 57
BERHOWE, 159
BERNARD, 55
BERNAW, 55
BERNER, 57
BERRY, 26 56 82 146 159
BERTRAM, 183 185
BERTWINGER, 30
BESCO, 57
BESHEER, 179
BESS, 132
BEST, 53 55 82
BETEBENNER, 159
BETTS, 82 153
BEZLEY, 132
BEZOLD, 159
BICKETT, 121
BICKFORD, 2
BICKLE, 54
BIEDENBACH, 57
BIEGER, 2
BIFFLE, 38
BIGGERSTAFF, 57
BIGGS, 82 159
BIGLER, 185
BIGLIENI, 159
BIGUS, 121
BILLINGS, 82
BINGHAM, 82
BINGLEY, 82
BINGMAM, 26

BIONDO, 160
BIRCH, 82
BIRD, 31
BIRDWELL, 47
BISER, 150 153
BISHOP, 57 160
BITTLEMAN, 82
BITZ, 54
BJORKBACK, 121
BLACK, 12-13 17-18 30-31 39 43-45 47-48 50-51 55 145
BLACKFORD, 174
BLACKMAN, 136
BLACKSTEN, 160
BLACKWELL, 33 82 130 152-153
BLAHA, 57
BLAIR, 57 160
BLAKE, 160
BLAKELY, 82
BLANCHARD, 134
BLANKENBAKER, 146
BLANKENSHIP, 21 31 38 82 128-129 160 174
BLANKINSHIP, 53
BLANTON, 82-83 128-129 160
BLASEY, 57
BLASSIE, 160
BLATT, 57
BLATTEL, 160
BLEDSOE, 54-55
BLENDERMAN, 57
BLESSMAN, 57
BLEVINS, 160
BLICK, 57
BLISS, 160
BLOCK, 83
BLODGETT, 2
BLONIGEN, 57
BLUMER, 57
BLY, 57
BLYTHE, 83
BOARDMAN, 55 83 160
BOATMAN, 160
BOATRIGHT, 38
BOBBITT, 173
BOBO, 160
BOCKEWITZ, 160
BODGER, 57
BOEVER, 161
BOGGS, 37 145 161
BOHALL, 55
BOHARTM, 55
BOHLEN, 57
BOHN, 57
BOHNERT, 25
BOHON, 161
BOIN, 131
BOLINGER, 55 83
BOLLINGER, 83
BOLLMAN, 57
BOLTINGHOUSE, 57
BOND, 45
BONDERER, 161
BONDS, 161
BONE, 13 40 53
BONEY, 185
BONNARENS, 161
BONNELL, 83
BONNER, 128
BONNEY, 49
BONNY, 41
BONO, 161
BOOE, 57
BOON, 83
BOONE, 175
BOOTH, 28 57
BOOTS, 57
BOOZARTH, 83
BORAWSKI, 161
BOROP, 58
BORRUSCH, 58
BOSLEY, 58
BOSTICK, 83
BOSTON, 26 161
BOSWELL, 53-54 161
BOTKIN, 21 27
BOTKINS, 26 51
BOTTS, 146
BOULWARE, 83
BOUNDS, 13

BOUR, 55
BOURNE, 161
BOUTON, 83
BOW, 54
BOWDEN, 55
BOWDERN, 161
BOWEN, 13 18-19 30 34 83 134 185
BOWER, 34
BOWERE, 22
BOWERS, 20-21 27 83 183
BOWING, 55
BOWLES, 28 32 48
BOWLIN, 36 83
BOWMAN, 10 83 152 161
BOWNE, 139-140
BOX, 131-132
BOYD, 13 29 42 51 55 146 161
BOYDSTON, 83
BOYER, 26 55 131-132 134-136 162
BOYLES, 162
BOZIKIS, 162
BRACY, 58
BRADBURY, 83 153
BRADEN, 83 162
BRADEY, 53
BRADLEY, 83 146 162
BRADSHAW, 84 131 134
BRADY, 84
BRAKEFIELD, 135
BRAME, 130-131 133-134 136
BRAMHALL, 136
BRANDOM, 162
BRANDT, 58
BRANHAM, 185
BRANK, 153
BRANNOCK, 54
BRANNON, 185
BRANSON, 124 162
BRASFIELD, 84
BRASHEARS, 162
BRASSFIELD, 124-125
BRATCHER, 135
BRAWLEY, 33 39-40 43-44 47 49-50
BRECKENFELDER, 58

BREDELL, 152
BREEDING, 162
BRENNAN, 162
BRENT, 180
BRENTANO, 153
BRESHEARS, 185
BRETZ, 84
BREWER, 34 39-40 42 44-45 52 128 131
BRIDGES, 58 134 186
BRIDGEWATER, 54
BRIDWELL, 58
BRIGGS, 146 186
BRIGHT, 162
BRIGHTWELL, 84
BRILL, 84
BRINK, 84 121
BRINKMANN, 58
BRISCOE, 53 58
BRITTON, 54
BROADHEAD, 53
BROADHURST, 84
BROCK, 84 142 162
BROCKMAN, 163
BRONOUGH, 55
BROOKES, 153
BROOKS, 22 24 29 31-32 35 39 41 44 47 52 84 151-152 163
BROTHERTON, 132
BROTT, 58
BROUGHTON, 146
BROWN, 9 12-13 26 29 31 37 40 42 44-45 47-48 50 54-55 58 84-85 126-127 131-132 137 146 163 183 186
BROWNING, 85
BRUCE, 58 177
BRUDAN, 36
BRUDEN, 16
BRUNER, 58
BRUNTS, 85
BRUSH, 58
BRUSTER, 22
BRUTON, 54 85 163
BRYAN, 56 58 85 126

BRYANT, 9 85 121
BRZEUKWICZ, 143
BUCHANAN, 9 53 55 85 133
BUCHANNAN, 137
BUCHER, 32-33 44
BUCKNER, 38 42 55 146 163
BUCSTEN, 34
BUCY, 133-134
BUDZINSKI, 164
BUELL, 164
BUERGER, 143
BUERNK, 144
BUFF, 85
BUFFINGTON, 28 164
BUFORD, 48 50
BULLERDICK, 164
BULLOCK, 85
BUMGARDNER, 135
BUMGARNER, 133
BUMILLER, 164
BUNCH, 164
BUNDY, 45
BUNEMANN, 85
BUNKER, 58
BUNTION, 164
BUNYARD, 22 45
BURCH, 58
BURDEN, 136
BURFORD, 164
BURGE, 85
BURGEN, 85
BURGER, 178
BURGESS, 1 55 85
BURKE, 49 58 85
BURKS, 164
BURNES, 55 85
BURNETT, 164
BURNEVICK, 10
BURNHAM, 23 28 135
BURNS, 1 58 85 130 164
BURRETT, 10
BURRIS, 135
BURROW, 164
BURRUANO, 165
BURRUS, 58

BUSBY, 58 85
BUSCH, 165
BUSH, 16 53 137 165 186
BUSHNELL, 58
BUSKIRK, 175
BUSTER, 85
BUTCHER, 11 58 85
BUTLER, 58 85 139 152 165 176
BUTMAN, 58
BUTRICK, 85
BUTTERMORE, 55
BUTTS, 86 137
BYERS, 55 58
BYRD, 31 51 86 165
BYWATER, 58
BYWATERS, 86
CABNESS, 55
CABRINI, 165
CADY, 165
CAFFERY, 165
CAGLEY, 165
CAHAIL, 58
CAHALL, 165
CAIN, 86 165
CALDWELL, 165
CALIHAN, 55
CALL, 137
CALLAHAN, 16 30 36 46 54 165
CALLIHAN, 166
CALLIWAY, 53-54
CALMESE, 166
CALVERT, 58 86
CAMDEN, 13 19 36 42 53 86
CAMEL, 23
CAMERON, 55 152
CAMPBEL, 186
CAMPBELL, 1 13 26 34 37 47 58 78
  86 166 174 176 179 186
CANDRL, 166
CANE, 86
CANNON, 86 125
CANTON, 137
CAPLAN, 166
CAR, 33
CARDER, 58

CAREY, 131
CARGILL, 180
CARLE, 53
CARLISLE, 54
CARLSON, 59
CARLYLE, 166
CARNAHAN, 25
CARNETT, 166
CARNEY, 55
CARNOSKE, 166
CAROL, 54
CARPENTER, 20 22-23 86 121 136
CARR, 59 86
CARRET, 55
CARRICO, 166
CARROLL, 59 166
CARSON, 59 86 136 166
CARTER, 9 14 17 24-29 45 53 55 59 86 131-134 137 167 176
CARTERAND, 47
CARTIER, 167
CARTY, 14 18 21-22 29 32-33 37 41 52
CARVER, 167 174
CARY, 86
CASE, 134
CASEBOLT, 167
CASEY, 20 33 54 146
CASH, 167
CASHINES, 55
CASINGER, 132
CASON, 167
CASSMEYER, 167
CASTEEL, 44
CASTILE, 52
CATES, 131 134
CATLETT, 86
CAUGHREN, 55
CAULLEY, 19 47
CAUSS, 135
CAVANAGH, 15
CAVANAUGH, 122
CAVE, 86
CAVENDER, 24
CAVESY, 52

CAVIN, 86
CAVNER, 59
CAWLEY, 167
CAY, 19
CEARNES, 86
CECIL, 59
CGURWELL, 94
CHAMBERLIN, 31
CHAMBERS, 53 167
CHAMERLAIN, 42
CHAMPION, 167
CHANBERS, 131
CHANCE, 32-33 52 54 59 86-87
CHANDLER, 59 87 145-147 149 167
CHANEY, 37 54 186
CHANNEL, 167
CHANSON, 135
CHAPMAN, 29 51 87
CHAPPELL, 41 167 180
CHARLTON, 37 39 54
CHASHINER, 55
CHASTEEN, 168
CHEATHAM, 55
CHENEY, 45
CHERRY, 168
CHESHIRE, 168
CHESTOCK, 59
CHILD, 168
CHILDERS, 168
CHILDRESS, 87 168
CHILOTE, 59
CHILTON, 20 24 26 46 55 132 135-137
CHINN, 59 87
CHIPLEY, 54
CHITTWOOD, 168
CHITWOOD, 11 15-16 20-21 23 25-27 33 35-36 39 45 48 53 168
CHORLINS, 168
CHRISMAN, 124 127
CHRIST, 54
CHRISTENSEN, 59 168
CHRISTISON, 87
CHRISTOFFERSON, 168
CHRISTY, 87

CHRONISTER, 15 39
CIESON, 85
CIMP, 136
CLAGGETT, 168
CLAPP, 59
CLARK, 24 37 42 46 51 53-54 59 87 128 132-133 135 168 186
CLARKE, 59 87
CLARKSON, 49 147 169
CLASBY, 181
CLASPILL, 169
CLAVERIE, 169
CLAXTON, 169
CLAY, 54-55 87 132 169
CLAYBROOK, 87
CLAYTON, 59 169
CLEAVER, 169
CLEAY, 55
CLEMENS, 87
CLEMENTS, 13 55
CLEMMON, 169
CLEMONS, 128
CLENDENNIN, 151 153
CLEVE, 169
CLIBURN, 136
CLIFTON, 169
CLINE, 87 186
CLINKEN, Beard 87
CLINKENBEARD, 87
CLINTON, 31 46 49
CLOINGER, 132
CLONINGER, 131 133
CLOUD, 53
CLOUGH, 147
CLOUSE, 48
CLOYED, 186
CLUBBS, 169
CLUSTER, 123
COAKLEY, 59 87
COATES, 59 183
COBB, 59 169
COCHRANE, 59
COCKRILL, 87
CODRELL, 53
COFFEE, 135
COFFMAN, 169
COHN, 39
COIL, 13 38 40 44 135
COLBERT, 169
COLCLASURE, 124
COLE, 25 40 42 59 87 136
COLEE, 59
COLEMAN, 22 53 87 132-133 137 170 182
COLINS, 132
COLLERD, 137
COLLETT, 87
COLLEY, 28 87
COLLINS, 10 47 87 125 128 134 152 170 175-176
COLLIT, 87
COLLMAN, 37
COLLYOUT, 33
COLMAN, 131
COLSTON, 186
COLVIN, 59
COLYOTT, 39
COLYOUTT, 18
COMBS, 170
COMLEY, 179
COMSTOCK, 151 153
CONARD, 59
CONAWAY, 87
CONDRAY, 131
CONDREY, 132 135
CONDRY, 131 137
CONEY, 176
CONGDON, 59
CONGER, 182
CONLEY, 13 18-19 186
CONLIN, 87
CONNER, 170
CONOWAY, 33
CONRAD, 59
CONWAY, 15 17 27 30-31 35-36 38 49 176
CONWELL, 87
COOK, 13-14 25 40 49 53 55 59 88 136 170
COON, 186

COONS, 88
COOPER, 55 59 88 170
COPE, 171
COPELAND, 11 18 20-24 26-27 37 40 43 46 135 171
COPELIN, 129
CORA, 14
CORBIN, 88
CORCRANE, 88
CORDELL, 53
CORDIA, 171
CORLAY, 1
CORNMAN, 53
CORNWELL, 59
CORP, 171
CORTOR, 171
CORUCH, 153
COSBY, 53
COSGROVE, 25
COSTELOW, 186
COTHER, 88
COTTRELL, 153
COUCH, 59 171
COULT, 171
COUNTS, 15-16 35-36 45 49 52 137
COURIER, 186
COURTNET, 59
COURTRIGHT, 59
COUTSELL, 134
COVIAN, 1 De Jesu Solares 1
COWAN, 21 51
COWEN, 9 132 171
COWIN, 21 26 132-134
COWMAN, 60
COWSERT, 171
COX, 15 35 39 49 60 88 130 133 171
COXEY, 5
COYOE, 60
COZINE, 30
COZMBS, 170
CRABTREE, 135 171
CRACRAFT, 88
CRADDICK, 186
CRAFT, 88
CRAGUE, 20

CRAIG, 171
CRAIGHEAD, 172
CRAMER, 172
CRANDELL, 137
CRANE, 172
CRANGLE, 152
CRANK, 125
CRAWFORD, 60 151 153 172
CRAWMER, 60
CRAYMON, 127
CREAMER, 60
CREED, 186
CREWS, 122-123
CRISMON, 196
CRITES, 88 130-132 137
CRITESER, 54
CRITTENDEN, 130
CROACH, 88
CROCKRAN, 172
CROLLEY, 132
CROMER, 38
CRONER, 22
CRONIN, 60
CRONISTER, 131
CROOK, 132 172
CROSBY, 172 179
CROSKEY, 60
CROSS, 60 172
CROSSER, 60
CROSSLAND, 30 38
CROTTY, 55
CROUCH, 78
CROUSE, 60 88
CROW, 133 173
CROWBARGER, 88
CROWDER, 173
CROWLEY, 16-17
CROWNOVER, 16 29 37 51
CROZIER, 37
CRUMBAUGH, 147
CUEASEY, 19
CULBRETH, 60
CULLERS, 173
CULVER, 151 153
CUMMINGS, 121

CUNDIFF, 32
CUNNINGHAM, 2 55 60 88 147 173
CUPPLES, 152
CURETON, 173
CURRIER, 173
CURRY, 60 173
CUSINGER, 135
CUTBIRTH, 173
DACE, 52
DAGNER, 21
DALE, 88
DALLAS, 55
DALTON, 21
DANIEL, 47 175
DANIELS, 21 88
DANIELSON, 60
DANSKIN, 60
DARBY, 186-187 189
DARDEN, 50
DARLING, 120
DASHER, 55
DAUGHERTY, 9 134
DAVENPORT, 60
DAVICE, 131
DAVIDSON, 35 49 52 55 88-89
DAVINSKI, 142
DAVIS, 15 20-21 28 33 35 46 49 51
  53-55 60 89 125 133-134 174
  178-180 184 187
DAVISE, 132
DAWES, 178
DAWSON, 39 43 54 89 133-136
DAY, 136-137
DEAN, 89
DEARING, 22 43
DEARMONT, 182
DEBS, 7
DECKER, 47 50 60
DEEM, 52
DEER, 178
DEFIGH, 140
DEFORD, 60
DEGEN, 60
DEHART, 187
DEJARMATT, 180

DELILA, 122
DENEKAS, 60
DENHAM, 27
DENHART, 60
DENISON, 28 136
DENNING, 60
DENNIS, 19
DENNISON, 19 32 34 40 42
DENNON, 136
DENTON, 55 60
DENVER, 89
DERIN, 16
DERKIN, 176
DERRIBERRY, 89
DERSHAN, 26
DESPAIN, 136
DESTAABLIER, 153
DETERS, 60
DETLEFSEN, 60
DEVIER, 147
DEVRIES, 60
DEWEESE, 187
DEWITT, 60
DIAL, 136
DICAS, 13
DICKEY, 60
DICKSON, 20 26 34 43-45 48
DIESTER, 89
DILDINE, 132
DILL, 20 23 27-28
DILLARD, 15 35-36 46
DILLER, 60
DILLERD, 36
DILLION, 123
DILLON, 123
DINGES, 55
DINGHAM, 121
DINKENS, 13 20
DINWIDDIE, 147
DINWIDEY, 137
DINWOODY, 137
DISKILL, 61
DITTEMORE, 11
DIX, 60 89
DIXON, 24 89

DOBBINS, 29 41 53
DOBRZYNISKI, 144
DOBSON, 60
DOBYNS, 1 180
DODGE, 145 149 152
DODSON, 41-42 46 89 178
DOEGE, 60
DOGGETT, 89
DOHRING, 138
DOLBOW, 120
DOLLAR, 133
DOLLINS, 89
DONIGAN, 132
DONNELLY, 54 182
DOOLEY, 55
DORAN, 147
DORLAND, 89
DORRIS, 26 78 89
DORRISS, 89
DORSETT, 120 148 150
DORTON, 26
DOTSEY, 55
DOUGHERTY, 89 179
DOUGLASS, 89
DOWDALL, 60
DOWNEY, 54 89
DOWNING, 60 89
DOWNS, 61
DOYLE, 61 89
DRAIS, 89
DRAKE, 34
DRENNON, 90
DREW, 90
DREWS, 61
DRIVER, 61
DROYER, 54
DRUM, 90
DRURN, 90
DRURY, 1 90
DUDLEY, 61
DUGGAN, 29
DUGGER, 32
DUGLAS, 13 55
DUN, 55
DUNAGAN, 90

DUNCAN, 11 24 26 53-54 61 90 148
DUNE, 19
DUNHAM, 152
DUNIGAN, 22
DUNIGIN, 23
DUNKLIN, 24
DUNLAP, 90
DUNN, 12 19 40 45 49 55 61
DUNNAGAN, 19 22
DUNNIGAN, 40
DURBIN, 90
DUREE, 47
DURHAM, 90 175
DURNING, 90
DURRETT, 90
DUTTON, 61
DUUNIGAN, 90
DWYER, 55 120
DYE, 90 127
DYER, 61 90 151
DYRE, 30
DYSART, 139
EADS, 22 37 90
EARLS, 31
EARLY, 90
EASMAN, 54
EASTBURN, 90
EATON, 43 90 136 187
ECK, 61
ECKLEY, 139
EDAMS, 37
EDDY, 61
EDEN, 61
EDGAR, 61
EDGELL, 151
EDINGTON, 135 137
EDMONDS, 14-16 20 33 39 45-46 61 136
EDMONS, 14
EDMONSON, 53
EDMUNDS, 122
EDMUNDSON, 90
EDWARDS, 61 90 133 151 153
EHLERT, 61
EHRIG, 61

EHRSIER, 90
EICKELBERG, 61
EILER, 90
EIVANS, 36
ELDER, 51 90
ELDRIDGE, 90
ELINGTON, 25
ELLEY, 90
ELLFRITT, 90
ELLINGTON, 90 136
ELLIOT, 14
ELLIOTT, 61 90
ELLIS, 21 53 90 127 132-133 135 145 148 183 187
ELLSWORTH, 90
ELMORE, 55
EMBRY, 90
EMERSON, 61
EMERY, 137
EMHOFF, 128
EMMONS, 177
EMRY, 134
ENGLAND, 136
ENGLISH, 90
ENTEMANN, 136
ERICKSON, 61
ESTEP, 30-31 47
ESTES, 44 122-123
ESTILL, 90
EVANS, 44 48-49 53 61 90 182
EWINGS, 90
EXCKLEY, 139
EYLER, 90
FACKERT, 121
FAGGA, 131
FAIRMAN, 61
FANCHER, 39
FANNING, 92
FARLEY, 51 90
FARMER, 55 90 177
FARNSWORTH, 90
FARRELL, 30
FARRIS, 14 17 23 26 52 78 92
FARRISS, 49
FAUBION, 92

FAULKENBERRY, 13 41 46 50
FAUST, 61
FE, 39
FEARS, 22 33 49
FEATHERGILL, 178
FEDDER, 14
FELLING, 78
FENIMORE, 61
FENNO, 121
FENTON, 54-55
FERGUSON, 61 92 121 179
FERGUSSON, 179
FERKING, 10
FERRELL, 27
FERREWLD, 11
FERSTL, 61
FICKLE, 92
FIDLER, 53
FIELD, 92
FILLING, 129
FILLMORE, 36
FINCH, 92
FINDLEY, 92
FINELY, 54-55
FINLEY, 92
FINNESTEAD, 61
FISHBURN, 61
FISHER, 61 135 142 148 187
FITCH, 141
FITTS, 21 33
FITZ, 50
FITZGERALD, 12 23 43-44 48 55 121
FLACK, 92
FLANAGAN, 120
FLANARY, 92
FLANNERY, 92
FLEEK, 10
FLEMANS, 92
FLEMING, 53-54 92 136 148 179
FLETCHER, 61
FLIPPO, 22
FLORA, 61
FLOYD, 187-188
FLYNN, 2 184

FOLLETT, 2
FOOT, 174
FOOTE, 61
FORBES, 61 92
FORBION, 92
FORBS, 54
FORD, 20 35 43 61 92
FOREAKER, 141
FOREE, 53
FORGASON, 36
FORREST, 92
FORSYTHE, 151 153
FORTNER, 19
FORTSCH, 61
FORTUNE, 21-22
FOSMIRE, 61
FOSTER, 13 19 44 54-55 92 124 153
FOUGHTY, 62
FOWLER, 54 129-130 188
FOX, 11 52 62 92
FOY, 62
FRAKES, 54
FRANANO, 121
FRANCIS, 41 62 92
FRANK, 62
FRANTZ, 62
FRAZELL, 2
FRAZIER, 53 55 92 134-135 137 188
FREDERICK, 62
FREDRICK, 131
FREELAND, 93
FREEMAN, 27 31 37 54 62 93 134
FREEZE, 25 47
FRESH, 93
FRIDAY, 62
FRIESE, 62
FRISTO, 56
FRIZZELL, 2
FRUSH, 62
FRY, 43 62 93
FRYE, 16
FRYER, 62
FUGATE, 188
FUGATT, 93
FULLER, 62 134

FULLINGTON, 131 174
FULTON, 93
FULTS, 62
FURGERSON, 132
FURNAS, 62
FURNESS, 78
GACKE, 62
GAINES, 93
GAINS, 93
GALBERT, 93
GALIAN, 52
GALLAHER, 12 14 21 41
GALLANT, 62
GALLEMORE, 181
GALT, 62
GAMBLE, 62 93 151 153
GANES, 132
GANN, 93
GANNT, 153
GANT, 30 41-42 44 183
GANTT, 151
GARDINER, 54-55 93 181
GARDNER, 62 132 146 148 150
GARFIELD, 62
GARGES, 93
GARGUS, 188
GARIGAN, 55
GARLAND, 153
GARNER, 62 148 180
GARNETT, 145 148
GARRETT, 180
GARTIN, 93
GARVIN, 62 122
GASKIN, 21
GASTEN, 11
GASTON, 42
GATES, 55 62
GAUSS, 152
GAYER, 93
GENTRY, 35 93 125 150
GEORGE, 11 41 44 46 182
GERBERLING, 62
GIBBONS, 55
GIBBS, 16 62 132
GIBSON, 93 183

GILBRAITH, 132-133
GILBRITH, 131
GILES, 131 133
GILHAM, 126
GILKERSON, 43
GILL, 55 93
GILLET, 54-55 62
GILLIAM, 93 150 153
GILLIS, 93
GILMER, 46 182
GING, 43
GINNINGS, 93
GISH, 62
GISSLER, 142
GIST, 93
GLAS, 133
GLASSCOCK, 93
GLEASON, 62
GLEEN, 188
GLENN, 188
GLIMP, 132
GOBER, 15
GOBLE, 62
GODDELL, 153
GODFREY, 188
GOEDDERTZ, 62
GOEKE, 62
GOELDNER, 62
GOESCHEL, 62
GOFF, 132
GOFORTH, 15 21 28 45 47 52
GOFOURTH, 38
GOGGIN, 12 19 21-22 29-30 34-35
　40-41 46-47 52
GOGGINS, 41
GOING, 48
GOKEY, 62
GOLDEN, 27
GOLSON, 153
GOOD, 53
GOODALL, 62
GOODLANDER, 93
GOODMAN, 26 93
GOODSON, 37
GOODWIN, 135

GOODYEAR, 93
GORDEN, 53
GORDON, 62 94
GORE, 36 52 79
GORSUCH, 62
GOSCH, 54
GOSSETT, 47
GOSZCZYCKI, 143
GOUCHE, 48
GOURLEY, 62
GOVERN, 63
GOWDY, 55
GOWEN, 23
GOWER, 49
GOWIN, 34
GOWING, 63
GRAGG, 94
GRAHAM, 48
GRANT, 55 178
GRAUL, 63
GRAVES, 94 178
GRAY, 63 94 130-131
GRAYHAM, 18-19
GRAYSON, 94
GREAZEL, 63
GREBE, 2
GREELEY, 27
GREEN, 23 53-54 63 94 133-134 136
　152 175
GREENFIELD, 63
GREENWOOD, 63
GREGG, 53 94
GREGORY, 63 94 181
GREOGRY, 148
GRESHAM, 79 130-134
GRIBBLE, 94
GRIFFETH, 53
GRIFFIN, 131
GRIFFITH, 63 94
GRIGG, 23
GRIGGS, 39
GRISHAM, 188
GROFF, 94
GROH, 94
GRONAU, 63

GROOM, 94
GROOMS, 94 121
GROSS, 11 135
GROTH, 63
GROVER, 94
GROVES, 139
GRUCHOW, 63
GUERIN, 3
GUFFEY, 39
GUILLIAMS, 50 94
GUINAN, 63
GUINN, 94 133
GUITAR, 148 150
GULLER, 134
GUMUT, 12
GUNDERSON, 63
GUNN, 131-133 153
GUNNETT, 12 18
GUSE, 63
GUSTION, 54
GUTHERIE, 94
GWIN, 94
GWINN, 94 184
GWYNNE, 3
HACKETT, 94
HACKMAN, 94
HACKWORTH, 18 32 37 39 50
HAGEMMANN, 63
HAGENSICK, 63
HAGUE, 94
HAHAN, 10
HAHN, 10
HAILE, 63
HAINES, 63
HAIR, 53
HALBERT, 188
HALDEMAN, 182
HALE, 50
HALET, 54
HALEY, 26 53
HALK, 30
HALL, 63
HALLEY, 148
HALLFORD, 94-95
HALSEY, 63

HALY, 40
HAMBLIN, 95
HAMERRICK, 136
HAMILTON, 63 95
HAMM, 95
HAMMEL, 3
HAMMON, 173
HAMPTON, 24-26 52 95
HANCOCK, 95 148
HAND, 63
HANDY, 7-8 55
HANGER, 23-25 27 132
HANNAH, 63
HANNINGS, 11
HANSEN, 63
HAR, 38
HARBERG, 63
HARBINSON, 55
HARBISON, 54-55
HARDCASSEL, 36
HARDCASTLE, 15 38
HARDEE, 63
HARDIN, 130 142
HARDY, 151 153 188
HARGROVES, 23
HARLAND, 95
HARMON, 44 63
HARMOND, 95
HARMS, 63
HARMSEN, 63
HARNES, 95
HARNIG, 144
HARRINGTON, 95
HARRIS, 11 63 79 95 145 148 178
HARRISON, 22 25 28 32-34 37-38 44 47 49 55
HARSTICK, 152
HART, 15-16 36 45 55 63 133
HARTLEY, 95 140
HARTMAN, 21 41 47 52 95
HARTRIDGE, 131
HARTWIG, 63
HARVEY, 63
HASTAIN, 188
HASTY, 12-13 42

HATFIELD, 95
HATHAWAY, 125
HATHEWAY, 181
HATRIDGE, 50
HAULKUM, 36
HAUN, 95
HAUSER, 63-64
HAUSERMAN, 120
HAVDAHL, 64
HAWK, 140
HAWKINS, 28 51 130 135
HAWN, 48 95
HAWNER, 95
HAYDEN, 176
HAYDON, 64 95
HAYES, 148 175
HAYNES, 64 79 95
HAYS, 95 178 180
HAYWOOD, 27 53
HAZLELIP, 137
HEAD, 54-55
HEARD, 95
HEARPST, 95
HEATH, 64 95
HEATHER, 64
HEATON, 38
HEBRON, 64
HEDDY, 37
HEDGEPETH, 133
HEDRIC, 33
HEDRICK, 22
HEETON, 20
HEGGEM, 64
HEIDEMANN, 64
HEINMILLER, 64
HEITLAND, 64
HELLUMS, 188
HELM, 48
HELMER, 55
HELPHREY, 64
HELSTEIN, 144
HELTIBIDAL, 45
HELTON, 27
HELVY, 24 46 50 52
HEMESATH, 64

HEMSLEY, 54
HENDERSON, 9 14 54-55 64 95-96
 150-151 153 174
HENDRICKS, 64 96 130
HENDRINSON, 40
HENDRIX, 51-52
HENLEY, 54-55 96
HENLYEY, 54
HENRICH, 64
HENRY, 34 46 64
HENSER, 64
HENSIN, 52
HENSON, 33 136
HEOFF, 153
HERIN, 38
HERMAN, 152
HERMANN, 151 153
HERMANSON, 121
HERNDEN, 96
HERNDON, 53 145
HERRING, 54
HERRON, 96
HERVEY, 53
HESER, 64
HESS, 53 55
HEVENER, 64
HEWETTE, 24
HEWEY, 130
HEWIT, 136
HEWITT, 64
HEYDEN, 54-55
HIATT, 64 96 133
HIBBS, 64
HICKEY, 96
HICKMAN, 53 145 148
HICKS, 15 50 64
HICKSON, 131
HIELSCHER, 139
HIENSON, 30
HIGGENBOTHEN, 38
HIGGINBOTHAM, 188-189
HIGGINS, 96 178
HIGHFIELD, 96
HILDRETH, 64
HILL, 11 31 33 36 50-51 54 96 134

178
HILLIARD, 64
HILLS, 28
HINDS, 121 178
HINES, 27 47 64
HINMAN, 64
HINSEN, 31
HINSHAW, 96
HIPSLEY, 64
HIRONS, 183
HIRSCHLER, 64
HIXON, 133
HOBS, 136
HOBSON, 189
HOCKADAY, 55
HOCKENBERY, 64
HOCKIDY, 54
HODGE, 148
HODGES, 14 17 46 96 128
HODGSON, 64
HOEPER, 64
HOFF, 64
HOFFMAN, 64 148
HOFMASTER, 64
HOGAN, 27
HOGJITT, 54
HOHL, 65
HOKENSON, 65
HOKIT, 96
HOLLAND, 25 27 96 134-135 180
HOLLINGSWORTH, 189
HOLLIS, 136
HOLLIWAW, 53
HOLLIWAY, 55
HOLLOMAN, 38
HOLLOWAY, 123-124
HOLMAN, 96
HOLMES, 18 120 184 196
HOLMS, 30
HOLROYD, 65
HOLSAPPLE, 65
HOLT, 96 189
HOLTON, 96
HOLUB, 65
HOMES, 18 152

HOMEY, 23
HON, 53 55
HONEY, 96
HONN, 55
HOOD, 20
HOOFER, 55
HOOK, 55 65
HOOLEY, 65
HOOPER, 65 96 132 134 189
HOOVER, 65 96
HOPE, 53 134 180
HOPKINS, 49 65 97
HOPPER, 131 148
HORN, 65 121
HORNBACK, 97
HORNBUCKLE, 97
HORSTMEYER, 65
HOSKINS, 24 131 134 136-137
HOSMAN, 65
HOUGH, 65
HOULEHAN, 120
HOUSDEN, 136
HOUSE, 97 132-136
HOUSER, 189
HOUSTON, 97
HOUTS, 97
HOWARD, 55 65 97 179
HOWELL, 26 30 46 178
HOY, 97
HUBBARD, 55 97
HUBBLE, 49
HUDSON, 97
HUETT, 26
HUFF, 33 37 45 65 97 122 136
HUFFAKER, 8
HUGHART, 65
HUGHES, 46 51 65 97 127 175
HUGHEY, 1
HUGHS, 97
HULETT, 177
HULL, 97
HUMPHREYS, 65 97 125 153
HUMSLEY, 54
HUMSTON, 65
HUNDLEY, 97

HUNGERFORD, 97
HUNT, 3 11 29 97 189
HUNTER, 31 40 44 46 52 55 98 128 134
HUNTINGTON, 98
HURLBURT, 98
HURST, 98
HURT, 34
HUSTON, 54
HUTCHESON, 65
HUTCHINGS, 37
HUTCHINSON, 179
HUTSON, 98
HYDE, 145
HYNES, 120
IATAN, 98
IBBOTSON, 142
ILER, 98
IMBODEN, 14 51
INGALLS, 4
INGRAM, 65 130
INMAN, 39 128
INMOM, 52
IRBY, 98
IRONS, 46
IRVIN, 14 53 131-132
IRWIN, 98 177
ISAAC, 98
ISHMAIL, 127
ISON, 55
ITTLE, 53
IVERSON, 65
IVES, 27
JACK, 98
JACKS, 27-28 98
JACKSON, 29 37 47 51 65 98 134
JACOBS, 148
JACOBSON, 120
JALOWICZ, 144
JAMES, 12 98
JAMESON, 148
JAMISON, 41
JANUARY, 14 33 46 51-52
JARRETT, 98
JARROTT, 53
JASPER, 59 98 121
JAYCOX, 34 42
JEFFERS, 98
JEFFERSON, 98
JENISON, 65
JENKINS, 47 128 189
JENNINGS, 17 46
JENS, 21
JERNEGAN, 65
JETER, 98
JETT, 136
JEWELL, 181
JININGS, 32
JOEGENSON, 66
JOHNSON, 13 17 20-21 27-28 30-36 39-40 42-43 45 47-49 51 53-54 65 79 98-99 121 133-134 178-180 182 189
JOHNSTON, 12 15 17 28 40-41 47 51 65 99 148
JOKAM, 106
JONES, 15 25 27-28 52 54 66 99 120 130 132-136 141 189
JOPLIN, 131 134 136
JORDAN, 23 38-39 51 66
JORDEN, 35
JORDGEWITZ, 143
JOY, 53
JOYLES, 131
JUCCO, 136
JURRENS, 66
JUSTICE, 40 99
KAFER, 66
KAISER, 181
KALLENBERGER, 66
KALTENHEUSER, 66
KANE, 66 99
KARG, 66
KASTER, 66
KAUBLE, 66
KAVANAUGH, 142
KAY, 30 99
KAZEE, 54
KEARBY, 132
KEARNEY, 189

KEATHLEY, 16 43-44
KEATING, 121
KEE, 17 29
KEEBAUGH, 142
KEEN, 54-55
KEENAN, 120
KEERAN, 66
KEESY, 66
KEETHLY, 18 52
KEETON, 99
KEITH, 125 127
KELLEHER, 66
KELLER, 66 99
KELLEY, 54-55 99 130-131 133-135 137 189
KELLOGG, 54
KELLY, 10 66 99 177
KELSO, 66
KEMP, 19
KENAN, 66
KENDIG, 179
KENEDY, 53
KENNEDY, 66 99 133-134 153 175-176 181 183
KENNETT, 53
KENSETT, 66
KERN, 66
KERNEN, 66
KERR, 66 99
KESSELS, 66
KESSLER, 100
KESTER, 66 79
KETCHERSIDE, 30
KETELSEN, 66
KETTLE, 66
KEVER, 135
KEY, 100
KEYES, 66
KEYSER, 148
KICENSKI, 189
KICHEL, 38
KIDD, 100
KILLEN, 39
KILLIAN, 66
KIMBALL, 66 176

KIMSEY, 100
KINARD, 130
KINCAID, 100 189
KINCAIDE, 121
KINEFELTER, 67
KING, 35 37 42 44-45 100 124 127 132 136
KINGSBURY, 66
KINNARD, 131-136
KINNEY, 66
KINSER, 66
KINSEY, 100
KIRBY, 3
KIRCHOFF, 66
KIRK, 100 124-125
KIRKPARTICK, 100
KISSIC, 54
KITCHELL, 35 52
KITCHEN, 100 175
KITE, 67
KJOSA, 67
KLEIN, 67
KLINE, 22 51
KLING, 67
KLINGEMAN, 67
KLINGER, 67
KNEPPER, 67
KNESS, 67
KNIGHT, 46 100 189-190
KNITTLE, 174
KNORPP, 55
KNUCKLES, 38
KNUDSVIG, 67
KOCH, 67
KOGER, 120
KOHN, 33
KOONS, 179
KOSKEY, 53
KOSZICKI, 142
KOTTKE, 67
KRACHT, 67
KREITLOW, 67
KRIEGER, 67
KROPP, 142
KRUSE, 67

KUKENDALL, 100
KUNTZ, 31 52
KUTHLY, 18
KUZMANN, 143
KYLE, 100
LACKEY, 141
LACY, 53 100
LAFFERTY, 100 130 132
LAFLIN, 153
LAGROVE, 153
LAHS, 67
LAIR, 176
LAMB, 100
LAMBERT, 130 136
LAMBLEY, 67
LAMERT, 135
LAMKEN, 67
LAMONT, 54
LAMPKIN, 54
LAMPSON, 100
LANCASTER, 100
LANDES, 54
LANE, 4 11 20 22 33-34 46 49 100 131
LANGLEY, 100 136
LANHAM, 100
LANIER, 100
LANK, 100
LANKFORD, 134
LANSBURG, 100
LARAMORE, 32
LARK, 67
LARKIN, 28 46 52 54 100
LARRABEE, 67
LARSON, 19 67
LARUE, 16
LASON, 101
LATAWSCHINSKI, 143
LATHAM, 33
LATHEM, 32
LATHIM, 51
LAUB, 55 67
LAUGHERY, 67
LAURIE, 184
LAUSON, 17
LAUTER, 101
LAVERTY, 101
LAWERENCE, 101
LAWNIN, 150 152-153
LAWRENCE, 67
LAWS, 11 40-41 180
LAWSEN, 16
LAWSON, 13 15 19 31 44 50 101 121 130-131 135
LAY, 16 51-52
LAYN, 28
LAYTON, 101
LEACH, 130 133-135 190
LEACHMAN, 101
LEADBETTER, 11
LEAMING, 67
LEBEAU, 67
LEBETTER, 51
LECOMPTE, 180
LECORNU, 67
LEDBETTER, 14
LEE, 21 31-32 40 47-49 51 67 101 136 175
LEIGHTON, 67
LEITER, 121
LEMMON, 146 148
LEMMONS, 123
LENEBERGER, 49
LENTZ, 67
LEONARD, 30 55 67 101
LEPPERT, 67
LESTER, 11 35 45
LETTINGTON, 67
LEVINGSTONE, 30
LEVORSON, 67
LEWIN, 144
LEWIS, 17 23-25 39-40 42-45 51-53 67 101 136 178
LIBBEY, 67
LICKEN, 127
LIECHTY, 67
LIENTZ, 150
LIGGET, 101
LIGHT, 12 51-52
LIGHTFOOT, 51 190

LIGHTLE, 190
LIMRICK, 180
LINDLEY, 9
LINDLSLEY, 101
LINDSAY, 32 49
LINDSLEY, 101
LINEAS, 101
LINGO, 136
LINK, 101 133
LINKOUS, 129
LINN, 101-102
LINSLEY, 54
LINSON, 18 31
LINTON, 55 68
LINVILLE, 101
LIONBERGER, 151
LIPFRET, 55
LIPPINCOTT, 68
LIPSCOMB, 101
LISTEN, 68
LITLE, 101
LITTLE, 28 53 68 102
LIVINGSTON, 18
LOBACK, 55
LOCKE, 190
LOESCHE, 68
LOFLAND, 55
LOFTIS, 179
LOGAN, 53
LOGUE, 102
LOLLAR, 102
LONES, 20
LONESS, 33
LONG, 55 68 102 130 132-133 137 150 153
LONGBOTTOM, 134
LONGMIRE, 142
LOOKABILL, 68
LORD, 129 135
LORENZ, 68
LOUDON, 68
LOUIS, 34
LOVAN, 178-179
LOVE, 47 68 102
LOVELADY, 102

LOVEWELL, 178
LOWDEN, 68
LOWE, 54 102 137
LOWELL, 28
LOWERY, 131
LOWMAN, 68 102
LOWRANCE, 68
LOWREY, 148
LOWRY, 14 136
LOY, 102
LOYD, 102
LUCAS, 128
LUCE, 68
LUDLOW, 102
LUHR, 68
LUMPKIN, 51
LUNDBECK, 102
LUTTA, 130
LUTTRELL, 190
LWIS, 101
LYDDON, 68
LYNCH, 53-55 102 120 150 153
LYNN, 54 102
LYON, 68
LYONS, 10
LYTLE, 102
MABERRY, 33 130-131
MABREY, 132
MABURRY, 43
MACEY, 104
MACHLAN, 68
MACK, 104
MACKEY, 50
MADDEN, 36 39
MADDIN, 39
MAGILL, 104
MAGNESON, 68
MAHAFFEY, 68
MAHAN, 54 68
MAHONY, 54
MAIDEN, 53
MAILLER, 10
MAJOR, 1
MALAND, 132
MALIN, 153

MALIS, 151
MALLETT, 68
MALLONEE, 190
MALLORY, 135
MALLOY, 131
MALON, 104
MALONOWSKI, 144
MALOTT, 104
MANARD, 132
MANK, 50
MANN, 10 16 22-25 27 37 39-40 42-43 45 50 104
MANNY, 153
MANSFIELD, 121
MANUEL, 190
MARBARY, 43
MARCHBANKS, 136
MARCONNET, 49
MARGOLIS, 143
MARIELS, 173
MARKHAM, 104 131
MARKWELL, 104
MARLER, 135
MARLOE, 14
MARLOR, 38
MARLOW, 14
MARNEY, 135
MARR, 104
MARRLER, 18
MARSH, 68 104
MARSHALL, 54 104 120
MARTEN, 29-30
MARTIN, 1 30 33 41 46 48-49 54 68 104 120 147 179 184 190
MARTINSEN, 68
MARTON, 51
MASCHLEWITZ, 143
MASLOWSKY, 144
MASON, 19 21 104-105 147 151
MASSIE, 40 105 134-135
MASTEN, 105
MASTERS, 33 39 105
MASTERSON, 105
MATHER, 68
MATHEWS, 42 53 55

MATHIS, 19 68
MATLOTT, 105
MATNEY, 105
MATSON, 68
MATT, 68
MATTHEWS, 147
MAUDE, 150
MAUK, 135
MAULSBY, 45
MAUPIN, 105 145
MAURER, 54
MAXWELL, 21 68
MAY, 68 105
MAYALL, 68
MAYFIELD, 151 153
MAYHEW, 68
MAYNARD, 105 132
MAYNER, 105 133
MAYO, 54
MAYS, 105
MAZE, 131
MCADOW, 102
MCAFEE, 55 147
MCALESTER, 45
MCALEXANDER, 102
MCALISTER, 24
MCALLISTER, 26
MCANINCH, 53-54 70
MCARTHUR, 54-55
MCAULIFFE, 122
MCBETH, 70
MCCABE, 41
MCCALL, 102 130
MCCANE, 133
MCCANNE, 175
MCCARNEY, 136
MCCART, 70
MCCARTHY, 102
MCCARTY, 102
MCCASKILL, 135
MCCASLIN, 190
MCCAULEP, 133
MCCAULEY, 70
MCCLAIN, 70 102
MCCLELLAND, 70

MCCLETCHEY, 102
MCCLOUD, 36 70
MCCLUEN, 132
MCCLUNEY, 153
MCCLUNG, 23
MCCLUSKEY, 134
MCCOIN, 132
MCCOLL, 122
MCCOMAS, 102-103
MCCONNAHA, 70
MCCORD, 103
MCCORKLE, 103
MCCOWN, 103
MCCOY, 103 190
MCCRACKEN, 103
MCCRARY, 103
MCCREADY, 136
MCCRILL, 70
MCCRON, 103
MCCULLOUGH, 70
MCCUMBER, 70
MCDANELL, 22
MCDANIEL, 103
MCDANIELS, 21
MCDONALD, 26 28 31 52 103 121 135-136
MCDONNEL, 54
MCENTRIE, 29
MCFADDEN, 54
MCFARLAND, 55 70 103
MCGACHAGER, 103
MCGEE, 23 103
MCGHEE, 181
MCGINNIS, 120
MCGLOTHLIN, 14 23 48
MCGOWN, 103
MCGRATH, 55
MCGREGGOR, 103
MCGUIRE, 70 103
MCHENRY, 51
MCKAY, 70
MCKEE, 54 103
MCKEEN, 130 136
MCKEIGHAN, 151-153
MCKERNAN, 120

MCKESSON, 54
MCKIBBIN, 153
MCKING, 134
MCKINNEY, 103 120 131 133 147
MCKINNIS, 12
MCKISSICK, 103
MCLAIN, 103
MCLANE, 70 103
MCLARNEY, 21 48
MCLAUGHLIN, 70
MCLAY, 127
MCLEARNEY, 32
MCLEOD, 70
MCMAHAM, 103
MCMAHAN, 14 121
MCMAHON, 70
MCMANIS, 70
MCMANUS, 103
MCMILLEN, 33 47 104
MCMILLIN, 18
MCMULLEN, 31
MCMULLENS, 52
MCMURRY, 41
MCMURTRY, 55
MCNAIL, 14 16 28-29 34-35 38 45 52
MCNAMARA, 120
MCNATT, 182
MCNEELY, 45 49
MCNEILL, 70
MCNICHOLS, 70
MCNIEL, 70
MCPHERREN, 70
MCPHERRON, 54
MCPHERSON, 104
MCPOLK, 48
MCQUEAN, 104
MCQUITTY, 147 149
MCSHANE, 70
MCSPADDEN, 133
MCSPADEN, 135-136
MCSPADIN, 132
MCTGERT, 70
MCWILLIAMS, 104
MEAD, 32 40

MEADOR, 29 147
MEADOWS, 32 68 130 134-135
MEANS, 68 105
MEDLEN, 41
MEDLIN, 105
MEDOR, 24
MEED, 35
MEEK, 105
MEEKINS, 68
MEESTER, 68
MEINERS, 68
MELOY, 69
MELTON, 105
MELVIN, 69
MENEELY, 69
MEREDITH, 69
MERIDETH, 56 129
MERIFIELD, 54
MERRET, 55
MERRIFIELD, 54
MERRIL, 24
MERRILL, 24 50
MERRIMEN, 69
MERS, 53 55
MESER, 19
MESHWERT, 46
METCALF, 122-123
MEYER, 69 138
MEYERS, 18-19 54
MICHEL, 69
MIDDLETON, 44 52 182
MIERS, 12 18
MILICAN, 134
MILLEA, 69
MILLER, 9 13 23 25 28-29 33 36 38 44 48 53 55 69 105-106 122 174 178 181 190-191
MILLIGAN, 106
MILLS, 13 22-23 34-35 37 39 51 69 136-137
MIMSEY, 190
MINER, 14 19-21 31-32 42 44 47-49 51
MINSHULL, 126
MITCHELL, 18 69 106 136-137 145 147 152
MIX, 176
MIZE, 106
MIZEE, 106
MOBLEY, 106
MODERSKY, 144
MOFFAT, 54
MOGUE, 38
MOMVE, 53
MONN, 69
MONSON, 10 69
MONTAGUE, 69
MONTGOMERY, 12 17 19 29-31 54 69 106 122 181
MOODIE, 69
MOODY, 106
MOON, 130
MOONEY, 15 36 69
MOORE, 13 19-21 32 34 48 50 53-55 69 79 106 130 132
MORAN, 69
MOREHEAD, 147
MORELAND, 106
MORETON, 175
MORGAN, 11 69 106 152
MORIN, 106
MORRIDON, 151
MORRIS, 26 32 48 50 106 122 132
MORRISON, 69 122 153
MORROW, 106
MOSBY, 106
MOSELY, 136
MOSES, 143
MOSHIER, 106
MOSIER, 147
MOSS, 32 49 134 147 150
MOTE, 69
MOTON, 54
MOTZ, 106
MOWER, 106
MOYER, 48 69
MUDD, 152
MULHOLLEN, 69
MULKEY, 106
MULL, 69

MULLANE, 120
MULLEN, 48
MULLIGAN, 18-19 52
MULLIKIN, 50
MULLINS, 16
MULVIHILL, 120
MUNGER, 22 32 34 37 48
MUNKERS, 106
MUNSE, 106-107
MUNSELL, 40
MURCH, 107
MUREY, 21
MURPHY, 69 107 135 149
MURRY, 16 55
MURY, 130
MUSICK, 174
MUTPHY, 107
MYERS, 39-40 43 49 54-55 69 107
MYNATT, 181
MYRICK, 24
NAHANM, 38
NANE, 107
NAPIER, 55
NAPPER, 21
NASH, 15 48
NAUGLE, 176
NAVE, 129
NAYLOR, 107
NEAL, 54 70 130 134
NEAVES, 122
NEEL, 107 135
NEFF, 55
NEILL, 16 36 38
NELSON, 54-55 107 182
NESBIT, 151
NETHERTON, 107
NETHERTOON, 107
NEWBY, 107
NEWCOMB, 107
NEWELL, 47
NEWMAN, 107 147
NEWTON, 23 42
NEYMAN, 53-54
NICHELSON, 54
NICHOLS, 56 70 107 124 153

NICKELL, 70
NICKLES, 135
NIEDRINGHAUS, 151 153
NIELSEN, 70
NIEUWENDORP, 70
NINE, 70
NISBET, 153
NIVINS, 132
NOEL, 107
NOFFINGER, 107
NOLAND, 107
NOLTA, 70
NONE, 132
NORCUTT, 70
NORMAN, 107 152 176
NORRIS, 49 53 107 136-137
NORTON, 70 131 133 135
NORVELL, 107
NOYES, 70
NUESSLE, 70
NUNN, 133
O'BANNON, 179
O'BRIEN, 9 12 45
O'CONNELL, 53
O'CONNER, 183
O'DELL, 23-27 29 32 45 70 130-131
O'FALLON, 152
O'NEIL, 71
OBERTHIEN, 70
ODOM, 126
OELTING, 141
OGBIN, 70
OGDEN, 54
OLDAKER, 191
OLDEN, 70 108
OLDEWORTH, 108
OLDHAM, 108
OLINGER, 108
OLIVER, 108 135
OLLIS, 17
OLSON, 54 56 71
ONSBEE, 11
ONSTOTT, 71
ORCUTT, 180
ORR, 152

ORRICK, 14-15 50
OSBORNE, 108
OSBOURNE, 108
OSMUN, 180
OSTIMYER, 54
OSTRANDER, 54-55
OVERGAARD, 71
OVERLY, 108
OVERTON, 55
OVIATT, 71
OWEN, 108 133
OWENS, 108 122 126 134
OWNESBY, 19
OWSLEY, 108
PACE, 71 108 133
PACK, 108
PACKWOOD, 108
PAGE, 15 54
PALMER, 108
PANTIER, 71
PARCELL, 71
PARIS, 135
PARIZEK, 71
PARK, 71 108
PARKER, 17 27-28 32 42 44 49-51 53-55 71 108
PARKS, 17 20 26 28-29 33 41 43-44 47-49 51-52 71
PARMER, 31-32 49-50
PARRETT, 135
PARRICK, 174
PARRISH, 71
PARROTT, 108
PARSONS, 8 108 130 152-153
PARTRIDGE, 153
PASCHALL, 52
PATE, 108
PATERSON, 71
PATRICK, 71 108 150 152-153
PATTERSON, 16 21 39 55 130 132 137 174
PATTON, 108
PAUL, 55
PAULE, 143
PAULEY, 108

PAULUS, 34
PAXTON, 108-109
PAYNE, 71 133 136 179
PEACHA, 175
PEAK, 181
PEANICK, 109
PEARCE, 54-55
PEAREE, 41
PEARMAN, 153
PEARSON, 23 71
PECH, 71
PECKHAM, 152-153
PEERY, 109
PELSOR, 53
PEMBERTON, 109
PENCE, 54 71
PENDERGRAFT, 71
PENICK, 109
PENICS, 55
PENNINGTON, 21 50 52
PERKINS, 71 109 174-175
PERRIN, 109
PERRINE, 122 150 153
PERRY, 30-31 46 50 71 109 153
PERTEAT, 131
PESTOTMIK, 71
PETERMAN, 71
PETERS, 109
PETERSEN, 71
PETERSON, 71
PETREE, 55
PETRSOL, 183
PETTIBONE, 109
PETTIGREW, 109
PETTIJOHN, 109
PETTIT, 71 153
PEVRIL, 27
PEYTON, 175
PHELAN, 71
PHELPS, 109
PHILLIPS, 71 109 142 150 182
PHIPPS, 71 147
PICKENS, 14 49
PICKETT, 109
PICKORAL, 109

PICKTHORN, 55
PIERCE, 45 71 130 177
PILE, 23 25 27 47
PILES, 20-22 25 27 34 36-37 47 51-52 133 136
PINCE, 130
PINKLEY, 42 51
PINKNEY, 37
PINLEY, 41
PIPHO, 71
PITCHER, 109
PITMAN, 71 109
PITTS, 54 109 191-192
PITTSS, 192
PLANALP, 71
PLANK, 11
PLANT, 151 153
PLASTER, 136
PLUEGER, 72
PLUMMER, 54
POCK, 153
POCOCK, 151
POE, 79
POGUE, 11 13 20 35 38 45-46 49 52
POLE, 54
POLK, 30 36-37
POOLE, 183
POORE, 72
POPE, 152
POPENSKY, 143
POPPLEWELL, 109
PORTER, 3 72 109 130
POTTER, 47 109 147
POTTS, 72 182
POUGE, 130
POULSEN, 72
POWD, 54
POWEL, 130
POWELL, 7 26 40 54-55 109
POWERS, 44 109-110
PRATER, 54 110
PRATHER, 147
PRATT, 20 26 37 41 150
PRENTIS, 72
PRESTON, 54-55 72 180

PREWITT, 145
PRICE, 1 11 20 28-29 32 47 72 79 110 128
PRIDE, 128
PRIESCHKOWSKY, 144
PRIEST, 123
PRIGMORE, 110 147
PRITCHET, 38 52
PRITCHETT, 36 135
PROEPSTEL, 110
PROFFITT, 28 41
PROSSNER, 56
PRUNTY, 110
PULLEM, 39
PULLMAN, 44
PUTNEY, 110
PYBURN, 53
PYLE, 72
PYRTLE, 23 29 34 49-50
QUERY, 72
QUICK, 9 192
QUIGLEY, 54
QUINLAN, 110
QUINN, 72
RACE, 53-54
RADFORD, 15-16 19-20 23 36-38 48 52
RAGSDALE, 53
RAIMO, 120
RAINES, 14
RAINEY, 110
RAINS, 13 38
RAKE, 192
RALLSTON, 110
RAMBO, 110
RAMER, 136
RAMEY, 110
RAMSEY, 110
RAMZY, 134
RANDAL, 178
RANDALL, 1 72 152
RANDOLPH, 15-16 36 43 110
RANKIN, 179
RAPP, 12 28
RAPPELYE, 9

RASDALE, 110
RASNIC, 137
RATLIFF, 18 42-43 49 52 110
RAY, 110
RAYBURN, 72
RAYFIELD, 11-12 14 17 20 22 27 29 40-41 46 49
RAYMER, 130 132 135
RAYMERI, 130
RAYMOUR, 131
RAYNOR, 72
REACE, 29-30
READ, 110
READMAN, 110
RECTOR, 133-134
REDDEN, 72
REDDING, 179-180
REDMAN, 27
REDMANS, 27
REECE, 72
REED, 11 22 26-27 29 34 41 46-47 49 53 55 72
REEDMAN, 21
REENEN, 77
REES, 127
REESE, 41-42
REEVES, 72 131 133 137
REID, 72
REIMER, 72
REIMERS, 72
REINHARD, 151
REINHART, 153
REITZ, 72
RENALEY, 137
RENTFROW, 192
RESER, 192-193
RESSINGER, 136
REYNOLDS, 19 46 72 110 122 175
RHADA, 110
RHEA, 53-54 152
RHEEM, 53-54
RHOADES, 72
RHODES, 54
RIBBLE, 175
RICE, 34 43 49 110 147

RICH, 11-12 37
RICHARD, 72
RICHARDS, 72 193
RICHARDSON, 55 72 193
RICHERSON, 152
RICHMOND, 12 30 40 133-135
RICKETT, 72
RICKEY, 72 147
RIDDLE, 110
RIDER, 145-147
RIDINGER, 128-129
RIEFENAUER, 34
RIGGINS, 147
RIGGLE, 120
RIGGS, 110
RILEY, 54 110
RING, 110 136
RINK, 130
RION, 16
RIPLEY, 152
RIPPEY, 184
RISK, 110
RITNER, 110
RITTENHOUSE, 72
RITTER, 111
ROBAT, 144
ROBBINS, 193
ROBERSON, 44 111
ROBERT, 153
ROBERTS, 23-25 72 111 139 174
ROBERTSON, 111 131 153
ROBESSON, 134
ROBINET, 29
ROBINETT, 40-41
ROBINSON, 12 20-21 28 54 72 111 125 144-145 147
ROBSON, 132
ROCKEFELLER, 72
ROCKETTS, 72
RODGERS, 55 137
ROE, 38
ROEBUCK, 55
ROEPKE, 72
ROGERS, 1 48 72 111 130-131
ROLLEY, 55

ROMAN, 72
ROMESBURG, 174
ROMINE, 73
ROOF, 53
ROOK, 43
ROORDA, 73
ROOSA, 73
ROOT, 40-41
ROP, 28
RORER, 111
ROSA, 16
ROSE, 111 135 137
ROSS, 37-38 48 111
ROSSANDER, 73
ROSSITER, 73
ROSSLER, 73
ROSSOW, 73
ROSTIN, 54
ROSTOCK, 9
ROTEN, 111
ROTHLISBERGER, 49
ROTHWELL, 111
ROUDEBUSH, 142
ROULEAU, 111
ROUSE, 32
ROUSH, 73
ROUTH, 73
ROUTT, 173
ROUVEYROL, 142
ROWE, 55 179
ROWLAND, 147
ROWLEY, 73
ROY, 111
ROZELL, 129
RUBENSTEIN, 144
RUBEY, 73
RUBINGER, 131
RUDY, 11
RUFFOLO, 121
RULE, 111
RUMBURG, 135
RUMMEL, 73
RUNYON, 111
RUPE, 112
RUPERT, 73

RUSSEL, 55
RUSSELL, 35 45 48 54-55 73 147
RUSSELLS, 112
RUST, 112
RUTLEDGE, 12 24 34
RUTTER, 13 33 35-36 40
RYAN, 73
RYKEN, 73
RYNOLDS, 72
SABIN, 34 73
SAFFORD, 73
SAGASER, 138
SAGASTURE, 27
SAINTJOHN, 112
SAMPLE, 73 112
SAMPSON, 146
SANDER, 47
SANDERS, 24 43 47 49 130-134 184
SANDHAGEN, 73
SANDS, 73 147
SANDUSKY, 73
SANFORD, 112
SANKEY, 182
SANTHUFF, 13 52
SAPP, 112 193
SAPPERSTEIN, 144
SARGEN, 21
SARGENT, 15
SARTIN, 37 135
SASS, 179-180
SATTERLEE, 177
SAVAGE, 112
SAVILLE, 73
SAWHILL, 73
SAWYER, 45 148
SAWYERS, 193
SAX, 55
SAXTON, 112
SAYEG, 121
SCAGGS, 22-24 42 45
SCANLAN, 181
SCANLIN, 112
SCARLETT, 45
SCEARS, 79
SCHADER, 54-55

SCHAMEL, 73
SCHERTZEN, 126
SCHMIDT, 73 143
SCHMOLL, 73
SCHOCK, 9
SCHOENE, 184
SCHOENEMAN, 73
SCHOFIELD, 4
SCHOOLER, 124
SCHOON, 73
SCHRAMM, 73
SCHREEVES, 34
SCHRIER, 73
SCHRODER, 121
SCHROEDER, 73
SCHULER, 54
SCHULTZ, 73 112
SCHWARMAN, 144
SCHWEITZER, 148 150
SCHWENK, 137-138
SCOBEE, 121
SCOGGIE, 73
SCOGGIN, 132
SCOTT, 45-46 54-55 112 127 177-178
SCROGGIE, 73
SCULLY, 73
SEAL, 16-17 23-24 42
SEAMSTER, 73
SEARS, 73-74
SEBREE, 55
SEDLACEK, 74
SEE, 74
SEGASTINE, 47
SEIDEWERK, 142
SEIEWRK, 143
SENTER, 151
SERVER, 153
SESSIONS, 153
SETTLE, 153
SEWARD, 112
SEXTON, 23
SHACKLEFORD, 112
SHADE, 53
SHAFER, 9 74

SHAFFER, 74
SHANER, 74 175
SHANK, 74
SHANKLIN, 112
SHANNON, 112
SHANSTROM, 74
SHARP, 112 132
SHARPE, 74
SHARPTON, 112
SHAVER, 112
SHAW, 17-18 44 53 112
SHEARER, 74
SHEDD, 177
SHEETS, 22 49 74 130
SHEETZ, 74
SHEILS, 123
SHELBY, 183
SHELDON, 74
SHELL, 74 112
SHELTON, 55 133 193
SHEPARD, 112
SHEPHARD, 54
SHEPHERD, 55 74 112-113
SHERALL, 14
SHERIDAN, 141
SHERILL, 14
SHERLOCK, 55
SHERMAN, 74
SHERRELLE, 14
SHERRIL, 37
SHERRILL, 37
SHETTERLY, 113
SHIBLEY, 179
SHIELDS, 74
SHINN, 74
SHIPE, 122
SHIRRILL, 28
SHIVELEY, 54
SHOBE, 148
SHOLAR, 133
SHORT, 54
SHORTRIDGE, 55 113
SHRICK, 113
SHRIVER, 32-34 38
SHRUM, 11-12 34 47

SHULTS, 113
SHULTZ, 173
SHUMATE, 134
SHUTTLEWORTH, 53
SHY, 14 22 26 33 113
SIBERT, 74
SIEBOLD, 113
SILVER, 74
SILVEY, 33
SILVY, 40
SIM-MONS, 55
SIMCOE, 148
SIMMONS, 53 113 122 153 193
SIMONS, 55
SIMPSON, 49-50 53-55 113
SINCLAIR, 40
SINGLETON, 113
SINNARD, 181
SISSON, 113
SKAGGS, 40 113
SKILE, 24
SKILES, 11 24-25 130
SKILLMAN, 53-54 113
SKINER, 138
SKINNER, 113 137-138
SLADE, 11 29 46
SLASOR, 74
SLAUGHTER, 113
SLAWSON, 150 153
SLOAN, 1 12 27-28 51 113 151 153
SLOWN, 55
SLUSHER, 26
SLUTCHER, 36
SMALL, 134
SMART, 177 193
SMELSER, 113
SMILLMAN, 193
SMITH, 12-13 15 18 20-21 23-26 28-29 31-32 36 38 40 42-45 49-52 54-55 74 113-114 121-123 127 130-131 134-136 138 141 146 149 176 193
SMITHER, 114
SMOCK, 114
SMOOT, 54
SMRCEK, 74
SMULL, 75
SMYTH, 114
SNEDEGER, 127
SNEED, 53-55
SNIDER, 75 130-136
SNIVELY, 75
SNODDY, 174
SNODGRASS, 20-21 28 32 136
SNOW, 193
SNYDER, 56
SOMERS, 34
SONGER, 75
SONNESCHEIN, 153
SORENSEN, 75
SOULTS, 75
SOUTHARD, 114
SOWARDS, 128
SPANGLER, 120
SPARKS, 54 75 123 184
SPEAR, 36
SPEARS, 26 35 54 131
SPECHT, 54 75 153
SPEED, 114
SPEER, 48 51
SPENCER, 114
SPIKER, 75
SPILLMAN, 131 193-194
SPIREK, 75
SPOONER, 75
SPRATT, 114
SPRINGER, 9 114
SPROW, 21
SPURLOCK, 114
SRITE, 114
STAATS, 114
STABB, 21
STACY, 54
STAFFORD, 22
STAGG, 114
STAGNER, 32
STALCUP, 130
STALEN, 55
STALNAKER, 54-55
STAMBAUGH, 75

STAMPER, 75
STANARD, 153
STANDIFORD, 114
STANLEY, 54 75 134 178
STANLY, 123
STANTON, 114
STAPEFELDT, 75
STAPP, 114
STARCK, 75
STARKEY, 194
STARRETT, 75
STARWEATHER, 75
STATLER, 114
STATON, 75
STAUFFER, 75
STAYTON, 114
STECKER, 75
STEELE, 114
STEEN, 23
STEFNER, 35
STEGALL, 29 46
STENBERG, 75
STENSON, 75
STEPHENS, 53 75 114 136 145
STEPHENSON, 55 75
STEVENS, 22 29 40 47 122
STEVENSON, 20 75 134 136 151 153
STEWART, 20 25 75 114-115
STEWHUM, 115
STIGALL, 11
STIGGERS, 115
STILES, 178
STILL, 115
STILLWELL, 115
STITES, 138-139
STITTH, 45
STIWERT, 20
STOCK, 75
STOCKHAM, 75
STOCKMAN, 4
STOKES, 115
STOLLER, 115
STONE, 26 55 115 146
STORM, 135

STORY, 75
STOUT, 31 46 49 75 130 194
STRAIN, 152
STRAW, 194
STRICKLAN, 27
STRICKLAND, 11 13 18 37
STRICKLING, 18
STRIEMER, 75
STRINGER, 41
STRIPE, 54
STRODE, 115
STRONG, 25
STROTHER, 28
STROUPTTO, 135
STROUSE, 115
STRUTHERS, 75
STUART, 22 40
STUCK, 175
STUCKER, 115
STUSHER, 26
STUTSMAN, 75
SUGGS, 115
SUITS, 75
SULLIVAN, 12 15-16 36 39 53 177
SUMMERS, 13 149
SUMPTER, 18 52
SUNDERLAND, 194
SURBER, 75
SURRITT, 115
SUTHERLAND, 75
SUTHY, 45
SUTTEN, 135
SUTTERFIELD, 16-18 29-31 33 36-38 46-47 137
SUTTON, 14 32 41 48 51 115
SWAFFORD, 40
SWAFORD, 27
SWAIM, 76
SWAIN, 76 115
SWANEY, 115
SWANSON, 194
SWARTZ, 140
SWEARINGEN, 115
SWEAZEA, 26 131 136
SWEAZY, 134

SWEENEY, 76
SWEEZEA, 131
SWEEZY, 17
SWEZEA, 130
SWEZIE, 137
SWIERS, 15
SWINEHART, 76
SWINNEY, 115
SWITZER, 179
SWOARD, 115
SWOPE, 115
SWYERS, 16
SYMINGTON, 55
TAAB, 34
TABOR, 22 125
TAHA, 76
TALBERT, 14 126-127
TALBOTT, 115
TALLEY, 28
TARLETON, 178
TATE, 115
TATUM, 149
TAWCZNSKI, 143
TAYLER, 53
TAYLON, 55
TAYLOR, 11-12 25 34 43 47 55 76 130-131 151 153
TEBBS, 115
TEDDER, 29 35 45
TEETERS, 76 141
TEHEROW, 115
TEMPLE, 44 48 76
TEMPLETON, 115
TEMPY, 44
TERRY, 47 115 181
TESMAN, 76
THARP, 17 76
THATCHER, 115
THIES, 76
THIESEN, 76
THOMAS, 38 54-55 115 125
THOMASON, 34
THOMPSON, 42 47 51 54-55 76 116 128-129 131 152 177 194-196
THOMSON, 149
THORN, 76
THORNBURG, 116
THORNTON, 20 22 24 28 53-54 76 129
THORP, 116
THORTON, 22
THROWER, 184
THURMAN, 38 194
THURMOND, 181
TICKLE, 116
TICKNER, 76
TIERNEY, 121
TILLERY, 150
TILLEY, 18 39 116
TILLMAN, 76
TILLY, 24
TILTON, 76 116
TIMBERLAKE, 116
TINCHER, 116
TINKER, 130 133-134
TINS, 131
TINSLEY, 76
TIPTON, 76 116
TODD, 116 149-150
TOFFELMIRE, 116
TOLIN, 142
TOLLIVER, 137
TOLSEN, 116
TOMPSON, 17
TOMS, 116
TORREY, 39
TOUGATE, 116
TOWNLEY, 76
TRAMMELL, 24 33
TRAPP, 116
TRAVIS, 133
TREACY, 116
TREADYWAY, 116
TRIBBLE, 116
TRIGGS, 194
TRIMBLE, 129 145 149
TRIMON, 136
TRIPP, 15-16
TROLINGER, 12
TROLLINGER, 21

TROMBO, 54
TROOP, 117
TROTTER, 54-55
TROUP, 53
TROUPE, 54
TROUT, 76
TROUTMAN, 18 29-31 38 44
TRUE, 76
TRUITT, 117
TRUMBO, 117
TUBBS, 134
TUCKER, 15 28 30 42-43 47-49 76 194
TUDER, 117
TULL, 117 124
TULLIS, 76
TURGEON, 76
TURLEY, 130-131 133 135
TURNBELT, 135
TURNER, 76 117 123 142 179
TURPIN, 53
TUTTLE, 54 149
TWINAM, 76
TYLER, 54
UHLENHAKE, 76
ULCH, 76
UNDERHILL, 25-26 117
UNDERWOOD, 53
URMY, 76
URRY, 76
VAINYARD, 130
VALENTINE, 76 136
VALLANDINGHAM, 117
VALLIERE, 76
VANARSDALL, 11
VANARSDELL, 54
VANBUSKIRK, 9
VANCE, 117
VANDENBERG, 76
VANDERFORD, 76
VANDERPOOL, 117 139
VANDEVANTER, 54
VANDIVER, 45
VANDOWN, 14
VANDYKE, 23 32 43 79 126

VANHOUTEN, 76
VANHOY, 54-55
VANHULTZ, 54
VANMETER, 121
VANNEMAN, 117
VANSICKLE, 55
VANSTON, 77
VAUGHN, 37 47-48 77 117 194
VELAND, 77
VENARD, 117
VETTER, 77
VICKERY, 55
VICKINBERG, 53
VICKREY, 18
VIERLING, 141-142
VIGNERON, 139
VINCENT, 132
VINEYARD, 26 50 117
VINSON, 13 22-23 33 45 48 117 131
VIRGIN, 55
VIVIAN, 117
VLEOXEY, 12
VONSCHRADER, 153
VOOHERS, 178
VOSBURG, 179
VOSS, 32-33
VOTTELER, 77
WADE, 77 180
WADKIN, 36
WADKINS, 15 31
WADLOW, 19 25 29 38-39 44 46-48 50 52
WAGEMAN, 177
WAILSON, 54
WAIT, 117
WALDO, 77
WALDRON, 117
WALKER, 28 35 37 41 46 53 77 117 149 174 181
WALL, 125
WALLACE, 77 117 145 149-150 182
WALLCE, 117
WALLEN, 17 29
WALLER, 117-118 133 179
WALLES, 35

WALLIS, 25 133
WALLS, 118
WALSH, 141
WAMBLE, 35
WANE, 124
WARD, 14 25 55 77 118 127
WARDEN, 54-55
WARE, 20
WARMICK, 19
WARNER, 13 118
WARREN, 15-16 31 35-36 38 44
WARSHAM, 48
WART, 50
WASHINGTON, 122
WATERS, 149 152
WATKINS, 53 118
WATKINSON, 55
WATSON, 32 34 149-151 153
WATTS, 153 177
WAYMEYER, 134
WEAVER, 118 142
WEBB, 17-18 20 24-27 47 51-52 77 134 151 153
WEBBER, 136
WEBSTER, 77
WEEB, 133
WEEKS, 51
WEEMS, 36-37
WEESNER, 118
WEEVER, 12
WEGER, 77
WEHLAND, 77
WEHRMAN, 77
WEIBLE, 28 50
WEINGARTH, 77
WEINTZ, 77
WEITGENENT, 77
WEIZMANN, 142
WELCH, 41 45-46
WELLER, 118
WELLS, 13 28 118 122
WELSCH, 118
WELTZIN, 77
WENCHELL, 134
WENTNER, 141
WER, 19
WERLEY, 19
WERNER, 141
WESEMAN, 183
WESLEY, 15
WESSLING, 77
WEST, 25 118 120 133 136 153 195-196
WESTBROOK, 176
WESTEN, 135
WESTFALL, 54
WESTHOFF, 141
WHALEN, 121
WHALEY, 55
WHALLEY, 149
WHAN, 77
WHEELER, 43 130 132-133 194
WHERRETT, 54-55
WHERRY, 4
WHISMAN, 118
WHITAKER, 182
WHITE, 13 30 33 48 54 77 118 126 130 132 153
WHITECOTTON, 28
WHITEHEAD, 10
WHITFIELD, 77
WHITLOCK, 118
WHITMAN, 179
WHITMORE, 183
WHITNEY, 52
WHITSEL, 55
WHITSETT, 54
WHITTAKER, 153
WHITTEN, 118
WHITTEY, 55
WHITWORTH, 37
WIDGER, 16
WIDNER, 123
WIGEN, 131
WIGERS, 132
WIGGER, 17
WILCOX, 77 118 121 145 153
WILDER, 4
WILHITE, 48 118
WILHITTE, 145

231

WILKERSON, 118 153
WILKEY, 77
WILKINS, 43 46 138
WILKINSON, 43 55 118
WILLBRAND, 141
WILLHELMES, 11
WILLIAMS, 12 14-15 20 32 37-39
  45-46 54-56 77 118-119 133 149
  176-177 194
WILLIAMSON, 53 194
WILLIANY, 51
WILLIS, 16 48 145 149
WILLOUGHBY, 77 119
WILLS, 119
WILLY, 11
WILSON, 7 12-13 33-34 41-42 44
  53-55 77-78 119 121 125 132
  149 153 184
WIMPY, 32 34
WINCHELL, 23 33 78
WINDES, 133
WINDFIELD, 54
WINES, 134
WINFIELD, 54
WINFREY, 55 194
WINKLEMAN, 38
WINN, 54
WINSCOTT, 139-140
WINSTON, 119
WINTER, 78
WINTERBOTTOM, 38
WISCARVER, 131
WISDOM, 30
WISHART, 153
WITHRO, 30
WITT, 78
WOLF, 18 129
WOLFE, 78 180
WOMBEL, 34
WOMBLE, 36
WOOD, 27-28 34 51 53 55 119 121
  135 137
WOODARD, 78-79 133
WOODRUFF, 136
WOODS, 78 119 130 133 149 153

WOODWARD, 78 176
WOODY, 149-150 184
WOOLFOLK, 1 149
WOOLRIDGE, 78
WOOTEN, 46
WORK, 78
WORKS, 127
WORLEY, 12 37
WORLOW, 79
WORMICKE, 34
WORNICA, 34
WORSHAM, 182
WOYE, 141
WRAY, 78
WRIGHT, 13 78 153 175 177 183
WULLBRANDT, 78
WYATT, 121-122
WYNN, 122
YANCEY, 149
YANCY, 119
YAPLE, 78
YARNALD, 54
YATES, 22 42 119
YEATMAN, 150-151
YOCAM, 119
YOCUM, 119
YODER, 78
YOHE, 119
YONKER, 179
YOUNG, 43 54-55 78 120 124 135
  149 183
YOUNGERS, 78
ZAKEWITZ, 143
ZAND, 120
ZANNELLA, 120
ZAVRISKEY, 120
ZEARRY, 35
ZECK, 78
ZEIGLER, 78
ZENOR, 180
ZICK, 53
ZICKEFOOSE, 78
ZINN, 121
ZOLLNER, 78
ZUKOWSKI, 144

Other Heritage Books by Sherida K. Eddlemon:

Missouri Genealogical Records and Abstracts:
Volume 1: 1766-1839
Volume 2: 1752-1839
Volume 3: 1787-1839
Volume 4: 1741-1839
Volume 5: 1755-1839
Volume 6: 1621-1839
Volume 7: 1535-1839

Missouri Genealogical Gleanings 1840 and Beyond, Volumes 1-9

1890 Genealogical Census Reconstruction: Mississippi, Volumes 1 and 2

1890 Genealogical Census Reconstruction: Missouri, Volumes 1-3

1890 Genealogical Census Reconstruction: Ohio, Volume 1
(with Patricia P. Nelson)

1890 Genealogical Census Reconstruction: Tennessee, Volume 1

A Genealogical Collection of Kentucky Birth and Death Records

Callaway County, Missouri, Marriage Records: 1821 to 1871

Cumberland Presbyterian Church, Volume One: 1836 and Beyond

Dickson County, Tennessee Marriage Records, 1817-1879

Genealogical Abstracts from Missouri Church Records and
Other Religious Sources, Volume 1

Genealogical Abstracts from Tennessee Newspapers, 1791-1808

Genealogical Abstracts from Tennessee Newspapers, 1803-1812

Genealogical Abstracts from Tennessee Newspapers, 1821-1828

Tennessee Genealogical Records and Abstracts, Volume 1: 1787-1839

Genealogical Gleanings from New York Fraternal Organizations
Volumes 1 and 2

Index to the Arkansas General Land Office, 1820-1907
Volumes 1-10

Kentucky Genealogical Records and Abstracts, Volume 1: 1781-1839

Kentucky Genealogical Records and Abstracts, Volume 2: 1796-1839

Lewis County, Missouri Index to Circuit Court Records, Volume 1, 1833-1841

Missouri Birth and Death Records, Volumes 1-4

Morgan County, Missouri Marriage Records, 1833-1893

Our Ancestors of Albany County, New York, Volumes 1 and 2

Our Ancestors of Cuyahoga County, Ohio, Volume 1
(with Patricia P. Nelson)

Ralls County, Missouri Settlement Records, 1832-1853

Records of Randolph County, Missouri, 1833-1964

Ten Thousand Missouri Taxpayers

The "Show-Me" Guide to Missouri: Sources for Genealogical and Historical Research

CD: Dickson County, Tennessee Marriage Records, 1817-1879

CD: Index to the Arkansas General Land Office, 1820-1907 Volumes 1-10

CD: Missouri, Volume 3

CD: Tennessee Genealogical Records

CD: Tennessee Genealogical Records, Volumes 1-3

www.ingramcontent.com/pod-product-compliance
Lightning Source LLC
Chambersburg PA
CBHW071430150426
43191CB00008B/1095